A HISTORY OF THE EARLY CHURCH

TO A.D. 500

A History of the Early Church to A.D. 500

by

J. W. C. WAND
Formerly Bishop of London

LONDON and NEW YORK

First published 1937 by Methuen & Co. Ltd
Second edition 1946
Third edition 1949
Reprinted four times
Fourth edition 1963
Reprinted 1965

First issued as a University Paperback 1974
Reprinted twice
Reprinted 1982

Reprinted 1994 and 1996 by Routledge
11 New Fetter Lane, London EC4P 4EE
29 West 35th Street, New York, NY 10001

Printed in Great Britain by
TJ Press (Padstow) Ltd, Padstow, Cornwall

ISBN 0–415–04566–5

PREFACE

ALTHOUGH this volume deals with the earliest period of Church History, it is actually the last member of a trilogy, the other two being Miss Deanesly's *History of the Medieval Church* and my own *History of the Modern Church*. It was almost completely written during my voyage to Australia in 1934, but so great has been the pressure of other duties since my arrival in this country that it has taken me sixteen months to add what little remained to be done before publication.

The delay, however, has had one advantage in that it has made possible a careful revision of the manuscript by the Rev. R. E. Sutton, the Vice-Principal of our Provincial Theological College. He has vastly increased the value of the book and my own indebtedness to him not only by making many corrections, but also by adding the comparative table of principal events and the two tables of the Councils.

Owing to the distance that separates us from England it will not be possible for me to see the volume through the press. That task has been kindly undertaken by my successor as Dean of Oriel, the Rev. J. F. Russell.

To both these scholars I desire to express my very deep gratitude.

✠ Wm. BRISBANE

February 1936

NOTE TO 1963 PRINTING

Revisions have been added in the form of extra notes. Passages in the text which are the subject of these notes are indicated by an asterisk.

CONTENTS

vii

CONTENTS

MAPS

(at end of book)

THE CHURCH IN THE ROMAN EMPIRE

PATRIARCHATES FROM 451

BARBARIANS *c.* 500

CHAPTER I

THE ENVIRONMENT

CHRISTIANITY in history may be studied as a form of religious belief, as a system of ethics, as a mode of worship, or as an inspiration that changed the fashions of art and life through many centuries. Each of these aspects of the subject must find some place even in so slight a sketch as the present. But our primary purpose is to consider the rise of Christianity as a society.

I

At the outset we are faced by the difficulty of deciding whether there is or ought to be in any real sense a Christian society at all. A common notion is that original Christianity consisted in a recognition of the vital truths of the Fatherhood of God and the Brotherhood of Man, and that all organisation is a departure from primitive purity. It is pointed out that in the history of most religious movements we find the first incentive given by some enthusiastic prophet, who with his immediate followers is swept forward on the crest of a wave of fanatical emotion. Those who come after him, however, are not able to maintain this exalted position, and endeavour to preserve what they can of the Master's spirit by reducing his teaching to a code and hedging it about with the protective barrier of an institution. But in the process a great deal of the original enthusiasm and freedom is inevitably lost. This, it is often contended, has been the fortune of Christianity. The original inspiration of Christ's teaching has been organised out of recognition. In so far as He can justly be said to have founded a society at all, it was an invisible society, the limits of which were set not by material rites but by moral and spiritual considerations alone.

This view, which threatened at one time to become popular, has in recent years received a deadly blow from the discovery of a definitely apocalyptic element in Christ's teaching. His eschatology shows too close an affinity with that of the general mass of contemporary apocalyptic literature to be easily ignored or confused with the usual prophetic idealism. Jesus was clearly no ordinary prophet, no mere preacher of moral righteousness and divine governance. He had come to usher in a Kingdom, and a kingdom is not only a rule but a society. It affected not only men's hearts, but also their lives: it might come on the clouds of heaven, but for its fulfilment it demanded a new earth. After the confession of Peter at Caesarea Philippi Jesus appears to have believed that the Kingdom had already begun: henceforth people need no longer wait for it; they could be brought into it.

Even those who are not willing to recognise any apocalypticism in Christ's teaching and still cling to the view that He founded no society are constrained to admit that the so-called degeneration had already begun before the New Testament was complete. Organisation is indeed the obvious background of all the epistles. It is therefore suggested that S. Paul was the dominating figure who changed the simple gospel into the Catholic Church. But this is quite unnecessary. On a sober and unprejudiced reading of the gospels it seems likely both that our Lord expected the world to continue in some form or other after His own death and that He made provision for a well-defined body to continue His work. Like the Baptist before Him He organised a faithful remnant which would inaugurate the Kingdom of the New Israel; the *ekklesia* which was to be so securely founded on a rock was to succeed the old assembly or church of the Jewish people. Initiation was by baptism; the young brotherhood was urged not to be diffident in the exercise of its functions; it was to make its arrangements in full confidence of the support of Heaven; the authority of Heaven would be behind its care for the moral well-being of its members, and the special favour of Heaven would be granted to its united prayers. And as if to ensure that

there might be no hesitation in the taking of the early steps, its leaders had already been chosen and close attention paid to their training.

It was within this clear-cut organisation that the new ideal was expected to have its full and perfect expression. Certainly it was to such a call that the original Christians believed themselves to be responding. They regarded themselves as the true Israel; the social element in their life was fundamental. The Church was not only a body but a corporation, which necessarily involved organisation and a law. It is indeed doubtful whether in the mind of the Jew, stored as it was with hopes of a coming Messianic Kingdom, any mere vague sentiment or disembodied ideal could ever have been received as a possible new religion.

II

Societies, like persons, do not live entirely to themselves; for both, environment counts for much in the development of character. It is therefore of first-rate importance that we try to obtain a clear picture of the surroundings of the early Church. We shall find that the Christian society was born at the place where two worlds met, the East and the West, the Semitic and the Graeco-Roman, the Jew and the Gentile. It is only as we grasp this that we shall be able to understand how the Church can claim to be the heir of all that was best in every section of ancient civilisation, and how Christianity can claim to be the absolute religion. We must therefore sketch the conditions that surrounded the cradle of the infant Church. It will be convenient to follow the widening circles as they stretch from Galilee to Rome.

What has been called 'the special seed-plot of Christianity' consisted of an apparently small section of the people, resident mostly in Galilee, who were distinguished by the fact that with especial earnestness they 'waited for the consolation of Israel', putting all their hopes in the promised Messiah. Their descent may be traced—although there are difficulties about this—through the 'humble and meek' of the Magnificat and Psalms, and the pious but pusillanimous

chasidim of Maccabean times, to the 'People of the Land', who had kept their homes in Jerusalem when the best of the nation had been carried into exile, had intermarried with the northern folk, and were consequently despised and castigated with remarkable vehemence by Ezra and Nehemiah. To this class apparently the Holy Family with Elizabeth and her husband and the bulk of the apostles belonged.

Christianity was thus, as Canon Streeter has said, mainly a Galilean affair. It is therefore necessary to remember that ever since the destruction of Samaria in 722 B.C. this country had had a semi-Pagan character, and was indeed known as 'Galilee of the Gentiles'. Together with Perea it had been brought under Jewish influences by the Maccabees. But it still remained largely heathen until Aristobulus conquered it in 103 B.C. and forced its inhabitants to submit to the rite of circumcision. The Judaism of Galilee could thus hardly be as orthodox as that of Jerusalem. This may account for some of the ease with which Christianity was able to adapt itself to Gentile needs.

At the beginning of the Christian era the Galilean 'People of the Land' had been responsible for the great reformation which was inaugurated by John the Baptist. This movement was the last effort of Hebrew prophecy to stem the corruption of the Chosen People and to recall them to a sense of the spiritual issues of their destiny. As we may judge from the case of Apollos, if not from that of the Mandaeans, it achieved some success even beyond the limits of Palestine. Nevertheless it proved ready to merge itself in the greater movement for which it had done so much to prepare the way. How serious had been the need for such a reformation can be seen at once from a glance at the religious and social conditions of Palestine.

The most notable feature was the turmoil of warring sects. The Pharisees, or Separated, had arisen as a protest against the attempt in the Maccabean period to Hellenise Judaism. For a time they had been an element making for true religious advance, and they had actually developed the doctrine of the resurrection of the dead. But they had now

degenerated into a body of fanatical formalists, who, though they rejected Hellenism, seem to have imbibed a good deal of Persian dualism, spiritism, and eschatology.

Their chief opponents were the Sadducees, the priestly and aristocratic party, who were conservative in matters of faith, stuck to the literal interpretation of the old written law, refused to accept the bolder speculations of the Pharisees, and adopted as their standpoint in life the somewhat despairing attitude of Ecclesiastes. The High-priesthood itself had long been subject to pagan political influence with the consequence that Hellenism had found stronger support among the official representatives of Judaism than among the lay-folk.

The extreme rivals to the priests were the Rabbis or teachers. They exercised tremendous influence among most classes of the people. Through their constant references to the judgments of their predecessors they exalted the claims of their whole body to the allegiance of the faithful, and they were already beginning to be regarded as wonder-working mediators with God. This development within Judaism offers an interesting parallel to the new type of religion with its emphasis on thaumaturgic teachers which had now taken root in the Hellenistic world.

The Herodians on the other hand were a political party who had accepted the subservient position of the national government as final, and were at pains to make themselves agreeable to the half-foreign Court. Arrayed against them were the Zealots, who were fiercely patriotic, would acknowledge no king but Jehovah, and had already given proof of their determination by revolting against the census of Quirinius in A.D. 7.[1]

It is a relief to remember that there remained one class, the Essenes, who had withdrawn from all this strife of factions and had retired into communities where they could serve God in quietness. It is true that they ran to extremes—they condemned marriage and animal sacrifice, and would

[1] This is the usual view, but the Zealots may not have become a separate party till A.D. 66 (see Foakes-Jackson, *Beginnings of Christianity*, Vol. I, p. 421).

not touch flesh food—but they provided a precedent for
much that was to be valuable in later religious effort.

The system of government to which all these parties
alike were forced to submit was the power of a foreign
conqueror exercised through native princes. Antipas ruled
in Galilee; Philip was his colleague on the other side of
Jordan; till A.D. 6 Archelaus had ruled in Judea, but at
that date he was deposed, either for misrule or because he
had appropriated the style and title of king, and then Judea
became part of the province of Syria under the authority of
a procurator. The foreign power was of course that of Rome.
Roman provinces were divided into two classes according
as they were under the rule of the Senate or that of the
Emperor. In the former case they were governed by pro-
consuls, in the latter by propraetors or legates. At this time
the legate of the imperial province of Syria was Quirinius,
and his subordinate, the procurator of Judea, was Pontius
Pilate. Judea had been subject to Roman overlordship since
63 B.C., the year in which Pompey had taken Jerusalem.
Even the three Herodian princes above mentioned were not
true Jews, but were the sons of an Idumean, Herod the
Great, whom Augustus had permitted to retain the throne of
Palestine after his victory over Antony at Actium in 31 B.C.
That splendid but tortuous monarch at his death in 4 B.C.
had left to his heirs the legacy of a divided kingdom and a
consolidated hatred on the part of patriot Jews, whom not
even his magnificent rebuilding of the Temple (begun 14 B.C.)
had sufficed to propitiate.

It was under this very unsatisfactory system that the
Romans organised the conquered country as an outpost of
their empire against the ever-threatening peril from Parthian
invaders. The birthplace of the Church thus stood on the
boundary between East and West. It is significant that this
infant religion, which is sometimes called essentially Eastern,
as soon as it was strong enough to leave the cradle marched
straight to the West.

III

The reason for this may lie partly in the fact that the way had already been prepared by the Jewish Dispersion, since the proselytising zeal of the Jews had met with more success in the Roman than in the Parthian empire. It is a remarkable fact that the number of Jews in the Roman world outside Palestine at this time cannot have been far short of five millions, that is to say about seven per cent of the total population. They had persuaded many of the more intelligent and moral of their neighbours that their presentation of an ethical monotheism was the closest approximation to philosophical and religious truth available at the time. Only a few of these were willing to go so far as to submit themselves to the rite of circumcision, without which they could not become full members of the Jewish community, but as 'God-fearers' they strove to live up to the Jewish moral ideal and became, like Cornelius, benefactors of the synagogue at which they received instruction.

The importance of the Dispersion for the spread of Christianity can hardly be exaggerated. It meant that the earliest preachers found in practically every town a religious community whose background was the same as their own. Here monotheism and morality had no need for apology; here also were people who had already the habit of regular worship and whose liturgical forms might become the basis of Christian services. Not only so, but through the medium of the Septuagint each worshipper was already familiar with the Jewish scriptures and with what may be termed the Jewish philosophy of history. This was a tremendous gain, of which Christian evangelism was not slow to take advantage.

But this was not the only way in which the Roman Empire affected the new religion. In it, as has often been pointed out, both material and cultural development had reached a stage peculiarly fitted to assist the advance of a new faith. The Roman power was now at its zenith, and was acknowledged from Carlisle to the Nile. This vast territory was crossed by roads along which private posts conveying

the letters of such a one as S. Paul could travel with as much safety as to-day. One coinage and one language would carry the traveller all the way. It is true of course that many dialects remained and that the Romans established Latin in Gaul, Britain, North Africa, and Spain. But Greek was a kind of universal language with which one could make shift anywhere: there would always be found someone who could speak it, and for most parts it was the official language. And everywhere the proud *Pax Romana* prevailed. Within the boundaries of the Empire there was no rebellion, and the legions could safely be packed around the frontiers. The Jews were the most turbulent of the subject races, but even in Judea it was enough to add a few legal and military powers to the financial authority of the procurator. This Roman peace was maintained for no less than two centuries.

The culture of the time was a palimpsest on which Rome herself had written little but the regard for law and order. Nevertheless this implied the political genius that had imposed a unity in diversity upon an amazing number of cities,[1] and welded them into one vast Empire, all obeying the common purpose though many of their individual peculiarities of organisation were carefully preserved. But the dominant influence was that of Greece. Even the old Greece, decadent as she was, had yet spread her language everywhere and put a torment of questioning in the minds of men. The great systems of Plato and Aristotle had proved a solvent in which the old myths disappeared or remained only as a conventional vehicle of poetic thought. The impress derived from the new Greece was not, strictly speaking, Greek but Hellenistic, the product of that commerce of the Greeks with the East which had followed upon the conquests of Alexander. Politically the new Hellenism had meant the fusion of races, the endowing of them with a common language and a common government. On the side of religion it had meant complete toleration and the absorption of many ideas from the East. This had resulted in a new type of Pagan piety which took the place

[1] *Civitas* = the town itself with the country lying around it.

of the old half-hearted worship familiar to us from our reading of classical authors. As Juvenal said, the Orontes had flowed into the Tiber, and the resultant mixture was supposed to confer upon its participants a guarantee of immortality together with some measure of success in the attainment of a sufficient morality. A famous saying of Professor Bury's, which is generally fathered upon other authors, suggests that this change in habits of piety was due to a 'failure of nerve'. In any case it was certainly a witness to the need of men for some assurance in face of the inscrutable mysteries of life and death. We shall have to consider later the way in which the Mystery Cults tried to meet this need, but it is well to remember from the outset how important a part they played in the life of the time.

All this was popular religion. Beside it we ought to place the spirits that in Rome itself looked after every phase of human activity, a separate one for each part of the house such as the threshold and the larder, and for each event in life such as the birth, the weaning, the health, the school-going of the child, and the love and marriage of the adult. It was inevitable that in such circumstances demonology and magic should play upon the superstition of the vulgar. For a reaction against this kind of thing one must turn to the philosophers. Among them rather than in religious circles could be found a school of virtue. Of this the highest example was the cold but duty-loving detachment of the Stoics. Stoicism indeed by this time had become moralism pure and simple. But if the ideals of a Seneca could lead to nothing better than suicide, it was not likely that lesser men would long think them worth pursuing. Nevertheless public office and philosophic study were still, in the failure of religion, the best opportunities for the development of the good life. To the Stoics ought perhaps to be added the Cynics as the professional representatives of virtue. At least they were often used as practical advisers in moments of difficulty, but their anxiety for the collection of alms laid them open to the charge of interestedness. Thus neither of the main philosophical schools could claim any large measure of success in ethical instruction.

Of all these religions and schools of thought the Government was quite willing to be tolerant, but in return it expected them to be mutually forbearing. And to them it added one necessary religious observance of its own in the shape of a blatant State-worship centring in the divine honours paid to Caesar. This was a ceremony without a creed, but it was a sign of loyalty, and it was the rock on which more than once the Church seemed likely to be wrecked. Its history is interesting. Although it came from the East it was Hellenistic rather than Oriental. Ancestor-worship made it possible, the honour paid to the dead emperor becoming attached to his living successor. It was natural that the Eastern peoples who had been saved from anarchy and oppression by the all-conquering Alexander should reverence that young genius as a god and pay him divine honours. The Greeks borrowed the practice from the peoples they had overcome, but the Romans thoroughly disliked it. A change came, however, under Julius Caesar, who no doubt saw the value of such reverence as an instrument in statecraft, and accepted it in Rome itself. Augustus also, although he disliked the attribution to himself even of the title Lord (*Dominus*), was politic enough to accept divine ascriptions in the cosmopolitan harbours of Italy. Tiberius, on the other hand, would have none of it; and that perhaps is why our Lord could tell His countrymen to render unto Caesar the things that were Caesar's and why they themselves in a moment of apostasy could say that they had no king but Caesar. The mad Caligula, however, definitely assumed divinity; and Nero demanded divine honours not only for the poisoned Claudius, but also for his dead wife and daughter. The rough old soldier Vespasian made a joke of it. 'I think I am becoming a god', was the way in which he announced himself to be dying. But there was already a regular body of ministrants, *sodales Flaviales*, who attended to the worship of the Flavian dynasty. Domitian took the final step and claimed the double title Lord and God (*Dominus ac Deus noster*). The Jews were known to be a peculiar people and they were exempted from this worship But there was no exemption for Christians. Thus of necessity

Christianity challenged the world to choose between two masters, imperial Caesar in his purple robe and the Carpenter's Son dyed in the purple of His own blood.

We may then sum up the position of affairs at the opening of the Christian era by saying that Judaism contributed to the best culture of the time monotheism and morality, Rome organisation, Greece philosophy, the East mysticism and a gift for worship. Of all these Christianity was to take advantage. But in other respects she appeared less fortunate. It used to be the fashion in books of this kind to say that Christianity appeared at the psychological moment when religion had died out of the world and atheism had left a void waiting to be filled. We know now on the contrary that there had been a striking revival of religious interest. The Church did not step forth on to an empty stage, but into an arena full of warring sects and rival faiths. But at least it remains true that religion and culture were in the melting-pot waiting to be fresh moulded, that men were conscious of a great need, that every question was an open question, and that if Christianity won in the end it did so not simply because of favouring circumstance but on its own merits.

CHAPTER II

THE APOSTOLIC CHURCH

I

A T whatever date we place the actual birth of the new society, whether on the occasion of S. Peter's great confession at Caesarea Philippi or on the evening of the Lord's resurrection, there can be little doubt that by Pentecost the Twelve were fully conscious of their mission as the propagators of a new religion, or at least of a new edition of the old religion. They had taken pains to maintain their own precise number and had filled the place left vacant by the death of the traitor. When they first began their propaganda under the leadership of Peter they announced that the long-expected Messiah had appeared in the person of Jesus, and that although He had been put to death as a malefactor His divine authority was proved by His resurrection. Shortly He would come again in glory to inaugurate a reign of righteousness and peace, and those who wished to share in the privileges of that new age should accept Him as Messiah, conform to His moral standards and enter His fellowship by undergoing the rite of baptism. Any difficulties that might be felt about a Messiah who conformed so little to the usual grandiose Jewish conceptions they swept away by declaring that the true Messiah had in point of fact been foreshadowed in the Suffering Servant of Isaiah, and by contending that, rightly understood, all the Jewish scriptures pointed to this ideal, which had been realised in Jesus of Nazareth. Such an interpretation of the national history they evidently expected their countrymen to accept, and they set themselves to build up on this basis a New Israel, in whom the divine promises should receive fulfilment.

Their disillusionment on this head is one of the most

pathetic features in the history of the Church. So far from finding their countrymen willing to receive this teaching they discovered to their surprise that in spite of many individual conversions fierce opposition was aroused. Jerusalem was naturally the headquarters of the new association and it was there that its struggles with official Judaism began. Trouble arose almost at once over the liberal teaching of Stephen, and it never died out so long as the city endured. Twice again during the period it came to a head. The first occasion was in the year 41, when Agrippa I, who had already acquired the territory of Philip and Antipas, succeeded also to the power of the procurator in Judea, thus reconstituting the kingdom of Herod the Great. Agrippa was anxious to achieve popularity with his Jewish subjects and started a fresh persecution, in which James, the son of Zebedee, lost his life. S. Peter escaped only by a miracle and the rest of the Twelve were scattered.

After the death of Agrippa there followed a renewal of the system of procurators, and they maintained an impartial peace. But when the procurator Festus died, the High Priest, Annas II, seized the opportunity of the interregnum to attack the Church again, and succeeded in putting to death James, the brother of the Lord, who was now at the head of the Christians in the city. For this Annas was deposed by the new King, Agrippa II, who does not seem to have been ill-disposed to the struggling society.

Four years later, in 66, there occurred an event which was to change the whole course of its history. In that year no fewer than 3,000 Jews were put to death by the procurator Gessius Florus and the nation was goaded into revolt. Nero sent Vespasian to deal with the trouble, but he, being proclaimed Emperor in 68, left the prosecution of the campaign to his son, Titus. After a seven months' siege, which has become a byword for tenacity and ferocity, the city was destroyed in A.D. 70. This of course meant the end of sacrificial Judaism. The Christian community had taken timely warning and found refuge in Pella, which was in Perea, a region already pacified by Vespasian.

This disaster to Judaism of the old type set a seal to the

effort which the Christian Church had long been making to disentangle itself from its connection with Jewish organisation. Originally, as we have seen, the Christians regarded themselves as the true Israel. To the outsider they appeared to be nothing more than a new sect in Judaism. Certainly they had their own synagogue in Jerusalem, but they attended the Temple and conformed to all Jewish ceremonies. But to what extent was the Jewish law really binding upon them? The question was first raised by certain Greek-speaking Jews of the Dispersion who had accepted Jesus as the Messiah. It is possible that their contact with philosophic thought had made them readily accessible to the new teaching and easily able to grasp its implications. At any rate Stephen argued that Judaism was not necessarily God's final revelation. As the tabernacle had been superseded by the Temple, so the Temple might be superseded by a new universalism. Of that supersession the prophet was none other than the Jesus whom official Judaism had done to death. The result of such teaching was seen in the action of Philip, who admitted to baptism not only Samaritans but also an eunuch, representatives of two classes who were barred from participation in the full privileges of Judaism. Philip's action was vindicated by the delegates of the Twelve; and Peter himself went even further in baptising the Gentile proselyte Cornelius and his household.

Stephen's teaching won a still more notable convert in the person of Paul. A centre of universalistic Christianity was founded at Antioch, whence were launched the great missionary undertakings of the Apostle of the Gentiles. He refused to demand circumcision of those non-Jews who accepted his interpretation of Jesus, and he thus brought to a head the vital controversy whether the Christian Church was any longer to be regarded as an inner circle within Judaism or was to be taken as a fresh organisation independent of all other religions whatsoever. The question was settled at a gathering held in Jerusalem and obviously regarded as representative of the whole Christian society. The letter in which its findings were embodied is not altogether easy of interpretation, but if we may accept the

longer form of its injunctions the arrangement was that while circumcision was not to be expected of Gentile converts, they were to conform to Jewish moral standards and when they entertained their Jewish Christian neighbours they were to see that only *kosher* food was provided, so that the susceptibilites of neither party should be wounded. Thus the infant Church won its freedom, and where the agreement was faithfully kept could address itself to its great mission, which was now to convert not the Jews only but the whole world to Christ. It can easily be realised that when, about twenty years later, Jerusalem was destroyed specifically Judaistic Christianity lost the reason for its existence, and ceased to be of any great importance in the development of the Christian Church.

II

While these events were proceeding in the East, Christianity was already obtaining a foothold in the West. Very early it arrived in the capital of the Empire. By what agency it was first carried to Rome we do not know, but inasmuch as in those early days each convert felt his own obligation in the matter of evangelisation we may conclude that it followed in the train of soldiers and merchants without special missionary effort on the part of any well-known leader. But once it became well established there, the all-important question soon arose what attitude would be adopted towards it by the Government.

At first the authorities in Rome seem to have had the same difficulty in distinguishing the new faith from Judaism as had been experienced by Pilate, Gallio, Felix, and Festus. It was apparently allowed to remain unmolested until in 51 a riot against the Christian teachers in the Jewish quarter induced Claudius to sweep all Jews, whatever their sect, out of the city. At least that is the inference we draw from the fact that Suetonius in his *Life of Claudius* tells us that the Jews were driven out at that time for rioting *impulsore Chresto*, 'at the instigation of Chrestus', which is probably Suetonius' effort to record the name of Christ. Six years later, so Tacitus tells us, Pomponia Graecina, the

wife of Aulus Plautius, had to appear before her husband's tribunal on a charge of superstition. She was acquitted, but passed the rest of her life in 'unbroken melancholy'. This is thought by many scholars to be a sufficient proof that she had embraced the Christian faith.

It is probable that long before this event Peter had arrived in Rome, and the fact that in writing to that city Paul expresses his unwillingness to build on another man's foundation suggests that Peter was already exercising apostolic functions there. In spite of his disclaimer Paul ensured for himself a visit to the capital by appealing to the Emperor's justice. He was allowed a considerable measure of liberty while awaiting his trial, and in characteristic fashion set about the proclamation of the gospel. If, as is generally believed, he was acquitted and made further missionary journeys, the Church must have been greatly strengthened on his return.

As a result, however, of its growing importance, the Christian community began to draw upon itself the dislike not only of Jews but also of Pagans. It was naturally difficult for them to understand the exclusiveness of a monotheist religion, and the secrecy that surrounded its ceremonies added to their suspicions. The mutual relations of married couples were often embittered when one of the partners was converted. People whose trade suffered by the spread of the new religion had a serious grudge against it. Social life was made very difficult when one's neighbour could not conform with the most ordinary convention on the ground that it implied the recognition of pagan deities.

This atmosphere of suspicion was adroitly used by Nero in the great disaster of 64. Fire had broken out in Rome, and disaffected citizens were beginning to say that the Emperor was himself responsible. In order to avoid losing the sympathy of the *plebs*, his last remaining supporters, Nero foisted the charge of arson on the Christians. Tacitus tells us that a '*multitudo ingens*' perished in the consequent slaughter. Nero naturally showed himself forward in the work, slaying his victims with barbaric cruelty and even using some of them as human torches to illuminate a fête

in the imperial gardens. Although Tacitus has a definite grudge against Nero, it is probable that his account is little, if at all, exaggerated. But we must remember that the suffering inflicted on the Christians would appear to the populace as a just punishment for a diabolical crime, and we cannot call it persecution in the technical sense.

Sometime during this period the Church suffered the greatest loss it had yet sustained in the death of the apostles Peter and Paul. The horror felt by the Christian society found expression in the lurid pictures of the Johannine Apocalypse, in which can be seen a wholly changed attitude towards the Roman State and a reflexion of the fear that the dead Nero might return to earth as Antichrist. But does this imply that the profession of Christianity had in itself become a crime, and that the State had now outlawed all Christians, holding them liable to punishment on this charge alone without the necessity of proving any further misdemeanour against them? That is a question by no means easy to answer.

It is generally agreed that Christianity was from this time forward regarded as a *religio illicita*. But this does not necessarily mean that it was an unlawful religion in the sense that there was a regulation against professing it. It need not mean more than that the Christian Church was an 'unincorporated society', that is, one which had not received the license or recognition of the State. Upon such a society suspicion would readily fall in any time of trouble. Tertullian, it is true, speaks of an *institutum Neronianum*, by which he seems to mean an edict of Nero putting all Christians to the ban. But there is no trace of any such edict having been published, and in the absence of evidence it is difficult to believe in the existence of such a document. Consequently many scholars have held that there was no actual outlawry of Christians until much later.

There is, however, one piece of evidence of a change of attitude on the part of the State at this time which needs careful consideration. The epistle known as 1 Peter draws a clear distinction between being punished for crimes against the laws and suffering 'for the Name'. If its contents may be trusted, it was written at the critical moment when

a change of policy on the part of the State seemed about to take place. And if the Petrine authorship can be accepted, it is clear that this change was threatened in the lifetime of S. Peter. On the whole we are inclined to think that this conclusion is correct. There is corroborative evidence for such a view. Tacitus after telling us of the charge of arson under which the Christians of Rome suffered, goes on to say that the people of this religion were regarded as 'enemies of the human race'. It looks therefore as if the hatred stirred up against the Christians on this occasion was such that they were henceforth reckoned as necessarily subverters of society. This may imply that without the publication of any edict they were placed beyond the pale, and were liable to police raids on any occasion. Generally, no doubt, when the first fury had spent itself they would be left alone, but the caprice of the mob, the jealousy of Jewish neighbours, the zeal of a magistrate or the will of the Emperor might at any time bring them before the courts; and then if they were unwilling to clear themselves by doing honour to the genius of the Emperor, which to them would be idolatrous worship, they could be summarily convicted as a common police measure. This was probably the precedent set by Nero which to some extent justifies the rhetorical phrase of Tertullian.

CHAPTER III

THE SUB-APOSTOLIC CHURCH

WHILE the Church was thus being ground between the upper and lower millstones of pagan hatred and Jewish intolerance, it might have been thought that its inner life and teaching would have been welded into a complete homogeneity. That, however, did not happen: then as always there was room for a wide divergence of opinion among the followers of Christ. Baur and the Tübingen scholars indeed have seen in the earliest history of the movement signs of an internecine struggle between the Pauline and Petrine interpretations of the gospel. According to their view the Christianity of the Twelve, with Peter at their head, remained always Judaistic. Against such an exclusivist Christianity the universalism of S. Paul waged a long conflict and ultimately triumphed. But the conquerors learnt something from the conquered and out of the combination of both schools arose the early 'Catholic' Church with its stereotyped organisation and worship.

This view is altogether too philosophical. It is built on the Hegelian system of thesis, antithesis, and synthesis. What substratum of historical truth it possesses we can judge from what we have already said about the existence and rapid decline of a Judaistic type of Christianity. There can be little doubt that although S. Peter was sometimes hesitant in his conduct he was really in agreement with S. Paul on fundamental principles, and even did much to open the way for the Apostle to the Gentiles. At whatever date we place 2 Peter it is probable that both in its acceptance of 'our beloved brother Paul' and in its caution against exaggeration of his teaching it expressed the characteristic mind of the 'Petrine' churches.

The trend of scholarship in late years has been to show

that instead of two clearly defined and opposed interpretations of the gospel such as were postulated by F. C. Baur
we should be prepared to recognise a wide variety. In the
New Testament itself we have not only a Pauline and a
Judaistic (Ep. James), but also a Johannine, and an Alexan-
drine (Ep. to the Hebrews) point of view, as well as a central
type of Christian teaching which can be deduced from the
Synoptics. It is sometimes suggested that in most of these
the influence of S. Paul can easily be seen, and Pfleiderer
was particularly fond of describing most early types of
Christian teaching as deutero-Pauline or diluted Paulinism.
But it is probable that the influence of S. Paul on the New
Testament writers has been exaggerated. We are apt to
regard his as the standard type because his writings have
come down to us in considerable bulk and occupy so large
a proportion of the New Testament. It would be interesting
to enquire whether it would not be better to accept S. Mark
and 1 Peter as representing the central core of Christian
teaching, and the rest as being individual interpretations of
it. In any case the responsible teachers whose writings are
gathered together into the canon of the New Testament
were certainly less uncompromising than some of their
followers on the extreme wings, and they certainly did not
find their interpretations of the Christ mutually incompatible.
Consciously or unconsciously their wise toleration made for
unity in diversity.

I

But in spite of this breadth of view there were certain
extremes that must at all costs be cut away. On the one
hand were the Nicolaitans rebuked by the author of the
Apocalypse, who were probably so called because they were
founded by a person named Nicolas (Irenaeus thought that
he was one of the seven 'Deacons', but it is impossible to be
sure). Of their doctrine we know nothing, but in practice
they obviously drove to excess the Pauline teaching of the
liberty accorded to Gentiles. This landed them in definite
immorality, and thus they show affinity with the libertines
castigated by Paul and Jude. It has been suggested that one

of their contentions was that Christians might be allowed to remain members of pagan clubs. It is possible that they later developed into a Gnostic sect.

At the other extreme was the Judaic school of the Ebionites. The name, meaning 'poor', has been variously derived from Ebion (the supposed founder), from our Lord's blessing upon the poor in spirit, from their enemies' gibes at their poverty in doctrine, and from their renunciation of worldly wealth. However this may be, their distinguishing tenet was a rejection of the divine sonship of Jesus. While they accepted Him as Messiah, they believed Him to be the son of Joseph and Mary upon whom the Spirit of Jehovah descended at His baptism, making Him the greatest of the prophets but not giving Him authority to abrogate the Law. These Ebionites seem to have used out of Christian writings only the Gospel of Matthew, and they showed themselves the strongest opponents of Paulinism. They appear to have been divided into two classes, one of which adopted a literal (Pharisaic) and the other an allegorical (Essene) view of the Law.

A third widely prevalent type of heretical thought was that of Docetism (from the Greek verb *dokein*, to seem). The Docetics taught that while Jesus was truly God His appearance as man was merely phantasmal. It is against such a view that the Johannine gospel and epistles emphasise over and over again the flesh-and-blood reality of the incarnate Son of God. Jerome believed that the Fourth Gospel was definitely written against the heretic Cerinthus, whose appearance in the baths at Ephesus is said to have caused a precipitate flight on the part of S. John. This Cerinthus seems to have stood midway between the last two types. Hort thought him to be the first clear example of the combination of Christianity, Judaism and Gnosticism. But these early doctrinal differences are extremely hard to define exactly. It is quite impossible to place accurately the various heresies that sprang up in S. Paul's churches after the circumcision controversy was over. In Colossians ii and the Pastorals it looks as if Judaism had taken to philosophy in order to commend itself to Western minds, and no doubt

Christianity found itself mixed with these elements in varying degrees.

Two examples of this combination call for special mention. The first is that of the Elkesaites. The name is probably derived from the *Book of the Hidden Power*, claiming to give a revelation direct from the Son of God. It appeared in Rome about A.D. 220, but professed to date from the first century. It produced a school rather than a sect, which stood for a more thorough-going Ebionism. Jesus, the Messiah, was a reincarnation of Adam, and as further reincarnations were possible Christianity could not be looked upon as the final religion. The Elkesaites rejected sacrifices, but they retained much of Judaism, including circumcision, the Sabbath, and purificatory ablutions; and together with this they incorporated a certain amount of astrology and magic. They are said to have originated in Parthia during the reign of Trajan. The chief authority for our knowledge of them is the *Philosophumena* of Hippolytus, a work that was discovered on Mt. Athos in 1842 and published in 1851.

The second example of this kind of teaching finds itself reflected in the *Clementine Homilies*. It is set in the framework of a romance narrating how a certain Roman, named Clement, wandered in search of lost members of his family. In the course of this we are given an account of some disputations of S. Peter with Simon Magus, under whose figure are thinly disguised the features of the Apostle Paul. Simon Magus is made the representative of a Gentile type of Gnosticism. Peter, who of course is victorious in the argument, represents a modified Ebionism. By him circumcision is given up, but Christianity is still made to appear as a mere republication of the old religion. Our present Greek form of the Homilies dates from the end of the third century, but the type of thought represented goes back much earlier.

The following tentative table may help to make a little clearer the probable connection between these heresies.

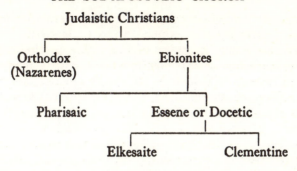

II

Against the unorthodox tendencies of such writings as have been mentioned above we should set nearly all the documents that have now been gathered together into our New Testament. But as these fall outside the scope of the present study, we content ourselves with a description of the two non-canonical writings that are generally agreed to belong to the first century. The first is the Epistle usually known as *1 Clement*, which can reasonably be placed about A.D. 96. It is a letter apparently drafted by the Roman Bishop (although there is no mention of him) and sent in the name of the whole Church of Rome to the Church of Corinth when some of the younger members of the latter community had cast off the authority of their elders and had started separate Eucharists of their own. Gwatkin speaks very slightingly of the Christian literature of the sub-apostolic age, but such strictures are certainly not deserved by this gentle but virile exhortation to unity. The writer has no diffidence as to the position of his own circle. 'If any be disobedient to the words that God hath spoken by us, let them know that they will be guilty of a serious fault. . . . Ye will afford us joy and gladness, if ye obey the advice which by the Holy Spirit we have written unto you.' The principle of authority in the Church is strongly emphasised in the beautiful closing prayer, and the establishment of the ministry is traced back through the apostles to Christ and God. The need for unity is based not only upon the evangelical teaching but also upon the peace of God as

manifested in the order of nature, and a particular point is made of the disorder which internal disturbances bring into the customary bestowal of hospitality by the members of one church upon visitors from another. The practical and orderly spirit that breathes in the whole letter is well seen in the exhortation, 'Let us venerate our rulers. Let us do honour to the older men. Let us bring up our young men in the fear of God', and in the terser phrase, 'Love has no parties'. It is clear that in the opinion of the writer unity and authority are two essential notes of the Church, but it does not appear that he claims any special authority for his own local church.

The only other book of this period is a kind of manual for communicants and clergy, called the *Didache*, or Teaching of the Twelve Apostles. This most interesting specimen of early Christian literature was discovered in 1875 and published in 1883, when it seemed likely to revolutionise beliefs hitherto held with regard to the early history of the ministry. Its date has been extraordinarily difficult to fix. Certainly it does not come, as it claims, from the apostles. and a measure of suspicion naturally attaches to it from the start. Nevertheless it reveals what seems like so primitive a condition of affairs in the Church that most modern scholars attribute it to the end of the first century. Dr. Bigg, however, thought it deliberately archaic, and believed that it actually belonged to the fourth century, being a stern Montanist reaction to the persecution of Julian. More temperately, but still in general agreement with him, Dr. Armitage Robinson believed that it could not be earlier than late second century. He pointed out that the Jewish document on the 'Two Ways', which forms the first part of the book, is used elsewhere in early Christian literature. Its original form, he said, is to be found in the Epistle of Barnabas from which it was taken by the author of the *Didache*. These views have not found general acceptance, and those scholars who believe that the conditions portrayed in the *Didache* are too primitive even for the end of the first century and who are nevertheless unwilling to give it a still earlier date, get over the discrepancy by supposing that it belongs to some backward

church in a remote situation, Syria being the most favoured place of origin. Recently, however, Canon Streeter has been bold enough to put forward a suggestion that instead of coming from any remote spot, it actually belongs to, and faithfully reflects the conditions of, the second great centre of Christianity and the fount of its missionary enterprise, namely Antioch itself. The effect of this suggestion on the * reconstruction of the early history of the ministry we must consider later; for the present we must content ourselves with giving some account of the contents of this enigmatic document.

The part of it taken up by the Two Ways describes the various moral conduct that leads either to death or to life. In this section the most interesting feature is the stress laid on the primitive penitential system. 'Thou shalt confess thy transgression in church, and shalt not come to thy prayer in an evil conscience.' The second section deals with asceticism, allowing different degrees of Christian attainment to be attempted. 'If thou canst bear the whole yoke of the Lord, thou shalt be perfect; but if thou canst not, do what thou canst.' This is the first instance of the recognition of a double standard in Christian ethics, and it was pregnant with great issues.

The same section deals also with the sacrament of baptism, allowing threefold aspersion where there is not enough water for the more regular immersion. Directions are given for the Eucharist, and here it is a nice question whether the love-feast or Agape is included or not. Most important of all, there is much information on the ministry, though what precisely it imports is still a matter of discussion. Christian fasts are to be observed on Wednesdays and Fridays, not on the Thursdays and Saturdays of the Jewish hypocrites.

The Eucharist is to be confined to the baptised, and is to be celebrated with the beautiful prayer: 'As this bread that is broken was scattered upon the mountains, and was gathered together and became one, so let Thy Church be gathered together from the ends of the earth into Thy kingdom.' Beyond such stereotyped prayers for the use of

the congregation, prophets are to be allowed the right of extemporisation.

Apostles and prophets appear to wander from one community to another, and there are careful regulations to prevent unworthy members of their order from imposing upon the hospitality of their hearers. 'Let every apostle that cometh unto you be received as the Lord. And he shall stay one day, and if need be the next also, but if he stay three, he is a false prophet. And when the apostle goeth forth, let him take nothing save bread, till he reach his lodging, but if he ask money, he is a false prophet. . . . And no prophet that orders a table in the Spirit shall eat of it, else he is a false prophet.' On the other hand, the prophets are 'your high priests', to whom first-fruits are to be paid, and what they say in the Spirit is not to be criticised by the ordinary Christian. The whole book closes with an exhortation to prepare for the coming of the Lord.

III

It was on our views as to the development of the clerical office that the influence of the *Didache* seemed likely to be most profound. What we want to know is precisely how the threefold ministry of bishops, priests and deacons came into being, and how arose the monarchical episcopate or the sole rule of a single bishop over each area.

Two opposed theories on this subject have been widely held. According to one the Church arranged for its own ministry, each local community electing its own officers as need appeared, arranging their functions and appointing them democratically, so to speak, from below. According to the other view the officers were appointed from above, the apostles having been set in authority by Christ Himself, and priests and deacons being ordained by the apostles or by the bishops whom they had appointed to succeed them. To the first view one might answer that there is no evidence of a self-governing power in the local community. Nearly every epistle we have in the New Testament shows how anxious were the leaders to maintain the close unity of all in one body, openly exercising their own authority where neces-

sary to that end. Unity and authority, as we have seen, were the two most characteristic notes of the primitive Church. To the second theory a great difficulty is presented by the fact that in the New Testament the terms bishop and presbyter seem interchangeable, nor is there anything to show how the former term came to be used for an office that had taken on apostolic functions.

There is, however, a third view of the origin of the ministry sometimes held, namely, that in the beginning men were called to the exercise of spiritual ministries by no other voice than that of the Spirit of God speaking in their own conscience. It was to this that the *Didache* seemed to lend unexpected support.

Enough has already been quoted from that document to show how high an opinion was held by its author of the position of apostles and prophets. With the above passages should be compared the following: 'Elect therefore for yourselves bishops and deacons worthy of the Lord, men meek and not covetous, and true and approved: for they also minister unto you the ministry of the prophets and teachers. Therefore despise them not, for these are they which are honoured of you with the prophets and teachers.' This presumably reflects a state of things in which the ministry of bishops and deacons has not yet as much prestige in the popular estimation as that of the prophets and teachers.

Professor Harnack, believing that it is in the light of such passages that we should interpret the two well-known lists given by S. Paul (1 Cor. xii 28 ff, Eph. iv 11 ff), evolved the following theory as to the beginnings of the ministry: 1, that in the Church of the first century a clear distinction was drawn between the ministry of preaching and that of administration; 2, that the former was filled by apostles, prophets and teachers, the latter by bishops and deacons; 3, that the former had received a definite gift from God (hence called a 'charismatic' ministry), while the latter was of merely human appointment; 4, that the former exercised a universal office, travelling from one community to another, while the latter had no authority outside the local

church to which it had been appointed; 5, that the former class was originally much the more important of the two, but that in the *Didache* we have evidence of a transition period in which the local ministry is beginning to succeed to the functions and authority of the charismatic ministry.

In criticism of this simple and clear-cut theory several things may be said. In the first place the lists in S. Paul do not look in the least like enumerations of different offices; they are rather lists of different gifts which the various members of the community may bring to the service of the whole body, and there seems no reason why one person should not perform more than one of the functions mentioned. Secondly, there is no hint in the New Testament that a gift for teaching implied any ministerial authority. Thirdly, there is no distinction drawn in the scriptures between a charismatic and an ordained ministry: in the Pastorals authority conveyed through the laying on of hands is itself described as a 'charisma'. And lastly, although it is true that from the beginning each local community had its own officers and that some apostles and prophets travelled about from place to place and won recognition everywhere, yet there is nothing to show that all ministry was not regarded from the first as a gift to the whole Church.

We are constrained then to conclude that the theory of a primitive charismatic ministry gradually displaced by an ordained ministry cannot be proved, at least in so far as it applies to the universal Church. Canon Streeter, realising this, has recently put forward the ingenious theory that local churches may have differed very considerably from each other in their method of administration. A foretaste of the later monarchical episcopate he would see in the position held by S. James at Jerusalem and by S. John at Ephesus. An example of a church governed by a college of presbyter-bishops he would see in Rome, for even when that church wrote officially to its sister community at Corinth, it did not mention the name of a bishop. It is possible too that in Alexandria the body of presbyters had more influence than they exercised in other churches. All these ultimately conformed to the common episcopal pattern, and an illustra-

tion of the way in which the process of change might go on is found in the story of the church of Antioch. The key-document for this story Canon Streeter finds in the *Didache*, which is found to fit in between the Acts and the letters of Ignatius (*c*. A.D. 112). In Acts we find Antioch under the dominance of a body of prophets. In the *Didache* we find the bishops and deacons just coming into recognition and the faithful exhorted not to despise them 'for they also minister unto you the ministry of the prophets and teachers'. In Ignatius, as we shall see later, we find a bishop who is himself a prophet doing everything he possibly can to stress the importance of the episcopal office.

This of course is extraordinarily interesting, but it seems hazardous both in its history of the ministry at Antioch and in its theory of variety in the Church at large. As for the first, we have already seen how uncertain is the date of the *Didache*, and in regard to Ignatius we confess that his injunctions read more like an effort to persuade the faithful to rally round an old and tried institution than an attempt to foist upon them something new. As for the second, we need not imagine that everything was managed in precisely the same way in all the churches, but it is very difficult to think that there would be a wide and fundamental divergence in so important a matter as that of organisation. The need for unity and for the maintenance of authority would make a similarity in office imperative.

For ourselves we regard it as extremely important to recognise the universal authority given to the apostles. It is possible that after the crucifixion they held themselves to have succeeded to the office of Jesus as Chief Shepherd or *episcopus* (cf. the Fourth Gospel and 1 Peter). In any case they certainly claimed and exercised the supreme office in the universal Church, the position of James at Jerusalem being easily conceded to a brother of the Lord. In facing their great task they had two main responsibilities, to build up the New Israel and to spread the gospel throughout the world. In the latter everyone would lend a hand, especially those who had particular ability as evangelists and teachers. The prophets were important not as exercising a particular

authority but as giving clear intimations of the divine will
and declaring the oracles of God.

In fulfilment of their responsibility for building up the
New Israel the apostles would naturally arrange the new
organisation on the lines of the old. Judaism had its main
centres of organisation in the Great Synagogue or Sanhe-
drin at Jerusalem and in a host of local synagogues scattered
throughout the Jewish world. Both types of synagogue were
managed by a small central committee with a number of
assistants. It was from this and not from any Greek source
that the Christian organisation was borrowed.

The deacons of the Christian Church, whether dating
from the Seven of *Acts* or an independent creation, were the
usual assistants who acted as almoners in the synagogue.

The elders appointed by S. Paul in all his churches
corresponded to the usual managing committee of the local
synagogue. It is possible that they may have represented
an 'undifferentiated ministry'—that is to say, they may
have been a committee of presbyter-bishops. Many circumstances, however, would combine to make one of them
exercise the presidency over the rest. It would be natural
* that one member only should preside at the Eucharist.
Correspondence with other churches must go through the
hands of one only. A head of the committee might be
purposely chosen, as in the Jewish synagogue. Or one of
them might be appointed as his delegate by the apostolic
founder. Or finally the apostle might leave one of his own
friends to take charge in his absence. By such means the
local church would never be left without a responsible
shepherd and the apostolic authority would be continued.

We have seen that already by the end of the reign of
Nero the State had settled down to an attitude of suspicion
towards the Church. This of course does not mean that
persecution was always raging, but that it might burst out
at any opportunity. For the sake of completeness we may
now sketch the relations of Church and State during the
remainder of the first century. For the reign of Vespasian
there is really no evidence. His son Titus at least knew the
difference between Jew and Christian, and at the siege of

Jerusalem set himself to wipe out the headquarters of both. On the other hand, the gloomy and suspicious tyrant Domitian seems not to have had a very clear idea of the nature of Christianity. It is said that the grandchildren of Jude, the Lord's brother, were brought before him on the ground that they claimed to be the descendants of David, and that they might therefore presume to demand the sovereignty of Judea. But when they explained that they aspired to no kingdom of this world, being only small yeoman farmers, and showed him their horny hands in proof, he 'treated them as simpletons with contempt, and commanded them to be dismissed'.

This Domitian is generally reckoned among the persecutors of Christianity. But the evidence is not altogether clear. It is known that when his own cousin, Flavius Clemens, was accused before him of 'atheism', he only waited for the end of his consulship before putting him to death. On the same charge was banished Clement's widow, Domitilla. As the latter's catacomb became a favourite burying-place for Christians, it has been concluded that their 'atheism' was really Christianity. It is possible that the same may be said of the other Consul who suffered the extreme penalty during his reign, Manlius Acilius Glabrio. But it has been objected that these were merely judicial murders intended to remove possible claimants to the imperial dignity. On the other hand *I Clement*, which was probably written about this time, speaks of present troubles, and a letter of the younger Pliny written about 112 speaks of Christians who had surrendered their religion twenty years before. This may be taken to substantiate the charge against Domitian as a persecutor. It is probable that the apocalyptic denunciations that had been written against Nero were now collected and re-edited in that indictment of the Roman government which we know as the Apocalypse of S. John the Divine.

CHAPTER IV

ATTACK AND DEFENCE

BY the end of the first century Christianity had spread far and wide through the Empire. At this time it had no obvious centre. Jerusalem had been destroyed and Antioch, although for a time the base of missionary activity, had never taken its place. Rome, as the imperial capital, was already rising to prominence among Christians, but it had not yet the same historic claim on their veneration as either Jerusalem or Antioch. The Church was thus in outward appearance a somewhat amorphous association, held together by its ministry. As its religion was not recognised by the State, it tended to take on something of the character of a secret society. Although the mere fact that it was not officially recognised was not enough of itself to set the police in action against it, yet many circumstances as we have seen might combine to provoke an attack. Above everything had to be considered the caprice or policy of the reigning emperor. In the first half of the second century we must notice the attitude of three remarkable rulers.

I

Trajan (98–117) was a soldier who had pushed the confines of empire beyond their former limits to the farther side of Dacia, Armenia, and Assyria. He had also inflicted a thorough defeat upon the Parthians. As a soldier he was not likely to be very partial to a class of people who had no great love for military service and were sometimes definitely opposed to it. Also he was a capable administrator with such a horror of societies, secret and other, that he had even refused permission for a fire brigade. Moreover, the Christians could not, like the Jews, claim any special consideration on the ground that they were a national cult of a peculiar exclusiveness. Trajan's attitude was therefore one of oppo-

sition. But was it worth while proceeding to extremes? That is the question that was put to him by the younger Pliny whom he had sent as governor to Bithynia in A.D. 110.

Pliny had found that the 'insanity' of Christianity had infected 'many of all ages and all ranks', that the temples were almost deserted and that consequently fodder for sacrificial animals was fast becoming unsaleable. This had surprised him. He had taken measures to bring delinquents to order. Some had been tried in court, some who had refused to sacrifice had been executed, some who were Romans had been marked down to be sent for trial to the capital, and two women had been examined under torture. These measures were proving effective; pagan worship was once more being restored; many had been won back to the old religion, and more might follow if opportunity were allowed.

This is a very illuminating document. It shows how much could go on in the name of justice without a responsible statesman knowing anything very precise about it. Pliny is aware that Christians are brought to trial, but he has never been present at such a trial. He is very anxious to humour the well-known dislike for societies manifested by the Emperor, but in doing so he has no desire to bring a hornets' nest about his ears and set his province in an uproar. In his dilemma he has very wisely thrown the responsibility on the Emperor. Trajan's reply is temperate and statesmanlike. After saying that in such matters it is impossible to lày down a hard-and-fast line, he goes on: 'They are not to be sought out; but if they are accused and convicted, they should be punished, but on the understanding that the man who denies that he is a Christian and gives proof of his sincerity by offering prayer to our gods, however much he has been suspected in the past, shall be pardoned on his repentance.' To this endorsement of Pliny's desire for leniency he adds a definite instruction that anonymous accusations are not to be received.

It is a pity that in a reign marked by so much reasonableness we should have to record two important martyrdoms. One was that of Simeon, the son of Cleopas, who had succeeded James as Bishop of Jerusalem. The other was

that of Ignatius, Bishop of Antioch. This hero of the faith was taken to Rome to perish in the arena. On his way thither he wrote seven letters to various churches and to Polycarp which have a special bearing on the history of the ministry. Nearly all of them insist in the strongest possible terms on the importance of the threefold ministry of bishop, priest and deacon. The bishop is the bulwark of unity against the disruptive forces of persecution: in each community there is only one bishop, and the faithful will know that they are helping to maintain the integrity of the Church if they keep in submission to him. This is the first clear emergence of what is known as the 'monarchical episcopate'. As we have already seen there is some doubt whether Ignatius is here seeking to enforce a new system or laying stress on an old one. As it seems unlikely that in a moment of such extreme peril any responsible leader would wish to commend untried experiments, we are inclined to the view that mon-episcopacy was already the custom and that the Bishop of Antioch is simply trying to make the faithful rally round their leaders at a time when steadiness was the most vital need of the Christian society. For the rest it must be said that he was the first example of that intransigent spirit which actually sought death. 'The nearer the sword, the nearer God', was his motto. He would permit no friendly intervention on his behalf, though it might apparently have been successful. 'I write to all the churches and charge them all to know that I die willingly for God, if you hinder not. I entreat you, do not unseasonably befriend me. Suffer me to belong to the wild beasts, through whom I may attain to God. I am God's grain, and I am ground by the teeth of wild beasts, that I may be found pure bread. Rather entice the wild beasts to become my tomb, and to leave naught of my body, that I may not, when I have fallen asleep, prove a burden to any man.'

The next Emperor, Hadrian (117–138), realised Rome's need of peace, and tried to secure it by giving up the newly conquered territory. He would have succeeded but for the last great revolt of the Jews under Bar-Cochba in 132. With immense difficulty and equal severity Hadrian quelled

the disturbance. By the end of the three years' struggle the site of the Temple had been defiled, Jerusalem had been totally destroyed, and its place was taken by a new pagan city, Aelia Capitolina, which a Jew might only approach under pain of death.

Hadrian was a man of many gifts and diverse interests. This fact, together with a certain mildness in his disposition, led to a new departure in Christian literature, an apology for the faith directed to the Emperor himself. How far the effort of Quadratus affected Hadrian's attitude we do not know, but what that attitude was comes out clearly in his rescript addressed to Minucius Fundanus, the new pro-consul of Asia. The ease with which the charge of Christianity brought punishment upon its victim had led to its use against quite good pagans whose removal was desired by unscrupulous foes. An enquiry on the subject had been addressed to the Emperor by Minucius' predecessor. Hadrian wished to stop the abuse and wrote apparently to reaffirm the principles laid down by Trajan. Anonymous accusations were not to be received. But if it were proved that the accused did 'anything contrary to the laws' they were to receive penalties 'in accordance with their offences'. At the same time merely libellous accusations were to be punished. This had the beneficial effect of preserving the Christians from the capricious incidence of mob law. That is not to say that it prevented persecution altogether. There were still martyrs, but the only one whose name has come down to us is Telesphorus, Bishop of Rome.

The policy of Trajan was carried out in the next reign also, that of Antoninus Pius (138–161). We have details of more martyrdoms this time. The apologist Justin mentions three, Ptolemy, Livius, and another, who were summarily executed on the mere confession of adherence to Christ. And now occurs the most famous of all, that of the aged Polycarp, Bishop of Smyrna. He was one of the last of the immediate disciples of the apostles and had known S. John. He had been the recipient of one of the letters from Ignatius, who speaks of his 'blameless face' but gives him plenty of good advice. The manner in which he met his end, together

with the sufferings of several others, especially the 'most noble youth' Germanicus, is narrated in the very beautiful letter from his own church of Smyrna to the church of Philomelium 'and all other parts of the Catholic Church'. A certain Phrygian, named Quintus, who had been forward in challenging notice, had given way before the final trial, but Polycarp remained unmoved at his post until, yielding to the desires of his friends, he retired to a neighbouring farm. There at night his pillow suddenly seemed to catch fire beneath his head, and this he interpreted as a sign of his approaching end. However, being pursued, he went still further into the country; but when he was at last discovered, he refused to flee a third time, ordered a meal for his captors, and begged only an hour's grace for prayer. On his way he was met by two officers who advised him to say 'Lord Caesar' and to sacrifice, and on his refusal thrust him so violently from their chariot as to graze his leg. Arrived at the tribunal, he was advised by the proconsul to have regard to his grey hairs and commanded to deny Christ. Then came the wonderful reply, 'Eighty and six years have I served Him and He did me no wrong, how shall I blaspheme my King who has saved me?' Further persuasion proving useless, the herald proclaimed that Polycarp confessed himself a Christian. The crowd thereupon demanded that he should be thrown to the lion. But that being refused on the ground that the games were over, they demanded death by burning. The flames licked round the stake in a hollow circle, not touching the body. At last, losing patience, the executioner plunged his sword into his victim, and so great a quantity of blood gushed forth as to extinguish the fire. The Jews, who had been gloating over the spectacle, urged that the body should not be given up 'lest the Christians, abandoning Him that was crucified, should begin to worship this one . . . not knowing that we can never abandon Christ . . . nor worship any other. For Him we worship as the Son of God; but the martyrs we deservedly love as the disciples and imitators of our Lord . . . of whom may we only become true associates and fellow-disciples'.

II

The somewhat milder attitude towards the Church which formed the policy of the Emperors during the first half of the second century induced some of the ablest Christian leaders to produce a crop of apologies in order to get their position better understood by the intelligent section of society. The writers of these tractates, unlike the Apostolic Fathers, were trained philosophers and rhetoricians, who, not content with a merely negative defence against the calumnies of their enemies, developed a positive method and tried to show that Christianity was in point of fact the most intelligent and intelligible religion that was anywhere practised. In thus trying to fit their belief into the moulds of the best contemporary thought they actually produced the first essays in scientific theology which had yet arisen out of the Christian faith. Their apologies took three different forms. First there was the open letter addressed to the Emperor, which was certainly read by the public, even if it never met the eye of the man for whom it was written. Secondly there were appeals to the public at large, like the *Address to the Greeks* of Irenaeus. And thirdly there were apologies addressed to some individual of less exalted rank than the Emperor. It must be remembered that the Christian apologist was still fighting on two fronts. He must defend his religion not only against the pagan but also against the Jew. Consequently we find that some apologies are intended for the one and some for the other, while a third class can be described as mixed, since it deals with the superiority of Christianity to both the others at once.

The first apologist was Quadratus, who, as already mentioned, addressed himself to the Emperor Hadrian. His work has come down to us only in a fragment preserved by Eusebius. Who he was we do not know for certain. There are references to a Quadratus who was Bishop of Athens and did good work there by recalling the church of the city from its lapse in zeal, and also to a Quadratus who was a missionary and prophet in Asia; but whether either of them is to be identified with the apologist is not clear. The tantali-

singly short extract in Eusebius simply tells us that some of those upon whom the Lord worked His miracles of healing were still alive in the writer's day. 'They remained living a long time, not only while our Lord was on earth, but likewise when He had left the earth. So that some of them have also lived to our own times.' The line of argument in this earliest apology thus seems to have been that the Christian miracles were superior to those of the pagan magicians.

The next writer of this class was Aristides, who wrote either in the reign of Hadrian or in that of Antoninus Pius. He was a philosophically minded Greek, and delighted to argue from natural religion to a belief in one God. He divides mankind into four classes: Barbarians, Greeks, Jews, and Christians. The errors of the first are easily exposed. The second, in spite of their undoubted culture and philosophy, have missed the way and gone astray after idols. The third, in spite of much theological and moral merit, have failed of the full revelation. The supreme excellence of the belief held among the last is evidenced by their lofty ethical code and particularly by their mutual love and self-denial for the good of each other. The Greek text of this work lies embedded in the curious story of Barlaam and Josaphat (a name that conceals the identity of the Buddha), but its modern study dates from the discovery by Dr. Rendel Harris in 1889 of the Syriac version in the S. Catherine monastery on Mt. Sinai.

Aristides belonged to the school of Athens. The same university produced another and more important philosopher-apologist in the person of Justin Martyr. Justin was a native of Neapolis in Palestine. His early passion for truth drove him from the Stoics, who denied the necessity of a knowledge of God, to the Peripatetics, who were anxious only about their fees, thence to the Pythagoreans, who over-estimated the value of intellectual knowledge, and so to the Platonists, who at last seemed likely to set him on the way of mystical attainment. But now, about 133, at Ephesus he was much stirred by the heroic fortitude of Christians under persecution, and an opportune conversation with a mysterious old man turned him from Plato to Christ. In spite of his con-

version Justin remained a philosopher to the end, not even abandoning his philosopher's cloak. He set up a sort of school in Rome and used metaphysics to explain the practical truths of Christianity. To him, as to the rest of these Christian scholars, religion was not only a redemption from sin but also an enlightenment from ignorance. The Prophet of Nazareth was not only the human Jesus but also the Divine Logos, Word and Reason, which had sown its seed even in the hearts of the pre-Christian patriarchs and philosophers. Truth was one, and proceeded from the same source whether it was expressed by Moses or by Heracleitus. 'So even if they are accounted atheists, those who lived with Reason are still Christians.'

The two books of Justin that have come down to us are his *Apology*, with its later supplement, addressed to Antoninus Pius, and his *Dialogue with Trypho*. The latter was a courteous Jew, returning from the fatal Jewish War, with whom Justin met and argued at Ephesus soon after his conversion. These books are of the greatest value for the study of the early development of Christian doctrine, and they also give many interesting details of Christian life and worship. But for our present purpose it is enough to notice that in his *Apology* Justin goes straight to the essential point, which was that the State had no right to punish except for proved crimes. Yet what actually happens? 'You do not examine charges, but, driven by unreasoning passion and scourge of evil demons, you punish without investigation or consideration.' If you did examine, he continues, you would find that these alleged crimes are non-existent. Christians are simply, like Socrates, putting a stop to the immoralities which these same demons (whom you call your gods) introduced into the world, and the vengeance which the demons wreaked on Socrates they are like now to bring on the Christians. Justin thus rounds upon the enemy by asserting that it is their own demon-gods who are the source both of all evil in the world and of strife (which he does not seek to disguise) in the Church. He even accuses the demons of having for their own purposes imitated the Christian sacraments, as witness the bread and water which play an

important part in the ceremonies of Mithraism. This is a type of argument which was to serve Christian apologists until quite recent times.

This ends the list of the first series of apologists; but there are two other specimens of Christian literature which fall to be considered in this period. The first is the *Epistle of Barnabas*, which is a somewhat curious effort to defend Christianity against Judaism. It has been thought by many ancient and modern scholars to be the work of the Barnabas who was a companion of S. Paul, and even Lightfoot placed it soon after the fall of Jerusalem in A.D. 70. But it is more probable that it belongs to the reign of Hadrian and the second Jewish War. It contains the Judaic document on the Two Ways already noticed in connexion with the *Didache*. The more original portion of the manuscript is taken up with the thesis that the Jews have all along mistaken the purport of their own Law, which was never meant to be taken literally but as a foreshadowing in every detail of the coming of Christ. This view is supported by the most extraordinary allegorical interpretations. Thus Abraham was commanded to circumcise 318 men because the Greek letters for those numerals stand for the name of Jesus (IH) and the sign of the cross (T). Also we here get some of those quaint analogies from a grossly misunderstood natural world which are repeated later in the medieval bestiaries. The hare, for instance, is a warning against lust, because it has as many places of conception as it has years to its age. The hyena is similarly unclean since it changes its sex at will. With this very doubtful method of combating Judaism should be compared the argument of S. Paul that the Law was a tutor to bring men to Christ and that of the *Epistle to the Hebrews* that the Law, while having a real truth of its own, was yet no more than the shadow cast by an eternal reality. The argument of Barnabas shows a distinctly worse feeling. The climax, as we shall see, was reached in Gnosticism, which taught that the God of the Old Testament was opposed to the New Testament God, and which consequently proposed to dispense with the Old Testament altogether.

The other book to be mentioned here was written about A.D. 150, although some parts of it may perhaps go back to the time of Trajan. It is the famous *Shepherd of Hermas*, a valuable specimen of Christian prophecy. Together with the *Epistle of Barnabas* it enjoyed great veneration in the early Church, and long struggled for a place in the canon. In fact both writings are to be found as part of the New Testament in the *Codex Sinaiticus*. Hermas appears to have been a freedman, who according to the Muratorian Canon *
lived at Rome and was brother to Pius, the bishop there. But the fact that the book is an allegory comparable to the *Pilgrim's Progress*—in fact the first Christian Romance— makes it difficult to decide whether autobiographical details contained in the narrative are fact or fiction. In the story Hermas was sold as a slave to a Christian lady named Rhoda, a mistress for whom he came to have a great regard. In his book he gives us five Visions, twelve Commandments, and ten Parables. The Shepherd is the Angel of Repentance, who appears in the fifth vision and dictates most of the rest of the book. The work differs from those we have been discussing in that it is addressed wholly to Christians. It is in fact a close examination of the moral state of the Church. The writer includes himself among the sinful and is rebuked in the opening vision for a sinful thought. This shows how deep the examination is going. But Hermas has not only thought evil, he is also reproved for not bringing up his family more strictly. If there was such evil in his own life no class in the Church was without its failings. Even the clergy were not exempt: the deacons were known to have appropriated funds given to them for charitable purposes, and the priests were sometimes proud and even negligent. Comparative immunity from persecution had evidently resulted in a considerable amount of moral slackness. Nevertheless Hermas' message is one of comfort. Sinners are not to despair because they fear that there is no forgiveness for sins committed after baptism. It has been revealed to the writer that one forgiveness will be shown, one act of repentance be allowed to be effective. But the opportunity will only be given once; the occasion is on them now and they

must seize it straightway. Yet they must realise that such a state of penitence is not easily achieved. 'Thinkest thou then that the sins of those who repent are straightway remitted? By no means; but he who repenteth must vex his soul, and humble himself mightily in all his conduct and be afflicted in all manner of affliction; and if he bear the afflictions that come upon him, He who created and empowered all things shall certainly be moved to compassion and give him healing.'

Hermas' theology was undeveloped, and his ideas on the Trinity were expressed with remarkable crudity. He suggests that the divine Being is only completed by the adoption of Jesus into the Godhead, and he actually speaks of the Holy Spirit as 'Son of God'. Perhaps he had never had occasion to think out his theology, inasmuch as doctrinal error was not rampant in his time. At least he shows no knowledge of any well-defined heretical system. That gap, however, in the list of the Church's misfortunes was already being filled.

CHAPTER V

GNOSTICISM

GNOSTICISM is a vague term covering a wide range of ideas. By derivation (*gnosis* = knowledge) it implies the pursuit of esoteric truth: common people knew the ordinary facts of religion, the wise had much private information that lifted them out of the ranks of the vulgar. This esoteric knowledge claimed to be scientific and cosmological as well as theological. We can thus understand why Harnack saw in it an 'acute Hellenisation of Christianity'. But in point of fact it was strongly dualist, combining a physical with a moral dualism, and its type of thought was far more Oriental than Greek. As a kind of theosophy it had affected most of the religions into the midst of which Christianity was born. It is therefore customary to trace Gnostic influence in many of the various types of heretical thought that arose around the cradle of the Christian faith. This is probably correct, although the latest English authority on the subject, Professor Burkitt, refuses to give the name of Gnosticism to any but the great outstanding systems that were known by that name in the second century. In his view, as in that of Dr. Schweitzer, Gnosticism was an effort to find a substitute for that apocalyptic hope of an immediate return of Christ which was now felt to be illusory. It was an attempt to explain on rational grounds how men came from God and can return to Him without cataclysm.

The point common to orthodox Christianity and Gnosticism was thus belief in a redemption through Christ. But the Gnostics thought the ordinary facts of the life of Christ as taught in the Church were only the vulgar conceptions that concealed the truth. Their own dualism precluded any belief that God could really become man.

In fact that was the real difficulty; granted both a spiritual and a material universe, how could the one be the source of the other? Not by direct contact, that was evident; for the one was altogether good while the other was altogether evil. Therefore between God, who is absolute spirit, and man, who is of the earth earthy, there must be a number of gradations in being, becoming less spiritual and more material as the steps descend from the higher to the lower level.

Like some theosophists of the present day, people with such views found no great difficulty in remaining within the Church. After all, they were denying no Christian teaching, only giving it a more scientific explanation. But in reality they had little in common with the Church of their day. Their aim was intellectual enlightenment rather than moral life; their desire freedom from the bondage of matter rather than from the corruption of sin; their system a philosophy rather than a religion. Ultimately they realised the incompatibility of their teaching with that of the Church, and began to form sects of their own.

According to our sympathies we shall judge them either as great Christian intellectualists born before their time, the only ones to encourage scientific research among a class of people by whom the wisdom of this world was too little valued, or as mere dreamers following not the exact methods of scientific enquiry but the vague speculations of a pseudo-scientific curiosity. In common fairness we shall remember that we know them less through their own writings than through the attacks of the orthodox Fathers, and that these latter were prone to confuse all heresies in a general and somewhat indiscriminate condemnation, and to attribute to the leaders the more extreme opinions and manifest errors of their disciples.

I

We may distinguish three main types of Gnosticism. The earliest appeared in Syria, where according to tradition the whole business began at Samaria with the teaching of Simon Magus. From the *Acts* we know that this Simon was

worshipped as being himself 'the great Power of God', which appears to imply a kind of rival Samaritan incarnation to that of the Judean Christ. From other sources we learn that Simon taught that this Power had caused the creation of the world through the instrumentality of angels and archangels, they having first been brought into existence by means of his Thought (Ennoia). Once having felt their strength they refused Ennoia the right to return to heaven, and she had perforce to remain on earth imprisoned in successive female forms. Formerly she had been Helen of Troy (a reminiscence of Selene, the moon goddess?), and now she was a woman of dubious reputation in Tyre. To deliver her the Power had appeared in Simon, who taught his followers that the way of freedom for all lay in a plentiful use of magical arts and a lordly disregard of the moral law.

This kind of teaching was handed down with embellishments through Menander, a fellow-countryman and follower of Simon. Another instrument in the transmission may have been the Cerinthus who had the encounter in the baths with S. John. From him we get the Gnostic teaching as to the creation combined with the Ebionite doctrine of Christ. The complete emergence of Christian Gnosticism may be dated from Saturninus, who taught at Antioch in the time of Trajan. The world, according to him, was made by seven angels, of whom the God of the Jews was one. It contains, however, a spark of life from the Father. The Saviour, who had no human birth or body, came down to assist the good, who possess this spark, against the evil, who are assisted by the demons. Salvation is by asceticism, marriage and the union of the sexes being the work of Satan.

This teaching had a local success in Syria. It was carried further by the Ophites or Serpent-worshippers. They taught that the inferior creator-spirit, the Demiurge or Ialdabaoth, as they called him, had given himself out to be the greatest of all spirits and was so incensed when the first created man gave thanks to the Father instead of to himself that he planned to beguile him through Eve and so bring about his undoing. From such a fate the Serpent rescued the primal man by introducing Eve to the knowledge of good and evil.

With this beneficent serpent the Saviour-spirit, descending upon the human Jesus, identified himself in the conversation with Nicodemus: 'As Moses lifted up the serpent in the wilderness, even so must the Son of Man be lifted up.' The serpent is therefore worthy of all veneration. It is easy to see that what we have here is an example of the resurgence of that belief in a primeval world-monster which appears in one form or another in nearly every creation story and dragon myth. The extreme reduction to absurdity of this type of thought is to be found in the sect of the Cainites, who acting on the happy suggestion succeeded in turning the whole of the Old Testament upside down by representing Cain and all the worst characters as the best. Even Judas Iscariot did a great work, since by betraying Jesus he hastened the redemption of the world. Beyond this no further progress could be made on these lines.

II

The second great centre of Gnostic teaching was Alexandria, where the mixture was more predominantly Platonic than elsewhere. Here the first name to demand attention is that of Basilides, who taught in the time of Hadrian; but it is not easy to say how much in his system belongs to him and how much to his disciples. De Faye thinks that Basilides was really a moralist, dependent both upon Plato and upon the Stoics, though with his own original doctrine of providence, surmising that the Christian confessors of his day were expiating offences committed in a former existence. Hippolytus thought him Aristotelian and a dabbler in the esoteric doctrines of the Egyptian priest-hood. What he actually taught was something like this. The supreme Godhead is non-existence. Below Him are the 365 heavens, which have emanated from Him and of which we see only the lowest and last. That is the home of the creating angels of whom the God of the Jews is chief. The long descent from non-existence to the material world, from the abstract to the concrete, has not been completed without hindrance. Confusion has entered in, and the present task is to restore harmony. With this object in view the gospel,

identified with the Nous, came down from the Supreme, passing through all the heavens, and rested upon Jesus, the son of Mary. Jesus, thus inspired, was taken without suffering from the earth, for at the crucifixion it was really Simon the Cyrenian who died. There was a practical corollary to this teaching. If Jesus did not suffer, there was no reason for His followers to do so either, and Christian confessors had no need to go to the extreme length of martyrdom.

Carpocrates also was an Alexandrian. He too believed in a Supreme and in a number of creating angels. It was these angels who had spoilt everything. The original plan of the Supreme had been a complete communism, but the angels had introduced the Law with all its invidious distinctions between good and evil and mine and thine. The wise ignored these differences. All souls had had a previous existence and were subject to many transmigrations until they had run through the whole gamut of possible wickedness. Their business then was to practise the communism of the original plan, and to have everything, even their women, in common. So only would they deliver themselves from the bondage of matter. But in so doing they have shown us a moral obliquity as bad as that of the Cainites.

The greatest of all the Gnostics was Valentinus. He also was an Alexandrian, but he taught in Rome during the reign of Antoninus Pius, that is to say somewhere about the time of the writing of the *Shepherd of Hermas*. Valentinus was the poet of Gnosticism, using his 'endless genealogies of angels' as personifications of the divine attributes. The Pleroma or Fulness of the Godhead was made up of thirty aeons. These were conceived as syzygies or pairs, male and female. The first pair were the Abyss and Silence, the second Intellect and Truth. The latter begat the Word and Life, and they in their turn produced Man and the Church, thus completing the first Ogdoad. By such steps we come down at last to Will and Wisdom. The latter of these two includes philosophy, but it also manifests itself as an irregular passion to comprehend the Highest. This passion produces a formless abortion, Achamoth, which is the usual Gnostic discordant element. Hence of Sophia's sorrows and passions

come the 'Ideas' which result in the material universe. To restore the lost harmony the system harks back to the second pair who produce two fresh aeons, Christ and the Holy Spirit. Similarly the disorder in Wisdom is restored by Horus (definition) and Staurus (the cross or exact division), both very salutary remedies for mistakes in philosophy. Out of the freshly established concord of the whole Pleroma comes the 33rd and last aeon Jesus. By him Achamoth gives birth to three classes of men, the carnal (non-Christians), the psychic (ordinary Christians), and the spiritual (Valentinians). The first of these classes is incapable of redemption and the last does not need it. The Redeemer comes for the benefit of the ordinary Christian alone; those who succeed in following him will be saved, the rest together with the merely carnal will be burnt. The Valentinians, being spiritual, will be saved whatever happens, and no sins or infirmities of the flesh can affect their salvation.

Valentinus had many followers in Rome, particularly Heracleon and Ptolemaeus. The former is known for his commentary on the Fourth Gospel, which was largely allegorical in its method of interpretation, but brought Valentinianism nearer to orthodox Christianity in its doctrine of redemption. Ptolemaeus wrote one of the few Gnostic works that have come down to us in a complete form, the *Letter to Flora*, called by Renan the *chef-d'œuvre* of Gnostic literature. It is a study of the Mosaic Law, which the author thinks due not only to Moses and the ancients, but also to the Demiurge, and in which nevertheless he discovers the whole system of Valentinus. The last of this school of Gnostics was Bardesanes, who carried the tenets of Valentinus to Edessa about the year 170.

We may now try to sum up what we have learnt of these two types of Gnosticism in so far as they can be reduced to a common system. The aim of such teachers seems to have been threefold: to attain to a superior science (*gnosis*) of the invisible world; to accomplish a return to God which should be not only individual but cosmic; and to assert the freedom of the soul in denying the power of the flesh.

In order to achieve this threefold aim they elaborated the intricate systems we have outlined. Behind these it is possible to discern some general ideas. (*a*) God in His essential nature is abstract, unknowable. (*b*) He is not the same as the creator-God of the Old Testament. (*c*) Between Him and creation there is an evolution through various grades of being. (*d*) Somewhere in this long process corruption has crept in, and the material world is the result of this corruption. (*e*) There can therefore be no real contact between divinity and matter. (*f*) Nevertheless there is something in humanity capable of redemption. (*g*) This redemption is won through Jesus Christ. (*h*) The way of it lies through escape from the flesh, which may be accomplished alternatively by rigid asceticism or by gross licentiousness. To contemporaries such a system might appeal because it offered a Christianity freed from the Jewish scriptures with their wars, barbarities, and animal sacrifices. It also made terms with the new thought of the day, combining a respect for philosophy with the fashionable religiosity. In trying to estimate the true position of the Gnostics we must also remember their constant resort to magical arts by which they believed themselves able to control the actions of the inferior divinities. Nor must we lose sight of the regular escape from criticism by appeal to an alleged secret tradition which was supposed to have been handed down among the initiates of their several schools.

The Gnostics were responsible for the production of a copious literature, some of which has recently been discovered in Coptic. *Pistis Sophia* and the *Books of Jeu* are two of the most important authorities, and many of our apocryphal gospels are of Gnostic origin, while the Hermetic literature is valuable evidence for pre-Christian Gnosticism. But what they relied on was the tradition to which they laid exclusive claim. In answer to this the Church set up a threefold defence. It began to fix a canon of scripture; it emphasised the importance of the bishops as the guarantors of tradition (after all, who was more likely to be in possession of an apostle's authoritative teaching than the man who had succeeded to his see?); and it condensed fundamental

Christian doctrine into a creed that could be easily memorised by all. This threefold defence of canon, episcopate, and creed seems to have been sufficient to preserve the orthodox doctrine from degenerating into a mere pseudo-science.

What was the ultimate fate of the Gnostics is not quite clear. Apparently they lingered on in diminished numbers until they found an even more strongly expressed dualism with Christian affinities in the sect of the Manichees and mingled their own fortunes with theirs. It is probable that the type of feeling they represent has always continued to lead a precarious and underground existence in the Church. And from time to time, as in the case of the Albigenses, it has risen to the surface and brought trouble in its train.

III

But we have not yet considered our third class of Gnostics. It was hinted above that the early representatives of this school did not form separate sects or leave the Church but formed confraternities within her pale. The first to organise a distinct body was one who is not, strictly speaking, a Gnostic at all but is generally reckoned as one because he borrowed some simple notions from them. This was Marcion, whom Polycarp dignified by the title 'first-born of Satan'. His career is interesting. He was born at Sinope on the shores of the Black Sea and was the son of the bishop of that town. He himself followed the sea and made a fortune as a shipmaster. He came to Rome in 140 and won favourable regard there on account of his munificence. He was also a keen student of theology. Abandoning metaphysics and cosmology, he confined himself to the more practical matters of ethics and exegesis. However, he was a man of only one leading idea. To him the key to all mysteries was to be found in the Pauline antithesis between grace and works. Indeed he wrote a book with the title *Antitheses*, the object of which was to expose the incompatibility of the Law and the Gospel. There are, he said, two Gods: the one is the God of the New Testament and is supreme, the other is the God of the Old Testament and is inferior. A strict literalism thus replaces the allegorising of true Gnosticism and results in a

fine, if short-sighted, distinction between love and justice. Jesus is the agent of the good God; He is therefore not the Messiah but comes to destroy the work of the Old Testament Demiurge. Marcion's conception of His person was frankly docetic: Christ was simply a manifestation of the true God without any actual birth or death. The way to apprehend His spirituality was to free the body from the desires of the flesh by a most rigid asceticism, including even the repudiation of marriage.

Marcion was not content, like other Gnostics, to propagate this teaching among more or less secret followers. The openness of his efforts to capture ordinary Christians led to a breach with the Church of Rome, which very properly returned the £1,600 he had given it. Thereupon the Marcionites resolved themselves into a separate sect, which speedily spread throughout the Empire, the more speedily in that its extreme asceticism was not demanded of catechumens. The Christian sacraments were retained with a difference, the married being excluded from baptism and water taking the place of wine in the Eucharist. The Marcionite scriptures were few and select. The whole of the Old Testament was rejected together with a good part of the New. S. Luke without the initial stories was regarded as *the* Gospel, and the Pauline epistles without the Pastorals completed the canon. 'Criticising with a penknife', Tertullian called it. Obviously Marcion knew of no canon of scripture recognised by the Church, and it was probably his efforts in that direction that turned the mind of the Church to the formation of a canon of her own.

The importance of Marcion may be judged from the fact that he was attacked by most of the Fathers, including Justin, Irenaeus, Tertullian, Hippolytus and Epiphanius. His difficulties were peculiarly modern. His antithesis between love and justice is still to be found in a popular sentiment that proclaims the inability of God and of the good man to punish. The reconciliation between the New Testament and the Old, which the early Church tried to establish by an abundant use of allegory, has only been accomplished in our own time by a scientific and historical

criticism that has taught us to see in the long education of the chosen people a gradual preparation for the fuller revelation in Christ.

Marcion's greatest disciple was Apelles, the author of the *Syllogisms*. He was bolder than his master and entirely rationalistic. He was a monotheist of the strongest type, regarding the Demiurge as nothing more than an angel. He recapitulated in himself the history of much later thought by beginning to doubt the efficacy of pure reason and finally becoming quite mystical. Towards the end of his life he gave utterance to a sentiment with which the cynical may well be glad to end the consideration of these strange vagaries: 'One ought not to dispute; each ought to cling to his belief; those will be saved who believe in the Crucified, provided that their works have been good.'

CHAPTER VI

THE SECOND HALF OF THE SECOND CENTURY

I

WE return now to the subject of persecution; and in doing so we notice a marked change in the temper of the times. The standing attitude of antagonism to the Church still held good. But it had always required three co-operating wills to make it take effect: the will of the Emperor, the will of the provincial governor, and the will of the populace. And the usual tendency was always to interpret the standing attitude in accordance with the views, expressed or divined, of the Emperor. Whereas in the first half of the century that interpretation had been consistently mild, during the second it swung from an extreme severity to a leniency hitherto unknown. We have only two emperors to consider: Marcus Aurelius (161–180) and his worthless son Commodus (180–192). It is the good ruler who was the bad persecutor.

Marcus' victims found it difficult to understand this. A circumstantial legend soon arose to prove that he did in point of fact relax the severity of his attitude towards the Christians. According to this story, in the war against the Marcomanni (174) the imperial troops were on one occasion cut off and without water. The Twelfth Legion, consisting mostly of Christians, thereupon betook itself to prayer, and was immediately answered by a downpour which saved the whole army. For this reason the name of the Thundering Legion was bestowed upon the troops who had rendered so great a service to their companions and to the common cause, and the Emperor himself wrote to the Senate ascribing his success to their prayers. That is the story. But as a matter of fact the name of the Legion was not Thundering

but Thunderstruck, a name that was derived long before this from their regimental crest, which was a thunderbolt. Further the miracle is ascribed by ancient historians variously to the Emperor's own magic or prayers, to the work of an Egyptian magician, and to the timely intervention of Jupiter Pluvius. About the storm there need be no doubt: the Christian embellishments of it remain a pathetic witness to their unwillingness to believe that a good ruler could persecute the saints of God.

Unfortunately there is abundant evidence to prove the ruthlessness of persecution in the reign of Marcus. On the whole it was natural. The Emperor was a thoroughly conscientious man, brought up in the straitest sect of the Stoic philosophy with prejudice against the Christians instilled into him by his tutor Fronto. He was harassed by troubles which could easily be ascribed to the 'atheism' of the increasing number of Christians. The walls of the Empire were being battered by barbarian hordes in the East and at the Danube. Troops returning from the Parthian War brought a pestilence that more than decimated the population. And in his own palace he had a faithless wife and a profligate son. The mildness of disposition that could shelter even them could not be extended to cover those who were the ultimate source of all public and private ills. So the philosopher carried principle to its logical conclusion.

The first notable martyr was Justin, the apologist. In addition to his writing he had engaged hotly in the work of public disputation, the chief object of his attack being the Cynic philosopher, Crescens. Apparently this Crescens, beaten in argument, sought surer means of accomplishing his opponent's downfall and delated him. Justin was compelled to seek safety in flight from Rome. He returned, however, in the early part of this reign and together with a mixed company of fellow-Christians met his end in 163.

A severe outbreak of persecution occurred in 177 at Lyons and Vienne. A graphic account of it has been preserved in a letter from those churches to the 'brethren

throughout Asia and Phrygia'. In this letter we see the play of every emotion on both sides, the fear of the Christians lest the fortitude of those about to suffer should break down, the ignorant hatred of the mob, the spiteful charges of unnamable horrors that turned friendly pagans into enemies, the ingenuity and baffled energy of the executioners. It began with the exclusion of Christians from places of public resort. Then the mob provoked a riot and succeeded in getting a public examination of certain Christians in the market-place, which resulted in the prisoners being remanded until the arrival of the governor. This official ordered a regular search to be made. The will of the Emperor was also consulted, and it was ordered by him that those who recanted were to be set free, Romans who remained obstinate were to be beheaded, and non-Romans were to be cast to the beasts. The most heroic figure of the company was Blandina, a female slave, who was tortured for a whole day and showed such courage that her tormentors were obliged to confess themselves beaten. Later with Sanctus, a deacon, and two others she provided a spectacle in the arena, being bound to a stake and exposed to the beasts, who would not touch her. After that she was brought out every day to watch the torture of other companions. Then on the last day she was led forth with Ponticus, a boy of fifteen, her brother, and taken through the whole round of torture. Finally after witnessing the death of the boy, after having been scourged, thrown to the beasts, seated on the roasting-chair, she was fastened in a net and gored to death by a bull.

This is an example of the way in which nearly fifty victims met their end. Some indeed, including Pothinus, the aged Bishop of Lyons, died in prison of suffocation. The bodies of those who thus perished were cast to the dogs, lest the Christians should get them and give them decent burial. The remains of the rest, such as they were, were carefully guarded by soldiers for the same reason; then after six days they were burnt and thrown into the Rhône.

How widespread was this persecution can be seen from

the trial and death at Carthage of seven male and five female Christians from Scilli. It is true that this took place three years later than the persecution in Gaul and occurred a few months after the death of Aurelius, but the policy is still that of his reign. Here we have an example of the way in which a humane magistrate would try to give the accused every opportunity of satisfying the law and escaping from the penalty of what seemed to him their obstinate folly. In the court the proconsul Saturninus pointed out that they could still 'gain the indulgence of our Lord the Emperor if they returned to a good mind'. When they protested that they had done no ill, he went on to say, 'We also are religious, and our religion is simple, and we swear by the genius of our Lord the Emperor, which you also ought to do.' Later, wearied of the argument, he suggested that they should have space for consideration, only to be met by the answer, 'In a matter so plain there is no need for consideration.' Yet again he offered them thirty days' grace, and only when they all contented themselves with the simple reply that they were Christians, did he proceed to give sentence.

Under the slack administration of Commodus the persecution gradually died down. Its end was hastened by the influence of Marcia, the Emperor's morganatic wife, who, if not a Christian, was at least friendly to the Christians, and managed to get a number of them released from the mines of Sardinia. This is not to say that severity was not still exercised in some parts of the Empire where a proconsul might not yet know which way the wind was blowing at Rome. Thus Arrius Antoninus is said to have put to death the whole body of Christians in one of his Asiatic towns when they all presented themselves together in his court and proclaimed their faith. Even in Rome itself a certain philosopher, Apollonius, was put to death on his confession of Christianity. But the careful exactitude of Marcus Aurelius was quite wanting, and on the whole slackness told in favour of the Christians.

II

Obviously in times like these the intellectual speculations of Gnosticism were not going to be much of a support. If

there was to be any exaggeration, such as periods of great stress have always produced, it would be of the mystical rather than of the liberal element in religion. That is what happened in the present instance. In Phrygia people began to react violently against the coldness and worldliness of the churches, and to declare that a new dispensation, that of the Paraclete, had begun.

Their leader was Montanus, a converted priest of Cybele. The date of his appearance is in dispute. Epiphanius puts it at 157, Eusebius at 172. He had brought over with him from heathenism a strongly developed gift of ecstasy. As a Christian it was very easy for him to associate this with the type of prophecy, or speaking with tongues, that had been dominant in the Corinthian Church of S. Paul's day and had probably never altogether died out. It was a marked feature of his utterances that they seemed to owe nothing to the independent reason or personality of the speaker, but to come by actual dictation of the spirit that possessed him. According to Montanus this was something quite fresh and evidenced the beginning of a new age in which the revelation of the Christ had been superseded by that of the Spirit. Indeed he spoke of himself in terms that implied that he was himself an incarnation of the Spirit as Jesus had been of the Logos. Associated with him were two women friends, Priscilla and Maximilla, who were the fortunate possessors of a similar gift. The three set out together on strange adventures, drawing many Phrygian Christians in their train.

The spirit speaking through these agents announced the speedy establishment of the New Jerusalem. This was to come down from heaven and alight upon a spot far removed from the populous places of the earth on a plain near the little village of Pepuza in the far west of Phrygia. Thither the prophet led out his followers to prepare for its coming. They formed a strange company in that far-away spot. They had broken all earthly ties and were not allowed to form new ones. Wives and private property were given up, and in the strictest asceticism and the practice of ecstasy they set themselves to the task of waiting for the new age. The heavenly city disappointed their expectations and failed to

appear, but with man's inexpugnable habit of making the best of things, they settled down in the new city of their own making, and declared that that was still the home of the Paraclete. A multitude of others believed and joined them until some of the towns of Asia were robbed of every Christian they contained. The rumour of these doings spread far and wide through the churches, so that even Lyons and Vienne in the midst of their persecution were compelled to take notice of it and pleaded for a lenient judgment on these fervent idealists.

All this was a difficult matter for the sorely tried Church. On the one hand great reverence had been paid to prophecy from the beginning, and the Fourth Gospel had certainly promised a descent of the Paraclete. Further in their zeal and their asceticism the Montanists, like the Methodists of a later age, seemed actually to surpass their contemporaries. Bishop Butler in the eighteenth century could say to John Wesley, 'Sir, the pretending to extraordinary revelation and gifts of the Holy Ghost is a horrid thing, a very horrid thing.' But no bishop of the early Church desired to kill enthusiasm or to earn the title of 'prophet-slayer'. Yet on the other hand a society founded on the Incarnation could not have the Christ superseded even by the Paraclete, nor could it have the standard set by the New Testament put on one side. But that is what the Montanists continued to do. They laid down in effect a third canon of Scripture, adding to the Old and New Testaments the utterances of their own prophets. And they did the same in respect of the moral standard; for even after they had begun to allow marriage they steadfastly refused to recognise second marriages, thus going contrary to the teaching of S. Paul. They were also charged with paying regular salaries to the clergy and admitting women to all ranks of the sacred ministry.

These departures from recognised Christian standards did much to discredit Montanist prophecy, and some bishops set themselves to test the power of the spirit by trying to exorcise it. This was the deadliest insult, and the voice of the spirit speaking through Maximilla was heard to protest:

'I am chased like a wolf from the flock. I am no wolf; I am utterance, spirit, and power.' Yet in that very saying there appeared just the kind of contention that seemed impossible to the Church, namely, that the prophet was the passive instrument of the Spirit. In earlier prophecy God had used the personality of man, not suppressed it. And so Miltiades wrote to contend that 'a prophet ought not to speak in ecstasy'. Meetings, which may well have been the beginnings of synodical action, began to be held in various parts of Asia to discuss and condemn the new prophecy. Condemnation led to excommunication, and thus at length a schism was begun.

This was the position by the end of the second century, at which time Rome also after some hesitation was to be reckoned among the 'prophet-slayers'. Indeed antagonism had run to the opposite extreme and produced a school of thinkers called the Alogi, who rejected S. John's Gospel with its teaching of Logos and Paraclete. That was particularly serious as it destroyed their hold on Trinitarian doctrine. But they were never driven out of the Church, which was fortunate as they sank at once to obscurity.

By this time the three Montanist leaders were dead. Nevertheless the movement took fresh root in Africa where it found a people very like in temperament to its native Phrygians, and where it also found a new leader in Tertullian, the first great Christian writer of Latin. His conversion took place in 205 and started a succession of Montanists in Africa, the last remnants of which were only won back to the communion of the Church by the efforts of the still greater Augustine.

The best defence set up by the Church against such conversions was to close the canon of scripture, and by so doing to deny any authority to the Montanist prophecies. As Harnack points out, if against Gnosticism the Church asserted the Apostolic-Catholic idea and made a collection of books with that character, against Montanism she declared that the collection was sealed. Thus the possibility of a new revelation was excluded by establishing an authoritative New Covenant side by side with the Old.

In our own day it has sometimes been claimed that Montanism was a return from a growing elaboration of organisation to the simplicity of original Christianity. But it must be replied that the claim of Montanism was to recognition as a new thing. The action of the Church of the second century, while not excluding the influence of the Spirit or belittling the importance of the individual, did secure for many generations the triumph of order and episcopal administration. It is only with difficulty that our own times have been able to raise the question whether Montanism or Catholicism is the true heir of Christ. Nevertheless while the doctrine of the 'inner light' is still with us it might be possible to prove that at least some elements of Montanist teaching have survived to our own day.

III

The second half of the second century produced a plentiful crop of Christian literature. The revival of persecution, the rise of Gnosticism and Montanism, as well as the attacks of pagan leaders of thought all demanded it. Two such leaders who attacked the Church in speech were Fronto, the tutor of Marcus Aurelius, and Crescens, the opponent of Justin Martyr: two who attacked it in writing were Lucian and Celsus, the latter of whom wrote the *True Word*, a book that was afterwards to be answered by Origen.

The necessities of the time called into being a second series of apologists. Apollinaris, Bishop of Hierapolis, and Miltiades, an Asiatic, wrote apologies against both Montanists and persecutors, but they have unfortunately been lost. It was from the former that Eusebius borrowed the story of the Thundering Legion, and the latter, as we have seen, inveighed against the habit of speaking in ecstasy. Melito, Bishop of Sardis, was himself a prophet, but wrote against exaggeration. He was on less secure ground in arguing against persecution on the assumption that it was only the bad Emperors, like Nero and Domitian, who persecuted. Nor would much be thought of his argument that the new religion, born in the great reign of Augustus, had proved itself so marked a blessing that no disaster had happened to

the Empire since its introduction. But at least he showed prophetic insight in affirming that Church and Empire were not necessarily incompatible with each other, and it was an excellent suggestion of his that the Emperor himself should take cognisance of the Christians under trial and see whether they had really committed crimes worthy of death.

This last was also the contention of Athenagoras, another of the great band of Athenian Christian philosophers, said, moreover, to have been the first great Christian teacher at Alexandria. In his *Legatio pro Christianis*, which is still extant, he sets himself to refute the three charges which were now regularly levelled against the Christians: atheism, Thyestean banquets, and Oedipodean incest. He too had an eye on the Montanists, but he agreed with them on the subject of second marriage, calling it a 'respectable form of adultery'. All these apologies were addressed to Marcus ∗ Aurelius, and show the desire of the Christians to take advantage of the Emperor's well-known leaning to philosophy and of his mildness of character.

Another writing that must be attributed to this period is the exquisite little *Letter to Diognetus*. Who was its author no one knows. It has been attributed to Clement of Rome, Apollos, Justin, Quadratus, Marcion, Apelles, Aristides. There are certainly similarities with the apology of the last named, and it is possible that both are dependent upon the 'Preaching of Peter', which is shown by its surviving fragments to have been a second-century narrative of S. Peter's work among the Gentiles. Diognetus was an enquiring pagan who wanted to know why the Christians made such fearless martyrs, why they would not recognise heathen gods or keep the observances of the Jews, why they loved each other so much, and why, if this was the true religion, it had appeared so late in time. These questions receive able answers. In particular the reply to the last affirms that God only waited until man had proved to demonstration his utter weakness and unworthiness before coming at the psychological moment to take Himself the burden of human sin. 'O sweet exchange. O inscrutable operation. O unexpected blessings: that the lawlessness of many should be hidden in

one righteous Person, and the righteousness of One should justify the lawless many.' The relation of the Divine Society to the world is set forth with equal nobility. 'In a word, what the soul is in the body Christians are in the world. . . . The soul dwells in the body, and yet it is not of the body; so Christians dwell in the world, and yet they are not of the world. . . . Yet it is they who hold the world together. . . . The soul when it is stinted of food thrives the better; so Christians when they are punished increase daily all the more.'

The calm temper and classical style of this writer contrast very strongly with the bitter invective of Justin's disciple Tatian. He was a barbarian from Assyria, and professed contempt for Greek culture. He had lived the life of a wandering Sophist before he came to Rome about 150 and was converted to Christianity. There he stayed for some time, but about 166 he went to Edessa and became a very important figure in that centre of Syriac Christianity. His best-known work is the *Diatessaron* or harmony of the Four Gospels. This sealed the exclusive canonicity of the four, but in the East at least it very nearly superseded them. His apologetic work is the *Oration to the Greeks*, which displays none of his master's desire to see in other faiths a preparation for the gospel. His violence led him astray, and in the end, like the equally violent Tertullian, he left the Church, founding the sect of the Encratites, a harshly ascetic body who combined the Valentinian aeons with the Marcionite distinction between the God of justice and the God of love.

From Antioch proceeded the apology known as Theophilus' *Ad Autolycum*. Theophilus was Bishop of Antioch about 180. In conversation with his pagan friend Autolycus he attacks idol-worship, defends the prophets, and affirms that the scriptures are more ancient than the pagan classical literature. This work is interesting for other reasons. It is the first book to use the term *Trias* of the Trinity, and it is also the first to affirm that the author of the Fourth Gospel is none other than the Apostle John.

Possibly it is to this period that we must also attribute the first apology to be written in Latin, the charming *Octavius*

of Minucius Felix, though some scholars prefer to put it in the reign of Alexander Severus. It is written in Ciceronian Latin and is indeed modelled upon Cicero's *De Natura Deorum*. It records a dialogue between a pagan and a Christian. The pagan Caecilius salutes the deity Serapis at Ostia and then proceeds to attack the Christian faith. Truth is and must remain unknowable, whereas Christianity is both secret and absurd: in the inevitable uncertainty the best thing we can do is to let religious enquiry alone. In reply to this Octavius defends Christians, painting them as a particularly pure and happy people. In the end Caecilius is converted.

By far the greatest of the Latin apologists is Tertullian, but him we shall keep for a later chapter, closing the present section with two writers whose main efforts were directed against internal heresy rather than external opposition. The first of these is Hegesippus. He was a member of the Jewish Christian Church and seems to have been in middle life about 160. He was able to preserve the traditions of James, the Lord's brother, and other members of the Jerusalem community, which have been carefully handed down to us in the pages of Eusebius. Hegesippus had a taste for travel and for collecting information as to the apostolic succession in the various sees. He knew well both Corinth and Rome, and it is significant that this travelled scholar saw no fundamental difference between the teaching of the Western churches and his own.

But even Hegesippus could not rival in representative character the greatest ecclesiastical author of the second century, Irenaeus, who is our best authority for the theology, orthodox and unorthodox, of the period. He was a Greek native of Asia, and at Smyrna had been a disciple of Polycarp. Later he moved to Rome, where he probably sat at the feet of Justin Martyr. It may have been the persecution of Marcus Aurelius that drove him to Gaul. There he settled at Lyons, acting as presbyter under the aged bishop Pothinus. It was probably Irenaeus who wrote the letter from the churches of Lyons and Vienne to describe their sufferings to the churches of Phrygia and Asia; it was certainly he

who carried it to Rome and the East. After his return he became Bishop of Lyons, and faced with courage the task of rebuilding the church there. Several of his writings have been lost, but his *Epideixis*, or Demonstration, a work on the apostolic preaching, has been recovered in an Armenian translation. This work first explains the Christian teaching and then proves it from prophecy. It was intended as a little handbook of apologetics for the use of the faithful.

An earlier but far more important work, the *Refutation of the False Gnosis*, generally known as the *Adversus Haereses*, has been preserved entire in an exact Latin translation. It is divided into five books, the first two of which are devoted to an exposure of the Gnostic heresy, chiefly that of the Valentinian school; the second two to constructive teaching based upon the canonical scriptures; and the final one to an explanation of the resurrection and the Last Things. Irenaeus knew some of the pupils of Valentinus and had read their commentaries. His practical experience had taught him the insidious nature of their teaching, which he describes as 'a glass imitation of the really genuine and highly prized emerald'. He apologises, unnecessarily, for the poverty of his own language. He explains that he had lived long among the Celts, and had used their language so habitually as to have forgotten the arts and graces of classical Greek. 'I have had no practice in writing books nor training in the art of composition; but my love urges me to reveal to you and your people teachings that have been kept dark until this present but have now in the grace of God been made manifest.'

His strongest argument against the Gnostics is that the true tradition is to be found already in the Gospels (of which nature itself with its four quarters teaches us that there must be four and only four), and has been handed down from the apostles, through apostolic men like Polycarp, and through the episcopal succession to the present day. As Ignatius had regarded the episcopate as the bulwark of unity against persecution, so Irenaeus regards it as the bulwark of unity against heresy. There is, he claims, no sign of any break in the succession or of any secret tradition which could

guarantee a better knowledge to the Gnostic sects than was to be found in the Church. 'According to these people Peter was imperfect and the other apostles were imperfect, and they must come to life again and become disciples of these men if they too wish to be perfect.' Thus Irenaeus begins the effort of the Church to keep its people in the way of salvation as laid down along the main path of historic Christianity.

But what is even more important about this writer is that with him, as with the apologists, a really serious effort is made to explain that central current of Christian tradition in the light of the secular knowledge of his own day. Whether we see in this 'Hellenisation' of Christian doctrine a gross corruption or a legitimate development of the Logos doctrine already found in the Fourth Gospel, we are compelled to recognise in Irenaeus, if not the pioneer, at least a staunch upholder of 'central Catholicism'. This he expresses in a 'recapitulation' theory, which is indeed the characteristic Eastern theory of salvation. The destiny of man is to be made like unto God. In order to achieve this end the Logos-Son became man, summing up in Himself all ages and classes of humanity. By sacraments and other appointed means this divine life of the God-made-flesh is actually imparted to us, and by our sharing in it we ourselves become divine. 'By His own blood the Lord redeemed us, and gave His soul for our soul, and His flesh for our flesh, and poured out the Spirit of the Father upon the union and communion of God and man, bringing down God to man by the Spirit, and raising up man to God by His Incarnation, and bestowing upon us incorruptibility in a real and true sense at His advent, through communion with Himself.'

CHAPTER VII

THE FIRST LONG PEACE

THE third century was a period of comparative quiet for the Church. A fierce and systematic persecution divided it into two long generations of peace. The Empire was mostly in the hands of non-Roman emperors, who looked down with scorn upon the ancient Latin traditions of culture. As the State grew weaker the Church grew stronger, until from its position as a semi-secret society it became more and more obviously an empire within the Empire. The emperors could no longer despise it, and began to fear it. Fear lent them cunning: some tried to make terms with it, and those who tried to stay its progress were careful to find the joints in its armour.

This was seen already in the partial persecution that preceded the first period of peace at the turn of the century. Septimius Severus (193–211) was an African soldier who with the aid of the army of the Danube had risen superior to the nonentities who scrambled for power after the death of Commodus. He himself was indifferent if not actually sympathetic to the Christians. His own household contained Christians and he had a Christian nurse for his son. The local churches assisted his mild intentions by representing themselves as burial and benefit clubs. Against such there was no law, and they were allowed in this guise to exist with impunity. It was probably to the Emperor's wife, Julia Domna, that a hardening of policy was due. She was the daughter of the High Priest of the temple of El Gabal, the sun-god of Emesa, and she led an effort on the part of the pagan world at this time to frame a faith and worship that should be a not unworthy rival of Christianity. The scepticism that had so easily disposed of the old myths had grown tired of itself, and philosophy and popular religion

alike were feeling the need to find the One, not by rejection of the Many, but through and beyond the Many. This Julia Domna tried to do by means of an elaborate syncretism. Essential monotheism was believed to be preserved by the worship of the Sun as the supreme god, and below him were collected together the gods of all religions in a kind of divine hierarchy. Even so there was no one to correspond to the Christ, but this defect was remedied by bringing forward the legend of Apollonius of Tyana, and making of it 'the story of the gospel corrected and improved'.

This Apollonius was a wandering Cappadocian ascetic and preacher in the latter part of the first century A.D. His story was written up by Philostratus, one of Julia's court philosophers, who drew attractive details with which to enhance the glory of his hero from many great religious figures, including Jesus Himself. According to the legend thus embellished Apollonius may have been the son of Jupiter. He received a great inheritance, the half of which he gave away, entering upon the Pythagorean five years' probation of silence, and then wandering about preaching many sermons and performing many miracles. His ministry was not to the outcast but to the virtuous, and there was about him none of the offence of the cross. When ultimately he was tried before Domitian he was miraculously delivered from the court, and it is hinted that he did not die but was received into heaven through the doors of a temple. After his ascension he appeared again on earth and discoursed on the immortality of the soul. This 'Life' had a great success and was remembered long after the syncretism that gave rise to it had been forgotten.

How far this kind of atmosphere influenced the gloomy soldier who ruled at Rome it is impossible to say, but about 202 Septimius published an edict which showed a desire rather to starve the Church to death than to persecute her in the old way. The edict forbade proselytism on the part both of Jews and Christians. It does not seem to have caused serious trouble elsewhere than on the southern shores of the Mediterranean, but there the two most important churches received severe blows. The rising school of

Alexandria, which was doing invaluable propagandist work, was dispersed, and at Carthage great execution was done among the catechumens.

At Alexandria the teacher Clement was compelled to flee, but his place was taken by a youth of seventeen, named Origen, around whom the pupils soon again gathered. Origen lost his own father Leonides in the persecution, and triumphantly led many others to their death. How he himself escaped is a mystery; once at least it was because his mother had hidden his garments so that he was unable to go out of doors. Eusebius gives us the names of seven catechumens who suffered martyrdom, numbering among them Herais, of whom Origen said that she received her baptism by fire. The most famous of them was Potamiaena, whose demeanour was such as to convert even Basilides, the soldier who led her away to execution. He later followed her example by confessing himself a Christian when his fellow-soldiers had demanded that he should take an oath which he felt bound to refuse. For this he laid down his life, the first example of a long line of military martyrs.

The attack on the church in Carthage took place in the same year 203. There were five victims, three young men, a matron Perpetua, and Felicitas a slave. Perpetua herself wrote the first part of the *Acta*, which show a strong Montanist colouring, and they were probably completed by Tertullian. Felicitas had a child born to her in the prison, and gloried in going straight from the midwife to the executioner's knife. Perpetua found the prison became a palace when her own infant child was allowed to be taken to her. The slave and the free-woman suffered their tortures side by side and bore striking witness before the intensely aristocratic society of the time that for the fellow-members of the Body of Christ all racial and social barriers were broken down.

This was the first official persecution by edict. After it there is no record of even partial persecution for a generation. The emperor Alexander Severus (222–235) imitated the religious syncretism of Julia Domna and even went one better, finding a place in his pantheon for the Christ, and

openly tolerating Christianity with all other faiths. He, however, was killed by mutinous soldiers. His successor was Maximin the Thracian (235–238), a military tyrant, who threatened to carry the ingenuity of Septimius a step further by aiming not at the catechumens but at the leaders of the Church, a policy that was to cost the Christians dear later on. But in his reign there seem to have been no executions. The bishops in Rome, Hippolytus and Pontianus, were banished to Sardinia, where they died, and at Alexandria Origen and some of his friends seem to have been imprisoned.

A later emperor in this period, Philip the Arabian (244–249), was said to be a secret Christian. There is a story that at Antioch he wished to join in the Easter services but was excluded from the church until he had made a complete confession, a thing which he hastened to do. Whatever credence is given to this story, it is at least obvious that we have travelled far from the state of things that was characteristic of the second century. The worst persecutions are yet to come, but we have seen sufficient gleams of toleration to guarantee the ultimate dawning of a better day.

During this first Long Peace the Church made great progress in the consolidation of her position. At the same time the period was remarkable for the growth of great local churches each with a decided individuality of its own. Unity of course was strongly maintained, and there were now some determined efforts after uniformity, but on the whole it is possible to compare and contrast various types of Christianity evolved in the great city churches.

I. ALEXANDRIA

The city of Alexander's foundation was at this time the intellectual centre of the world. It was the place where East met West, and where Judaism had been most closely affected by Hellenic thought. It was the home of the Septuagint and of Philo's religious philosophy. The close proximity of the famous Museum and the free Jewish colony numbering nearly a million had brought about an alliance between the noblest religion and the widest learning of the day. This alliance once established had been carried over into the

Christian Church, the foundation of which is assigned by an unsupported tradition to S. Mark. We see the alliance at work in the *Epistle to the Hebrews*. The philosophical side of it was pushed to an extreme by the Gnostic leaders, Basilides, Carpocrates, and Valentinus. Equilibrium was restored in the wonderful catechetical school, which shared with the apologists the honour of capturing the most advanced learning of the time and bringing it into subjection to Christ. It is possible that in the first two centuries, before doctrine had fallen under complete episcopal control, the office of teacher in such a school was both important and to some extent independent. A somewhat similar position of authority is claimed by Jerome for the presbyters of Alexandria, who, so he says, were accustomed to appoint their own bishop. But Harnack is perhaps right in saying that the worst gap in our knowledge of early Church History is our almost total ignorance of the history of Christianity in Alexandria and Egypt till A.D. 180.

Perhaps it was the apologist Athenagoras who founded the catechetical school, but the first master of whom we have certain knowledge is Pantaenus. He was a native of Sicily and a converted Stoic, who had been on a mission to India, had found there a gospel in Hebrew said to have been carried thither by S. Bartholomew, and on his return took up teaching at Alexandria. He was not an official of the university but probably taught privately any members of it who wished to learn something of the Christian faith. The school was thus in its origin not for native Christians but for converts. He must have worked very quietly, for it was only with difficulty that an enquirer who was destined to become his successor was able to find him at all. This enquirer was none other than the scholar who was later known to fame as Clement of Alexandria.

Clement was probably the descendant of one of the freedmen of the Christian consul Clement in the reign of Vespasian. He himself may have been brought up as a pagan, but he had had several Christian teachers before he came to Alexandria about 180 (the year of the death of Marcus Aurelius), and sought out Pantaenus. With him he

taught in the school until ten years later he succeeded his leader as its head. This position he occupied till Septimius' prohibition of proselytising, when in obedience to the evangelical injunction rather than to imperial command he 'fled to another city'. Fortunately enough of his writing has come down to us to make possible a complete judgement on his position in the development of theological thought. F. D. Maurice said of him that he was 'that one of the old fathers whom we should all have reverenced most as a teacher, and loved best as a friend'. Hort said that 'with all his very manifest defects there was no one whose vision of what the faith of Jesus Christ was intended to do for mankind was so full or so true'. Certainly he has had a great influence on modern theologians, and it is hardly too much to say that if it had not been for Clement of Alexandria, *Lux Mundi* with its effort to reconcile Christianity with evolutionary theory, could never have been written.

Clement's favourite theme is that the world was prepared for the coming of Christianity by Greek philosophy as much as by Judaism. He starts from Justin Martyr's position that all knowledge flows from Christ. There is thus a true *Gnosis* as well as a false, and Clement's object is quite frankly to lead his pupils to become real Gnostics. He had in his pre-Christian days been initiated into the Eleusinian mysteries, and his chief writings follow the successive steps of such initiation, interpreting them as stages in the Christian life. First in the *Address to the Greeks* comes the purification, an effort to show how the Word of God draws the heathen to Himself. The initiation proper is represented by the *Tutor*, the title of which designates Christ Himself teaching the convert from paganism what changes his conversion will necessitate in certain practical matters such as food, manners, language and personal adornment. The revelation, or third step, comes in the treatise called *Miscellanies* (*Stromateis*, literally carpet-bags in which bedding and odds and ends were kept). In this a Christian philosophy is developed at length. There is also a fourth big work of which fragments have been preserved called *Sketches* or *Outlines*. In this the instruction is extended by a com-

mentary on the scriptures. Finally there are specimens of his popular style, of which the best known is, *What rich man can be saved?* It is in this that we find the beautiful story of S. John and the young man who became a bandit chief but was restored by the apostle's love.

The glory of Clement is that in spite of much opposition he rescued learning from the disrepute into which the Gnostics had driven it. He clung to the belief that all truth is one and comes from one and the same Father of light. The truths of secular science must be one with the truths of revelation. For the vulgar to 'believe and obey' may be enough, but for the intelligent it is necessary to use the reason. Difficulties there are in plenty, even within the pages of scripture. But the way to be rid of them is not to cut out the Old Testament, as the Gnostics had done, but to make a plentiful use of the allegorical method of interpretation. This had been introduced by Philo and now becomes a fixed characteristic of the Alexandrian school. 'The true scribe brings all kinds of learning into the gospel net', said Clement, and he is most conspicuous through his attempt to carry out his own ideal. From the starting-place in the ineffable One, who has neither body, parts, nor passions, he endeavours to form a system which shall include the whole multitude of truths whether of religion or science. He does not succeed, because his great learning was not sufficiently accurate, nor his retentive mind sufficiently synthetical. But it was much that the attempt should have been made.

Clement's reputation was thrown into the shade by that of his pupil Origen. Origen was more fortunate than most of the early Church writers in that he had Christian parents. We have already seen how he lost his father in the persecution of 203. From that time he began to support his mother and six brothers by teaching. Although only seventeen years of age, he was sought after in the absence of Clement by heathen enquirers and was soon made formal head of the catechetical school by Bishop Demetrius. He sold his secular books and supported his family on the pittance that they brought. A less worthy piece of asceticism was an attempt to secure perfect chastity by an act of self-mutilation in a

mistaken application of our Lord's words about those who make themselves eunuchs for the kingdom of heaven's sake, an act that was to cause him endless trouble later.

There followed many years of toil in Alexandria at learning, teaching, and writing. He made a study of Hebrew for the better understanding of the Old Testament, and also attended the lectures of the pagan Ammonius Saccas in order to keep in touch with the new movements in philosophic thought. About 215, on the occasion of some disturbances in Alexandria, he left that city and paid a visit to his friends the Bishops of Jerusalem and Caesarea. In the latter city he was invited to give an address before the bishops, an invitation that so incensed his own diocesan that he was ordered home. This trouble between himself and his bishop came to a head twelve years later. This time Origen had answered a call from the churches of Achaea to go and refute certain heresies that were springing up in their midst. On his way through Palestine his old friends ordained him to the priesthood. This was a much more serious breach of discipline, especially as Origen had gone without leave. Accordingly on his return he was summoned before an assembly of bishops and presbyters by whom he was banished from Alexandria. The rancour of Demetrius pursued him still further, obtaining from a later gathering of bishops what the earlier synod had refused, a declaration of the invalidity of his ordination. The cause alleged was no doubt his mutilation, but jealousy and doctrinal disagreement had probably something to do with it.

For the rest of his days Origen lived at Caesarea, carrying on his work as teacher and writer, and paying visits to other churches that needed his help in combating false doctrine. Famous people came under his influence, such as Mammea, the mother of the emperor Alexander Severus, Julius Africanus, his regular correspondent, Pamphilus, his apologist, and Gregory of Neocaesarea the Wonder-worker, who on leaving him delivered a panegyric which still survives. At length in the great persecution of Decius Origen was thrown into prison and received such treatment that he died two years later at Tyre (254).

In his early days Origen had not attempted to write much, being content with oral instruction, but while still at Alexandria he accepted the offer of his wealthy friend and convert Ambrosius to pay for the services of shorthand writers and copyists. It is to this fact that we owe the preservation of so much of this great scholar's work; but even what we have is only a very small part of the six thousand volumes for which Epiphanius gives him credit. We may divide his works into three classes, Biblical, Miscellaneous, and Doctrinal.

Origen was the first of the Fathers to insist upon a good text as the foundation of all work on the scriptures. For the purpose of establishing such a text he compiled his famous *Hexapla* (six-fold), where were given in six parallel columns the Hebrew text, the same in Greek letters, the Septuagint, and the other Greek versions of Aquila, Symmachus and Theodotion. Other Biblical works include commentaries on practically the whole Bible, which were given either in the form of short notes or in expository sermons or in commentaries proper. Here in full accord with the allegorical method of his school Origen distinguishes no less than three senses in scripture—body, soul and spirit: the body is the literal interpretation which served for the ancients; the soul is the moral meaning which is to be searched out in the present; and the spirit is the allegorical meaning which may be known in part now but is reserved in its full understanding for the life hereafter.

Under the head of Miscellaneous we must include not only the ten books of *Miscellanies*, but also the letters, of which Eusebius collected a hundred. And to these must be added works *on Prayer*, *on the Resurrection*, and also the *Exhortation to Martyrdom*.

The most important division is that on doctrine, which includes the reply to Celsus (*contra Celsum*) and the *De Principiis*. Celsus' *True Word* had made little impression when it was published towards the end of the reign of Marcus Aurelius, and it was fated to be preserved only in the book of the man who refuted it. But Origen saw that the foe was worthy of his steel. Celsus had taken the trouble to

make himself familiar with Christian literature and was even aware of the existence of divisions in the Church. His two main arguments are the absurdity of the Gospel and the need of preserving the peace and unity of the Empire in face of its enemies. An Incarnation seems to him derogatory to the majesty of God, and the loss is emphasised if the Incarnation takes place in so obscure a corner as Judea and has to be guaranteed by miracles that can be outclassed by every conjurer. It is true that the Christians' morals are good but their best ideals are borrowed from the philosophers, and spoilt in the borrowing by being made to depend not upon reason but upon a blind obedience: such a religion can only appeal to fools and the low-born. Here then is the offence of the cross set forth plainly by one who felt it most keenly. Origen replies with great pains and an admirable spirit of restraint. Although the Incarnation took place late in time, the Word had always been helping the souls of those who were willing to receive Him. He came to the Jews because they had been carefully prepared by prophecy, and the intention was that from that one nation the light should go forth to lighten every man. Certainly the Word does call the foolish, but only that He may make them better, 'and He also calls those that are much better than they, since Christ is the Saviour of all men, especially of them that believe, whether wise or simple.'

In the *De Principiis* Origen sets forth his theology on the grand scale. What Clement had only suggested Origen succeeds in accomplishing, and his is the first great Christian theological synthesis. He holds that philosophy is in general agreement with Christian teaching but that it differs in three particular respects: in saying that matter is co-eternal with God, in confining God's providence to the sphere above the moon, and in affirming that man's destiny is governed by the stars. The basis of Origen's system is the Catholic rule of faith, but where the Church had not definitely spoken, Origen felt himself free to speculate; and that he did with such boldness as later to incur the charge of heresy. Origen took a more positive view of the nature of God than did Clement. To him the Deity is the

source of all existence. Although He is one and indivisible He cannot be arrived at by a mere process of abstraction. He is goodness itself and goodness demands creatures. These came into existence through the Word, who though subordinate to the Supreme Being partakes of His nature and is divine, being begotten of His Father by an eternal generation. The created spirits sinned and the material world was made for their correction. According to the measure of their fault they are found as men or demons. But the Word became flesh and suffered for them upon the cross, paying there the price that alone could redeem men from the power of the demons. So great was that price that it availed even for the demons, so that ultimately all spirits will be saved. To this end there operates in those who are being saved the Holy Spirit; but here Origen is not very clear, and he leaves the relation of the Spirit to the Father and the Son undefined. Such sin as is not removed in this life is destroyed in a purifying fire beyond the grave, after which the soul is clothed in an immaterial body, while the physical body returns to earth in order to house still other spirits.

Such is the system that was to form the practical basis of discussion for the next hundred years. By it Origen destroyed millenarianism, and made a great advance in the understanding of the being of God. But he left behind many difficulties. The difference between Father, Son and Spirit was clearer than their unity; and the Son was too definitely subordinated to the Father; while the pre-existence of souls together with the theory of a pre-natal fall was more than the Church could accept. Nevertheless it was a magnificent effort. Of its author it has been well said that 'no name of equal lustre appears in the records of the early Church'. His greatness is most clearly seen in the fact that we still think it worth while to be trying to solve some of the questions that he raised.

II. ANTIOCH

The great rival of Alexandria as a city, a mart, a garrison and a centre of learning was Antioch, and soon it was to be

its rival also as a theological school. After having been the
capital of the old Seleucid Empire, in which the total
Hellenisation of all culture had been so ruthlessly attempted
by Antiochus Epiphanes, Antioch had become under Roman
domination the greatest Greek city in the world. Its importance in Christian progress was early seen when it became
the centre of missionary effort and succeeded to the leadership left vacant by the persecution in Jerusalem. At the
beginning of the second century it had given to the world
the martyr bishop Ignatius. Later, like Alexandria, it had
produced its own type of Gnostic heresy, of which Saturninus
was the chief exponent. By the time of Marcus Aurelius, in
common with most other important churches, it had
developed its own catechetical school.

This school appears to have had a more usual history than
that of Alexandria; it arose not out of the needs of propaganda in association with a university, but out of the need
for preparing native catechumens for baptism. For this
reason it was probably from the beginning more definitely
under the control of the bishop. It is probable that the idea
of a school for instruction was originally taken over from the
common practice of the synagogue. The instruction given
would be that suited to those who were to become full
members of the Christian Church, and would consequently
deal with morals, methods of worship and the doctrine of
our Lord. It would be given by the local clergy under the
guidance of the bishop, sometimes by the bishop himself.
More than one bishop actually published his catechetical
lectures. In so important a centre as Antioch this would
inevitably be expanded to meet the needs of the *intelligentsia*,
and would take on a university character very like that of
Alexandria. In this higher flight the subjects dealt with
would be dialectics, physics, philosophy, ethics and theology.

We have already seen that the Bishop of Antioch in the
Aurelian period, Theophilus, wrote a defence of the faith
addressed to a certain Autolycus. He is also important in
the history of theological thought in that he was the first to
use the term Trias or Trinity of the Godhead, including
within that term God, and His Word, and His Wisdom. So

far there is no opposition to Alexandrian teaching. Theophilus even borrows Philo's distinction between the 'immanent' and the 'proceeding' Word and applies it to the Son of God, and his explanation of the manner of the Son's proceeding has a good deal in common with Origen's doctrine of the eternal generation. Nevertheless there was a considerable difference in the spirit with which leaders in the two schools approached the question of the Being of God. While both parties of course held firm to the original tradition of Father, Son and Holy Spirit, the Antiochenes, with their Semitic connexions, took a highly individualised view of God. He was the Jehovah of the Jewish people who had been revealed by Christ as a triad; consequently it was the unity of God that was always uppermost in the minds of the Antiochenes. But the Alexandrians, as we know, stressed the multiple character of God's Being. The two views have been distinguished by certain modern scholars who call the Antiochene teaching 'Economic Trinitarianism' and the Alexandrian 'Pluralistic Trinitarianism'.

But this was not the only point of difference between the two schools. The Christians of Antioch as a result of their close association with Galilee and Jerusalem and the scenes of the Lord's earthly life had always resisted every tendency towards Docetism. Thus Ignatius had insisted upon the flesh-and-blood reality of the Crucified, and Serapion, who was bishop in the time of Septimius Severus, refused to allow the use of the *Gospel of Peter* in divine service on account of its Docetic view of Christ. This led to a twofold departure from the Alexandrian type of teaching. By Antiochenes the Son was very strongly subordinated to the Father. Although this had also been done by Origen it never became the rule in Alexandria, where preoccupation with philosophical questions, and particularly with the Logos doctrine, led to a characteristic emphasis on the divine element in Christ. Thus Antioch stressed the human side of Christ in opposition to what appeared to be the Docetic tendency of Alexandria. This led to a difference in method of exegesis, Antioch rejecting the allegorical method of Alexandria, and substituting for it a hard and literal inter-

pretation. Thus there was much in the Antiochene method which modern scholarship finds agreeable. The importance of this will become clear as the story proceeds.

III. CARTHAGE

We have been thinking of two great cities of the East where speculative questions were always most hotly discussed. We find ourselves in a different atmosphere when we turn to the West, an atmosphere of moral and practical effort rather than of intellectual subtlety. Carthage was not a typical African city. It had its indigenous population, which consisted of descendants of the ancient Berbers, but it had been colonised repeatedly by Phoenicians and Romans. Latin culture had succeeded to native and Canaanite customs. The Christian Church consequently used the Latin language, and Carthage rather than Rome became the first centre of Latin theology. But the Carthaginian church also drew from its soil and surroundings a certain measure of African heat and fervour. That zeal had been exhibited in 180 by the martyrs of Scilli and again in 202 by Perpetua, Felicitas and their companions. In other directions it was also characteristic of the first great Latin father, Tertullian.

Tertullian (c. 155–225) is the Thomas Carlyle of early Christian literature, full of enthusiasm, bitterness and invective, and with a style whose fiery and rugged eloquence is unsurpassed. He was born somewhere about the middle of the second century of heathen parents at Carthage. He was trained in his native city and in Rome as an advocate, and when he became a Christian he brought the legal phraseology and the lawyer's habit of special pleading into the Church. His conversion was due to the constancy he had seen so splendidly displayed by the martyrs; and it was he, as we have seen, who helped to write the *Acta* of Perpetua and Felicitas. He was ordained a presbyter, but afterwards was attracted by the intense zeal and hard rigorism of the Montanists, finally leaving the Church to identify himself with that sect. Beyond the fact that he lived to old age we know nothing more of his history.

With him we pass at once from the broad and inclusive

spirit of Alexandrian Christianity to the exact and legal spirit of the Latins. Where Clement and Origen wish to claim all truth as leading to Christ Tertullian rules out everything pagan as pernicious and will not allow to heretics even the right of appeal to scripture. 'What then,' he asks, 'has Athens in common with Jerusalem?' The faith has been handed down in the Apostolic churches and it admits of no addition or diminution. 'Faith is posited in a rule and it has a law. . . . To know nothing contrary to the rule is to know everything.' He dislikes infant baptism because of the danger of post-baptismal sin. He admits the rightfulness of prayers for the Emperor, but will not allow service in the army. Of Praxeas, who opposed Montanism and taught that God really suffers, he said, 'Praxeas did two bits of business for the devil in Rome; he drove out prophecy and brought in heresy; he put to flight the Paraclete and crucified the Father.' Tertullian's wit was made all the sharper by a hot temper of which in one of his most moving passages he shows a truly Christian abhorrence. It occurs in his tract *on Patience*. 'It will be some sort of consolation to dispute about what it is not given me to enjoy. . . . I, most wretched of men, must sigh for and call after and discourse about that health of patience which I fail to possess.' After such a confession we may be prepared to find that this first great Puritan of the West could be tender and playful and had a love of nature beyond most writers of his time.

His most famous books are the *Apology* and the *Prescription of Heretics*. The former was written about 197 soon after his conversion, while he was still a layman. It is a good example of his special pleading, for he asserts that only the bad emperors have been persecutors and actually claims Tiberius and Marcus Aurelius as protectors of the Christians. It is the first apology to be developed on legal lines. It complains that the procedure employed against Christians is both illegal and absurd; it goes on to assert that the laws against Christianity are contrary to common and natural right; it proceeds to refute the charges of secret infamy and of treachery; and it claims that the Christian society is law-abiding, its doctrine true and its conduct irreproachable.

With regard to the second book mentioned it is to be noted that 'prescription' is a legal term of the Roman courts and connotes a plea that was entered in order to limit an action to a particular point. In this case Tertullian limits the whole discussion with heretics to the one point of their appeal to scripture. He first asserts that heretics have no necessary connexion with Christianity but are the offspring of pagan philosophy. He then contends that the body of essential truth must have been known to the apostles and must have been delivered by them to the churches of their foundation. Its continuance in those churches is guaranteed by the episcopal succession. Heresy, however, being of later date than the Church, has no such succession. Therefore its appeal to scripture has no authority, and consequently its teaching has no claim to credence.

Besides these books there are about thirty other writings ✱ on apologetic, controversial and practical subjects, the tone of which varies according to the author's position at the time of writing, whether orthodox or Montanist. The chief theological importance of Tertullian is that he established the terminology of the West. By his use of the terms 'substance' and 'person' in their legal sense of property and an individual with the right of holding property he made possible that belief in Three Persons and one Substance that formed at once the starting-point and goal of Western Trinitarian doctrine. His influence on sacramental doctrine was also great, for he set that type of thought which laid great stress on the precise repetition of the words and acts of the Lord in order to produce the sacramental effect. In some respects his doctrine came dangerously near the magical. He believed, for instance, that the water of the sea had the power of spontaneously generating the fishes that lived within it; and so he taught that the water blessed in baptism has the power of spontaneously generating the spiritual life of the catechumen.

In morals he was a rigorist, and on this point crossed swords with the Bishop of Rome. The usual view in the Church ever since the *Shepherd of Hermas* had been that for sins committed after baptism only one repentance was

possible. Tertullian adopts this view and describes the one repentance as a period of public penitence. For three sins, however—idolatry, murder and fornication—the Church will take no responsibility at all. Callistus, the Roman bishop, believing that such severity was defeating its own ends, decided to modify it and declared that sexual sins could be regarded as subject to the same penitential system as availed for lighter sins. Those guilty of such sins might be admitted to communion after a period of *exomologesis* or public penance. This seemed to Tertullian an unwarrantable lowering of the Christian standard, and, as we shall see later, he was not alone in his opinion.

IV. ROME

The mention of the Bishop of Rome has brought us to the greatest of all the churches. Here we must notice that what we have to deal with is not a special school of thought but a centre where every school of thought met for discussion. As in modern London, so in the capital of the ancient Empire, representatives of every nation were to be found; everyone with any sort of axe to grind came to Rome sooner or later; every teacher hoped to have the authority of Rome at his back. This naturally placed the Roman church in the position of a judge, and its attitude on any question was a matter of vital importance. The genius of Rome was practical rather than intellectual, a fact that enhanced its judicial authority, while at the same time producing a fresh crop of difficulties for settlement. A church that welcomed so many visitors from all parts of the world, each tenacious of his own customs, was bound to feel these practical issues most keenly.

The first of such difficulties to arise for settlement was the date for keeping Easter. Special importance had been attached to this season from apostolic times. But a difference had arisen between East and West. In Asia the all-important date was the 14th Nisan, the day on which the Passover lamb was slain and, according to the Fourth Gospel, of the crucifixion. On that day, in whatever part of the week it fell, Christians were accustomed to fast until three in the

afternoon and then celebrate the Eucharist. In the West, however, the fast was maintained until the Sunday following the 14th Nisan and then only was the paschal Eucharist celebrated, on the ground that that was the day of the week upon which the Lord rose from the dead. Thus in Rome it frequently happened that visitors ended their fast several days before members of the local church. Various attempts were made to put a stop to this obvious inconvenience. In 155 Polycarp argued the question with the Pope Anicetus, but as neither could persuade the other they agreed to differ. At Laodicea in 167 the Quartodecimans, as those who observed the 14th Nisan were called, fell out among themselves. The reason is not clear: probably some of them regarded the commemoration as nothing more than a continuation of the Passover. Dr. Kidd calls them the Ebionite or Judaising Quartodecimans and designates them as the only heretics in the various groups. Their immediate opponents probably contended that the true commemoration was not of the Passover but of the crucifixion.

A more important stage of the controversy took place in 197 at Rome. There the Pope Victor, a man of much more dominating temper than Anicetus, determined to put a stop to all confusion and to compel the whole Church to accept the Dominical rule, i.e. observe the feast on the Sunday. Conferences were held at various places in East and West, with the result that the Dominical rule was accepted everywhere except in Asia. Victor thereupon pursued his advantage and excommunicated the recalcitrant churches. This, however, raised a storm of protest. Irenaeus tried to act as mediator. Polycrates, the Bishop of Ephesus, sent a dignified letter in which he claimed for his use the authority of S. Philip, S. John, and a host of other Asian saints, and contended that as he was himself the eighth of his family to hold the office of a bishop, he at least ought to know what the correct rule was. Victor seems to have accepted the position with a good grace and to have withdrawn his excommunication. It was well that he did so, as the Quartodecimans seem to have died out by the fourth century. Of course there were still difficulties with regard to the determination of the date

of the full moon, upon which the 14th Nisan depended, but they were met by authorising the Bishop of Alexandria for the East and the Bishop of Rome for the West to send out an annual notice of the day to be kept. This custom lasted until a proper calendar was fixed, which was not until the sixth century.

Other Roman controversies, theological as well as practical, circle round the name of Hippolytus, 'the most obscure of all the early church writers.' Of the origin of this enigmatic figure we know nothing. He was a disciple of Irenaeus and surpassed his master in learning. He was a great figure in Rome during the early third century, but was banished together with the Bishop Pontianus to the Sardinian mines, as already mentioned, by the Emperor Maximin. As a result of his sufferings he died, and received the seemingly unique honour of a statue, which was unearthed in 1551, a headless figure seated in a chair, his cycle for determining the date of Easter and the names of his books engraved upon it.

As to Hippolytus' actual position in the Church of Rome we are very uncertain. He writes as a bishop, but there is no record that he was ever Bishop of Rome. It has been suggested that he was Bishop of Portus at the mouth of the Tiber, the port of Rome, but there is no evidence. A list of the bishops of Rome belonging to the middle of the fourth century speaks of him as a presbyter. He was certainly a very bitter opponent of the Bishop Callistus. But the silence of other writers as to any schism made Lightfoot believe that he might have been the Bishop of the foreign congregation at Portus. At best, however, that is only a guess and it is generally believed that he was in point of fact the first anti-pope. At all events he was a fellow-sufferer with the later Pope Pontianus, and the Roman Church to-day reckons him as a saint and martyr.

The quarrel between Hippolytus and Callistus was largely personal, and Hippolytus found no difficulty in raking up sordid memories of Callistus' past. But there was also a real difference in point of view. Hippolytus took up the rigorist attitude of Tertullian towards moral questions and was genuinely shocked at what he considered Callistus'

concessions to wickedness. 'He was the first to adopt the plan of condoning the sensual pleasures of men, saying that all men had their sins absolved by him. . . . In his time began bishops, priests and deacons twice and three times married to be appointed to clerical office. And if one already in office should marry, he was allowed to remain in office as if he had committed no sin.' It was not only to his penitential system that Hippolytus objected, but also to the arrangements made by Callistus for recognising the unions with slaves or freedmen of well-born Christian women who did not wish to forfeit their rank by a servile marriage.

Another subject of controversy was that of the divine unity. We have already noticed the difference between pluralistic and economic views of the Trinity. Each contained an element of truth, but each might be pushed to an impossible extreme. The danger was particularly pressing for those who stressed the economic view. Its extreme upholders were called Monarchians because they believed in one only fount of divine being. There were two opposed sections of them, and representatives of both appeared and clamoured for recognition at Rome. The one section consisted of Modalist Monarchians and the other of Adoptianist Monarchians.

To take the latter first. The Adoptianist school was represented by Theodotus, a leather merchant from Byzantium, who came to Rome just before the end of the second century. He believed in one original undifferentiated Deity, who had sent His spirit upon the man Jesus at His baptism and given Him the power to work miracles. The perfect co-operation between the divine and human in the Christ led to His adoption into the Godhead after the resurrection. This teaching brought prompt excommunication, but it was revived and a sect made to foster it by a second Theodotus, a banker, with the assistance of a certain Artemas, somewhere about 230. The latter of the two sectarians claimed in face of all the facts that this had actually been reckoned orthodox teaching until the time of Pope Victor. Indeed it must have passed for such long after, since we know that the great Augustine just before his conversion

still thought of it as the common view of the Church. With Paul of Samosata, the best-known exponent of this type of thought, we shall have to deal at a later stage.

It is to be noticed that on the Adoptianist view the distinctions in the Godhead, once made, were permanent. The Modalists solved the problem in a very different way. In their view there never were any permanent distinctions within the Godhead but only three temporary phases in the operation of one divine Person. Thus the one God acted as Father in creation, as Son in redemption, and again as Spirit within the world and man. But when the need for these modes or phases of activity was passed the Godhead assumed its undifferentiated character once more. This teaching had the advantage of preserving the full divinity of Christ, which seemed to be endangered by the Adoptianists, but it had the paradoxical result of making it appear that God sat on His own right hand. It also meant that it must have been the Father Himself who died upon the cross. Praxeas indeed taught that doctrine, which was dubbed Patripassianism, at Rome, and as we have seen earned on that account the biting sarcasm of Tertullian. Consequently when he tried to spread the same teaching in Tertullian's own town of Carthage he was compelled to sign a recantation. Noetus was also condemned for teaching the same views at Smyrna, but he too appeared at Rome and modified the doctrine by explaining that the Eternal God had by the exercise of His own will put Himself into a condition of visibility and passibility. The fully developed doctrine appeared with Sabellius, the head of a school founded at Rome for the expounding of Modalist principles. He said that the one God worked sometimes as Father, sometimes as Son, and sometimes as Holy Spirit, there being one substance and three activities (*prosopa*). The relation between the activities he likened to the body, soul and spirit of man and to the roundness, heat and light of the sun.

This teaching seems to have been welcomed in Rome by Pope Zephyrinus as an aid in defending the faith against the Adoptianists. Hippolytus, however, with great boldness attacked both types of Monarchianism, and when Callistus,

a protégé of Zephyrinus, succeeded his master, Hippolytus scored off his enemy by declaring that as a presbyter he had been a supporter of Praxeas. Callistus was thus driven to condemn Sabellius. It is possible indeed that he had never gone further than the theory of 'compassion', according to which the Father suffered together with the Son. It is also possible that he was unfavourable to the Logos doctrine with its tendency to a pluralistic theory of the Trinity, which to Callistus might savour too much of tritheism. It is perhaps Hippolytus' greatest claim to distinction that he, the last Roman teacher to write in Greek, did something to preserve this characteristic Greek doctrine of the Logos in the central church of the Empire. This he did in his doctrinal books written for the purpose of refuting heresy, of which his work commonly known as *Philosophumena* and his *Homily against Noetus* are the best known. He was also a great Biblical scholar and wrote commentaries on most of the books of the Bible. In these he steered a middle course between the allegorism of Alexandria and the literalism of Antioch. His *Commentary on Daniel* dating from about 204 A.D. is the earliest Christian commentary on a book of the Bible still remaining to us. The only other class of his writings that need be specially mentioned is his contribution to apologetic literature. Two such works are known, one addressed to Jews, the other to Greeks. But he was also responsible for a collection of ecclesiastical canons, though not in the fully-developed form that goes by his name.

CHAPTER VIII

CHURCH LIFE AND WORSHIP

I. The Church Orders

THE mention of the Canons of Hippolytus leads naturally to the consideration of a fresh type of Christian literature. This is the group of Church Orders, to which increased attention has been given in recent years, and from which we derive much valuable information as to the inner life of the Church in early days. They are manuals that give instruction on the celebration of the sacraments and the general ordering of the Christian life. They are obviously pseudonymous, purporting to give the injunctions that were uttered by the apostles for the regulation of the churches. They exist in a bewildering series of editions, and it is not altogether easy to trace the stages by which they were built up. The prototype may be found in the *Pastoral Epistles*, but the first actual example is certainly the *Didache*.

Of this work we have already said sufficient. It was followed sometime during the third century by a similar manual which has no original title but is now generally known as the *Apostolic Church Order*. Harnack thought that it emanated from Egypt, but it is more likely to have been composed, like the *Didache*, in the more remote parts of Palestine or Syria. It attributes each section of the *Two Ways*, which it includes, to a separate apostle, makes no mention of S. Paul, and appears to know no other Gospels than those of Matthew and John.

Next in order of time comes the *Apostolic Tradition*, a genuine work of Hippolytus, formerly known as the *Egyptian Church Order*, which belongs to the period about 220. It, however, is the only set of these canons that comes from the West. It is our richest source of information for the Roman

church of the second century, and it set the standard in the East for many generations. Easton says of it:

In the East, especially in Egypt and Syria, Hippolytus's work was accepted as possessing high authority. It was of course not treated as infallible, for later legal writers do not hesitate to amend or omit laws disagreeing with local usage. Yet the title Hippolytus chose for his work was taken really seriously, and he, more than any other Church Father, gave the laws and the liturgy of the Eastern Church their permanent form.

In the East a new edition appeared about 230 to 250, known as the *Didascalia*, which has survived in a Syriac text. In character it is somewhat reminiscent of the Jewish Christians, descendants of whom may easily have survived and given themselves to reconstructions of the Law. The compilers of this book dislike the spirit of Deuteronomy, and give an elaborate account of the Council of Jerusalem. They appear deliberately to minimise the importance of S. Paul.

The *Didascalia* was the basis of the first six books of the *Apostolic Constitutions*, a comprehensive edition of this type of instruction which appeared in the second half of the fourth century. This work belongs more clearly to the regions of the Great Church, whether in Syria or Palestine. Caesarea is more likely to be its place of origin than Antioch, for although S. Paul is mentioned in the later chapters, he nowhere has the importance of the other apostles. It has been suggested with a good deal of probability that the author was Acacius of Caesarea (340–366).

There are two other editions of the *Apostolic Tradition* which must be mentioned. The one is the *Testament of our Lord*, which attributes the regulations to the risen Christ and adds instructions on church architecture and clerical duties. It was probably produced in Syria soon after 360. The other is the so-called *Canons of Hippolytus*, which is really a more conservative revised version of the *Tradition*. It belongs to the fifth century and its place of origin was probably Egypt.

The Church Orders in the East thus seem to have been the product of circles which, without being consciously

anti-Pauline like those which produced the Clementines, yet attached little importance to the life and work of S. Paul. That is to say that they were in some faint sense Judaistic. This may create some prejudice against their testimony, yet they contain material of very great value. If we combine them with writings of Tertullian and Justin and with the Sacramentary of Serapion, Bishop of Thmuis (337–370), which gives us the oldest extant written liturgy, we shall have a considerable store of information on the more intimate details of Christian life in the early centuries.

II. Daily Life

Beginning with the Christian in the home, we realise at once how different was his life from that of the pagan. It would be very hard for that difference to escape notice for long. Basilides, the soldier martyr, was betrayed as a Christian because he refused to take an oath with his fellow-soldiers. Tertullian gives a graphic picture of the difficulties that might arise between a Christian wife and a pagan husband. 'If a station is to be made, her husband will arrange to meet her at the baths; if fasts are to be kept, her husband will be giving a feast on the same day; if she has to go out, never will family business be more hindering. For who would allow his wife to go round to other people's houses, and especially to all the poorer cottages for the sake of visiting the brethren? Who would willingly let her be taken from his side for meetings at night, if it should be her duty? Who, in short, would put up with her absence all night at the Easter solemnities without misgivings? Who would let her creep into a prison to kiss a martyr's chains? or indeed to meet any one of the brethren for the kiss?' Such differences in families often embittered the last hours of martyrs. Perpetua's one grief was the thought of the sorrow that her sufferings would bring to her pagan father.

The division persisted outside the home in the world of business. There were some trades, such as idol-making, acting, fighting in the arena, and those connected with immorality which were forbidden to the Christian. Others, like the army, were at best regarded as doubtful and by the

rigorists were condemned. And these key-trades carried with them a host of allied trades. Thus no Christian could become a cutter of bone tickets for the arena, nor a polisher of sacrificial knives. Even the holding of civil office under the Government was difficult, when the ceremonies connected with office involved the recognition of heathen gods. Indeed in all his public and private life the Christian was surrounded by the tokens of another worship, and no day passed during which he had not to settle with his conscience the doubtful line beyond which lay actual betrayal of the Christ.

The social life of the Empire, based as it was on an intensely aristocratic theory, was completely overturned in early Christian practice. No effort indeed was made to put a stop to the system of slavery, but its sting was drawn by the glad recognition of the fact that all were brothers in Christ. Slaves came with their masters to the Lord's Table, and suffered by their side in the persecutions. They were eligible for the highest offices in the Church: Callistus was not the only example of a slave who became Bishop of Rome. The same independence of view was seen in the treatment of children. In Roman law the father had a right of property in his children up to any age, and although the power of life and death was seldom exercised except in the case of exposure, it was still there. The custom of exposing children was one of the most terrible evils of contemporary life. A well-known letter from an Alexandrian soldier to his wife shows how, after promising to send her some of his pay when he gets it, he goes on to remark that if the still unborn child turns out to be a girl she had better expose it. That was a thing absolutely forbidden in Christian communities. 'Christians marry', says the author to Diognetus, 'like the rest of the world. They beget children, but they do not cast their offspring adrift.' A new conception of the sanctity of human life had entered into the world.

III. Worship and Penitence

Until the third century services and meetings were held in private houses, as they had been originally in the upper room at Jerusalem. The church in a particular house would

include the members of the family, the slaves and dependants, together with other Christians situated conveniently near. There might be several such small communities in one city. The insistence on the authority of the Bishop, which forms so marked a feature of second-century writings, had as part of its purpose the bringing of these various bodies under one central control. In the reign of Alexander Severus, about 222, we begin to hear of special buildings being used as churches. The *Apostolic Constitutions* recommend an oblong structure looking to the East. Later a sanctuary and a narthex were marked off, and during the more peaceful parts of the third century some of these ecclesiastical buildings became of considerable importance. Within the church was the Holy Table, behind which facing the people and with his presbyters on either hand sat the Bishop. Men and women sat apart, and each class had its own place assigned to it, Tertullian being particularly horrified if a virgin should stray among the widows. Places were found for visitors befitting their rank and condition.

Worship from the earliest times consisted of the singing of hymns, reading of scriptures, prayers and Eucharist. It is generally thought that the Agape or love-feast was an original accompaniment of the Eucharist. But it is more probable that the Eucharist was always a purely ritual meal, and that the holding of a semi-sacred full meal began in unorthodox circles, not being introduced into the main stream of Church life until towards the end of the second century. Then it seems to have been a kind of community meal to which all contributed, and to have become a gift of charity from the rich to the poor before it was finally abandoned.

The attitude of the Church to the sinner within her fold was dictated by the threefold need to uphold a good example to the flock and to bear a good witness to those who were without as well as to restore the wrong-doer. The most difficult cases were those of people who had given way in persecution, and they provided controversies with which we must deal later. The other great difficulty was the case of those guilty of fleshly sins. We have already traced the

development of the Church's practice in this respect from Hermas to Callistus. The *Didascalia* endeavours to keep the mean between harshness and laxity; it warns the Bishop against being afraid to bring the sinner under discipline and at the same time tells him that his business is not to condemn but to save. 'Judge severely, O Bishop, like Almighty God, and receive those who repent with compassion like God.' The guilty are to be excommunicated, and to be received back only after due penance.

Excommunication involved literally staying outside the church during the service. 'When he is put out, be not angry with him and contend with him, but let him keep outside of the church, and then let them go in and make supplication for him. . . . Then thou, O Bishop, command him to come in and thyself ask him if he repents. If he be worthy to be received into the Church, appoint him days of fasting according to his fault, two or three or five or seven weeks, and thus allow him to go, saying to him all that is proper for admonition and doctrine.'

An important element in this penitential system was the *exomologesis* or public confession of sin before the assembled congregation. This was part of a period of penance voluntarily entered upon. Where a sinner did not know whether he ought to submit to such a period of probation or not, advice could be sought in a private confession. If a sinner did not voluntarily seek discipline but was charged by a fellow-Christian (no charge from a heathen being admitted), the case was tried by a sort of court presided over by the bishop but so representative of the whole Church that even the laity seem to have taken a share in pronouncing judgment. It will be remembered that not only S. Paul but also the organisers of pagan clubs and *collegia* condemned the practice of resort to the civil courts: it was held that the members of any brotherhood ought to be able to settle their differences among themselves. Cases that might come before the Christian bodies for jurisdiction were those of fraud, false witness, fleshly sins, homicide, heresy, schism, idolatry and magic. The severity of the period of penance imposed varied with different churches. The most elaborate system

comes from Asia Minor, where we hear of three successive stages through which the penitent must pass. The first was that of the Hearers, who were dismissed from the Eucharist after the sermon; the second was that of the Kneelers, who stayed only a little longer while the congregation prayed over them; the last was that of the Consistents, who remained throughout the service but were not allowed to join in the oblation or to make their communion.

IV. Special Days

Penitential days and seasons to be observed by the whole Church came in very early. Already in the *Didache* we have found Wednesday and Friday set apart as station days, that is, days on which a special stand was made against the enemies of the soul. The custom was no doubt borrowed from the Jews, who kept Tuesdays and Thursdays in memory of Moses' journey up and down the Mount. The Christian days were those of the betrayal and crucifixion. 'When the Bridegroom shall be taken away then shall ye fast in those days.' The fast ended at three o'clock in the afternoon. In addition, a fast was kept annually on the Friday and Saturday of Holy Week. In the *Didascalia* this fast lasts for the whole of the week. Those who were to be baptised at Easter began their period of fasting forty days before, and it was probably this that led to our present practice of Lenten observance.

The earliest feasts to be observed were those of Easter and Sunday. The Easter festival lasted until Pentecost, and Tertullian mentions the custom of not kneeling for worship during that time. The Sunday was an Easter day in every week and was carefully distinguished from the Jewish sabbath. Until the time of Constantine there was no obligation to refrain from labour on that day, although Tertullian mentions the beginning of a pious effort in that direction. The characteristic note of the day was worship, and the essential element in that worship was the Eucharist.

V. The Eucharist

The Eucharist or Thanksgiving was something quite different from the grace which Aristides tells us was said at

every meal. It was the repetition of the rite which it was believed Jesus had instituted at the last meal of which He partook with His disciples. It is necessary to say this, as a modern historian has stated that in the New Testament and in the *Didache* it is the solemn grace which closed an evening meal. When the practice of morning celebration began is not clear. Pliny's letter is indecisive, but by Justin's time the custom was established, and by Tertullian's day there was a general rule of fasting communion. The *Apostolic Constitutions* reveal the fact that children were accustomed to be present and to communicate. Non-communicating attendance was imposed upon the Consistents or highest class of penitents. For others than penitents and catechumens it was a highly prized privilege to receive the Sacrament each Sunday. Those who were sick were communicated at home, not by a special celebration but by distribution from the central Liturgy, the ministrants being deacons in the case of men and deaconesses in the case of women. During the times of persecution this duty exposed the messengers to special danger. There is a moving story of the young Tarcisius, who allowed himself to be done to death rather than deliver up the sacred Host that he was carrying. It was probably on account of this danger that there arose the custom of allowing the laity to take to their homes a sufficient supply of the consecrated Bread to last for some time. This was kept in a special 'ark' and used each morning before other food was taken. Tertullian urges it as one of the disadvantages of a mixed marriage that the husband would not know what the wife was about while this ceremony was being performed; no doubt he would be inclined to suspect magic. Probably this custom did not last long. At any rate it was ultimately superseded by the practice of reserving the Sacrament in church.

As for the Liturgy in church, the central act began after the exclusion of penitents and catechumens. Then came the 'common prayers' and the kiss of peace. At the offertory the faithful brought their gifts of bread, upon which, together with the mixed chalice of wine and water brought by the deacons, the Bishop and presbyters laid their hands. The

Bishop recited the Thanksgiving, to the precise words of which he was not tied down, and the whole congregation took their share in the act of consecration by reciting the great Amen. The Elements were then administered by the Bishop, priests and deacons. In the *Didache* there is given a form of thanksgiving 'after ye are filled', which includes a beautiful prayer for the Church and for the coming of the Kingdom. 'Remember, Lord, Thy Church, to deliver her from all evil, and to perfect her in Thy love, and gather together from the four winds her that is sanctified into Thy Kingdom which Thou didst prepare for her. For Thine is the power and the glory for ever. Come grace and let this world pass away. Hosanna to the God of David. If any is holy let him come: if any is unholy let him repent. Maranatha. Amen.'

VI. BAPTISM

Baptisms were normally held only at Easter; and this sacrament of initiation, occurring only once in the Christian's life, was held in even greater esteem than was the Eucharist. It was led up to by a long preparation, though of course there was an exception to this in the case of infants. Evidence for infant baptism becomes strong before the end of the second century. Polycarp, for instance, who had served Christ for eighty and six years, was probably baptised in infancy. But there were some, like Tertullian, who objected to the practice. By the middle of the third century Cyprian and others will not have children kept without the rite so long as eight days after their birth. They might be baptised at any time by clergy or, in case of necessity, by lay folk, and only those born just before Easter were brought to the great service. For adults a long period of catechumenate was necessary.

Even before being admitted to the catechumenate the postulant went through a long examination at the hands of the catechists. If he were the slave of a Christian, his master's consent and testimonial must be obtained. If he had a pagan master, he must be careful to please him. If he were a married man, he must be faithful; if he were unmarried, he

must be chaste. If he were of unsound mind, he could receive no instruction until the malady was over—a provision that will not seem harsh if we remember the close connexion thought to prevail between insanity and demoniacal possession. The examination ended with a determined effort to see that the candidate was not pursuing any unlawful trade or profession. Then, if accepted, he was admitted to the catechumenate with the imposition of the hand.

After this ceremony the catechumen was considered as a Christian and had his own place in church, where he was allowed to remain for the Eucharist up to the end of the sermon. At the Agape he was not allowed to sit down with the faithful but was given a special cup and bread that had been exorcised. Normally he was kept under instruction for two or three years. The teaching would be twofold, moral and doctrinal. Of the former a sufficient example is given in the document on the 'Two Ways' already mentioned as incorporated in the *Didache*. Of the latter no complete example exists earlier than the fourth century, but its character can be judged from the Rule of Faith and its summary in the Apostles' Creed, the original form of which was the pattern for all baptismal creeds in the West.

Before Easter came round the catechists selected those sufficiently advanced for baptism, and put them through a second examination in which sponsors were called upon to witness to their moral fitness. Then throughout the forty days of Lent they were given more advanced instruction; also they were daily exorcised and subjected to fasting and penitential exercises. On the Wednesday in Holy Week the final examination took place before the Bishop. On Thursday they bathed, fasted on Friday, and on Saturday they were solemnly exorcised by the Bishop, who laid his hand on them, breathed on their face, and signed them with the cross. Before the Sunday there was an all-night vigil, and at cockcrow they were all taken to the baptistery where they undressed while the Bishop blessed the water and the oils.

After this each candidate in turn pronounced a renunciation of the devil and all his works. Then he was again exorcised, in Rome with oil and in Africa with the laying on

of the hand. Finally he was taken down into the font, where he made a short confession of faith. The Bishop put to him the three main articles of the creed in question form, after each of which he baptised him, either by plunging him beneath the water or by pouring water over his head or by placing him beneath a jet. Then the newly baptised ascended from the font, and was anointed with the oil of thanksgiving, which by Tertullian is interpreted as giving him a share in the sacerdotal character of the Messiah.

Confirmation followed immediately upon baptism and was indeed a part of it. When all had been baptised, they repaired with the Bishop to the church. There he laid his hand upon them, prayed, anointed them with consecrated oil, signed them with the cross, and kissed them. This represents the Roman use. Elsewhere in the West there seems to have been no unction, while in the East it was the imposition of the hand that disappeared.

After the Confirmation the Liturgy was resumed, the new members now for the first time taking part in the central act. A special feature introduced for their benefit was the offering with the bread and wine of two cups, one of water and the other of milk mingled with honey. After the thanksgiving these were administered to the new communicants to signify respectively their inward washing and the Promised Land into which they had entered.

CHAPTER IX

RENEWED PERSECUTION

THE third century, as we have seen, consisted of two long periods of peace set in a framework of persecution. The comparative quiet of the first half had witnessed great growth and consolidation of the Church. The Christian society had become that terror of the State, an empire within the Empire. But success had brought also a weakening of moral fibre. There had been heresy and schism, and in spite of all precautions there had crept into the Church a number of merely nominal Christians. It was perhaps a providential judgment that the worst persecution yet endured was about to fall.

Such peace as the Church had enjoyed had rested on no legal basis, but had arisen out of the love of succeeding emperors for Oriental mysteries and the consequent religious syncretism. In the State this departure from the old standards synchronised with much moral corruption and national decay. The thousandth anniversary of the founding of Rome had just been celebrated, but, as Gibbon points out, twenty years of shame and misfortune for the Empire were now beginning. It was not to occur, however, without a gallant effort to stop the rot. This effort was undertaken by the Emperor Decius (249–251). He felt that improvement must come by way of a return to the cleaner morals and purer religion of the old days. Taking Trajan as his model he revived the office of Censor, appointing Valerian with extraordinary powers, and attempting through him to remove all traces of those Eastern religions which he felt had weakened the national strength. As against the Church this meant persecution. That popular feeling would be with the Emperor had been shown by a rising of the mob against the Christians at Alexandria towards the end of the

reign of Philip the Arabian. The issue once fairly set, Decius did not shrink from making the attempt to root out Christianity as thoroughgoing as he could. The stress of feeling under which he laboured is well shown by Dr. Bigg, who enumerates the actual causes of the persecution as four, viz. the fear that the Christians would foment disloyalty at the moment of extreme danger from external enemies; the terror induced by a new visitation of the plague; the reaction against the old syncretism; and the personal keenness of the Censor.

The actual edict that announced the beginning of this war of extermination has been lost, but there is abundant evidence of the unique character of the persecution. Three points about it should be especially noticed: it was an official campaign, having nothing to do with that mob-law which had frequently been the cause of trouble for the Church in the past; it was universal throughout the Empire, not confined to one particular province as such outbursts often were before; and thirdly, it was systematic, beginning on a fixed day and leaving nothing to the initiative of the local magistrates. So much for the general character of the persecution. It was equally unique in its method of procedure. Aiming to destroy the prestige and influence of the Church, it endeavoured to make apostates rather than martyrs. The leaders bore the brunt of the attack. The bishops, if caught, were severely dealt with, and the question was forced upon them whether flight were legitimate.

Cyprian of Carthage answered in the affirmative and acted upon his opinion. Dionysius of Alexandria, after having been captured, allowed himself to be rescued. To have rushed into captivity would have played into the enemy's hand. It was necessary that the leaders should survive, if possible, in order that they might at least direct their flocks from a distance; otherwise the whole organisation of the Church might have broken up. As for the rank and file, everything possible was done by government to make them apostatise. On a fixed day every citizen was to appear before the local magistrate and a special commissioner at some temple with sacrificial crowns on their heads. Either they

must sacrifice or they must at least throw incense upon the altar. If they had been under suspicion but now conformed, a certificate (*libellus*) was given them. This consisted of a statement by the accused that he had sacrificed, countersigned by the officer in charge of the ceremony. A typical certificate is as follows: 'To the officers in charge of the sacrifices of the village of Alexander's Isle, from Aurelius Diogenes, the son of Satabus, of the village of Alexander's Isle, aged about 72, with a scar on his right eyebrow. I have always sacrificed to the gods; and now in your presence according to the commands I have sacrificed and made a libation and tasted of the victims: and I desire you to subscribe. Fare ye well.' Then follows the date, together with the signatures of the villager and the witness. It goes without saying that such certificates were often granted on inadequate grounds, and that many whose consciences would not allow them actually to apostatise obtained a *libellus* by bribery or favour. In case of complete refusal to conform there would follow imprisonment with repeated efforts at persuasion, backed up by torture. Origen, for instance, suffered so much in prison that he never recovered. After complete and final obstinacy there followed execution, as in the case of Fabian, Bishop of Rome.

The result was as might have been expected. At first there were many apostates, but as the persecution proceeded and the waverers were weeded out, resistance became fiercer until it bordered upon fanaticism. Commodianus in Palestine, who wrote at this time the first Christian Latin poem, gives in rough and uncouth verse what must have been popular sentiment. He enumerates seven persecutions from which the Church has suffered and likens them to the seven last plagues of the Apocalypse. The end of the world is at hand: Rome is Antichrist, and this last persecution represents the return of Nero. But Nero is destroyed by a Jewish Antichrist marching at the head of a Persian host. He in his turn is slain by angels and cast into the lake of fire. The Lost Tribes then return to Zion, and God comes to judgment and to destroy the wicked. The situation, however, was not saved by such prophetic denunciation, but

by the cool caution of leaders like Cyprian and by the calm courage of the faithful. The persecution grew less and less successful until it was stayed by the death of its instigator.

Decius died in battle against the Goths, 'the first Emperor who died fighting against a foreign enemy upon Roman soil'. This defeat was followed by a period of anarchy within the Empire, the effects of which were made more terrible by the continuance of the plague. In this visitation the Christians distinguished themselves by their humanity. While the pagans only too often fled at the first sign of sickness, deserting even friends and relatives, the members of the Church remained not only to bury the dead but to tend the afflicted whether friend or foe. Dionysius in Alexandria and Cyprian in Carthage gained an honourable name in this connexion. But this did not avail to save the Church from further persecution.

The riot of anarchy was at last ended by the choice of Valerian (253–260) as Emperor. He had been Censor in the reign of Decius, and in character was somewhat like his master. For the first three years of his reign he was constrained to leave the Church in peace, but increasing difficulties may have made him feel that the Christians were not doing their share in the defence of the Empire. In the midst of his struggle with the barbarians he decided to bring them to heel. Like Decius he made the leaders his special point of attack, but he added to his predecessor's ingenuity by confiscating the property of the wealthy and so endeavouring to make Christianity the religion of the outcast and poor. Another point that showed the Government's advancing knowledge of Church customs was the refusal to countenance gatherings for worship in the catacombs. Sixtus II, the Bishop of Rome, disregarded this injunction so far as to translate the relics of SS. Peter and Paul to the catacomb on the Appian Way on June 29, 258; whence arose the custom of observing the feasts of both apostles together on that day. But Sixtus paid the penalty with his life. He was beheaded as he sat in his episcopal chair, and four of his deacons were slain beside him.

This is the first persecution in which we find a carefully graduated scale of punishments. The details are preserved in a letter of Cyprian. 'Valerian had sent a rescript to the Senate to the effect that bishops, priests and deacons should immediately be punished: but that senators and men of importance and Roman knights should lose their dignity and moreover be deprived of their property; and if when their means were taken away they should persist in being Christians, then they should lose their heads; that matrons should be deprived of their property and be sent into banishment; but that people of Caesar's household, whoever of them had either confessed before, or should now confess, should have their property confiscated, and should be sent in chains by assignment to Caesar's estates.' The great Cyprian himself perished. He was first sent into exile and then summoned by the proconsul to stand his trial at Utica. Cyprian, however, was unwilling to die out of Carthage, and was there found in his own house when the proconsul came to that city. His speedy arrest, trial, and execution by beheading followed. 'An easy death', says Gibbon. At this time also occurred the death of the deacon Lawrence on his gridiron, and probably also of the boy Tarcisius whom we have before mentioned. Valerian gained nothing by his severity. He managed to drive back the Parthians on the Euphrates, but as he returned he was treacherously taken by the Persians and died in captivity.

The lesson was not lost upon his successor Gallienus (260–268). In the break-up of the defence of Asia, with the Persians conquerors of Antioch and a rival preserving the integrity of Gaul, he declared the persecution at an end, and actually restored to the Church her confiscated property. This meant the official recognition of practical toleration. We have no edict in which this new attitude is prescribed, but Eusebius gives a rescript which outlines it clearly enough. It is addressed by Gallienus to Dionysius and other bishops. 'I have ordered the bounty of my gift to be declared throughout the world that the places of worship be restored. And for this purpose you may use this copy of my rescript that no one may molest you. And this that you

may now lawfully do has long been conceded by me. And therefore Aurelius Cyrenius, the chief administrator, will keep this copy which I have given.' So was inaugurated the second great peace, which lasted till the end of the century.

CHAPTER X

CYPRIAN

THE greatest Christian figure in the West during these times of persecution was Thascius Caecilius Cyprianus. He was not converted till middle life; before that he had been a successful and wealthy barrister or professor of rhetoric. He was baptised in 246, and tells of the access of joy that the change brought into his life. It received practical expression in the sale of his pleasure gardens in order that he might give the proceeds to the poor. But his popularity was such that his friends bought the gardens and gave them back to him. Shortly afterwards he was ordained to the priesthood, and within two years he was elected Bishop of Carthage. This was a compliment to his fame and a witness to the affection he had inspired among the laity; but it left him implacable enemies among the presbyters.

As a Christian he took for his hero his fellow-townsman, Tertullian. Indeed he went even further than Tertullian in his refusal to study any literature that was not Christian. We should naturally therefore expect on his part a fierce and hot-headed fanaticism; but in point of fact he was a really great ecclesiastical statesman, who was ready to endanger if necessary his own reputation so long as he secured the best end for his society. We have seen his courage in time of plague and his caution in time of persecution: it is evident that we have here a great individual spirit subdued to the ability of a great administrator. We see the same combination at work in the three important controversies in which he was the central figure.

I. The Lapsed

The Decian persecution, which broke out the year after Cyprian's consecration, had gained both by the cowardice

of some Christians and also by the exaggerated respect paid to the courage of others. It was held that those who had remained staunch and consequently suffered had acquired sufficient merit to atone for those who had been weak and had given way. As the persecution died down the frailer brethren began to creep back to the Church's services. With them they brought, not their *libelli* signed by the presiding officer at the sacrifice, but another sort of *libellus* bearing the signature of some hero who had gone to prison, to torture, or to death for the faith. Such a confessor or martyr, it was alleged, having won the victory for himself could hand the fruit of it to his weaker brethren; and so he had granted a certificate of readmission to those who with tears had applied for it.

How difficult this made things for the Church can easily be imagined. In some cases the certificates had been granted wholesale, and if their authority had been accepted it would have meant the breakdown of all discipline. Thus there would have been no prospect of presenting a united front to the enemy at the next attack. What outrageous fraud the system might lead to can be judged from a letter of Cyprian's in which he tells how a certain Lucian had continued writing such certificates in the name of the confessor Paulus even after Paulus was dead. 'In order in some measure to put a stop to this practice, I wrote letters to them . . . in which I did not cease to beseech and persuade them that some consideration might be had for the gospel and for the law of the Lord. In reply to which Lucian, as if some more moderate and temperate step were being taken, wrote in the name of all the confessors. . . . For he wrote in the name of all that they had all given peace and that he wished this decree to be notified by me to the other bishops.'

Cyprian's own action in seeking safety by flight was hardly understood by those who were doing everything possible to nerve themselves and others to the limit of endurance, and it gave a handle to those who had resented his elevation to the episcopate. Chief among the latter was the presbyter Novatus, who made a great point of the apparent coldness shown by the Bishop to the confessors.

It was a delicate situation and it was made worse when to Novatus was added one of the most wealthy and influential laymen in the diocese, named Felicissimus. An open breach occurred and both parties to the dispute sought support at Rome.

In the capital a curiously parallel state of affairs had arisen. The personal spite of Novatus against Cyprian had its counterpart in the feud between the theologian Novatian and his diocesan. This Novatian was an able man and the first Latin writer in the Roman Church. His work on the Trinity, in the form of an exposition of the three main articles of the creed, written in reply to the Sabellians and other heretics and characterised by much lofty eloquence and knowledge of the Scriptures, was a valuable contribution to theological studies. His career, however, had been stormy. *
Baptised during an illness, he found afterwards that there were some who on that ground objected to his ordination to the priesthood. He seems to have been a catechist of the type of Clement and Origen, and he had a close friend in Pope Fabian. It is possible that on Fabian's martyrdom Novatian hoped to succeed him. The choice of the Church, however, fell on another presbyter, Cornelius; whereupon Novatian was elected bishop by his own faction and became an anti-pope, a schism of some importance being thus started.

Novatian's original attitude on the subject of the lapsed was very like that of Cyprian, but as this moderate line was also taken by Cornelius, Novatian, in order to show his superiority, must needs become the champion of an extreme rigorism. Nevertheless it was with him that Novatus, the champion of laxity at Carthage, formed an alliance. In opposition to this combination Cornelius and Cyprian recognised and supported each other. The whole effort of the two bishops was to regularise the attitude of the Church towards the lapsed. The question was at first kept open until it could be dealt with by a council. Then at Carthage in 251 it was decided to ignore the certificates obtained from confessors and to consider each case on its merits. Those who had actually sacrificed were not to be readmitted except

in extremis. In judging other cases extenuating circumstances were to be taken into consideration. There was to be a public confession, a period of penance commensurate with the fault, and then readmission by imposition of hands. Clergy might be restored on these terms to communion, but never again to the exercise of their functions.

These measures were at least strong enough to emphasise the evil of apostasy. They were very effective at Carthage, where the council condemned Felicissimus and upheld his excommunication. They were accepted by a council at Rome, where the confessors returned to the communion of Cornelius; but the schism spread to the East and lingered on some time there under the protection of the Bishop of Antioch. A fresh turn was given to the problem of the lapsed in 252, when there seemed likelihood of another persecution. Then in order that they might be strengthened to face the new trial Cyprian proclaimed a general pardon to all who at that time were doing penance.

II. Baptism

In the next controversy Cyprian was not so successful in carrying his point. A difficulty had arisen over the readmission to the Church of repentant heretics and schismatics. Adherents of the Gnostics were examples of the former, and Novatianists of the latter. Where such people had originally been members of the Catholic society and had been baptised therein, the custom was to readmit them after penance by imposition of hands. But when they had received their baptism from some schismatic or heretical body, ought that baptism to be regarded as valid or not? Custom in this case had apparently varied, the usual practice being to accept their baptism and not to expect them to be re-baptised. But there were exceptions: Tertullian had strongly opposed this usage and the African bishops at least had followed him. To Cyprian the matter seemed of fundamental importance: the very soul of the penitent was at stake, for baptism removed all sin, and those who wished to return should have this benefit. They could not have had it in schism, for 'baptism there is none outside the

Church'. Nor could it be replied that their baptism must be valid on the ground that schismatics baptised with the same creed as the Church, for they had no true Church and that made the last clause of the creed meaningless. The truth is that the Church is God's instrument for man's salvation. There is thus no salvation outside the Church, for 'he cannot have God for his Father who has not the Church for his mother'. It is no answer to say that re-baptism is contrary to the age-long custom of Christians, for since the schismatic baptism is no baptism, the penitent is not re-baptised but baptised for the first time.

Cyprian's view was warmly supported in his own country, where the Novatianists had embittered local feeling by presuming to baptise those whom they won over from the Church. However, Stephen, the new Bishop of Rome, was known to be of a contrary opinion, and a deputation of bishops from Carthage waited upon him. He refused to see them, and answered an official letter by excommunicating those who did not agree with him. This aroused intense indignation in Africa and the East. A council of eighty-seven African bishops in 256 was unanimous in urging the necessity of a fresh baptism, and there was general agreement with them in Asia Minor. Dionysius of Alexandria, who shared Stephen's views but not his temper, tried to mediate. Each church seems in practice to have retained its own custom and the matter was allowed to drop after Stephen's death in the following year. But in the end his view won general acceptance, because it was the more charitable, and because it refused to go beyond the words of the Lord. For the West the controversy was settled in this sense by the Council of Arles, 314. Yet Cyprian's refusal to excommunicate those who were unwilling to adopt the same line of action as himself has won him the greater respect, and Christendom as a whole agrees with Jeremy Taylor's verdict that he 'did right in a wrong cause'.

III. EPISCOPACY

It was natural that these troubles should impel Cyprian to state his whole theory of the Church and ministry. Not

only had he to take sides in the Novatianist schism at Rome, but he had also to face a rival in his own see. Felicissimus, who had been ordained deacon, had been instrumental in getting a certain Fortunatus consecrated as bishop, thus starting a schism at Carthage. Out of this situation two questions arose, the method of a bishop's election and his precise position in the Church.

With regard to the first point Cyprian held that three things are necessary for a valid election: the bishop must be chosen by the bishops of the province, he must be accepted by the people, and he must be supported by the judgment of God. This requires a little explanation. The frequent mention of the part played by the laity in the election of bishops and the actual circumstances of Cyprian's own election might have led us to suppose that the primary choice lay with the people. It has therefore been suggested that Cyprian was making an innovation and that Novatus in his revolt stood out as a champion of the popular rights against episcopal tyranny. There is not likely to be much truth in this, but it must be confessed that Cyprian's statement does seem to represent some change of emphasis. The real choice now lies with the comprovincials; the laity must be present and their acquiescence is necessary because they have knowledge of each man's life and conduct and can therefore prevent the election of immoral persons. There can be no doubt, however, that in some instances the laity by their acclamations, if in no other way, actually initiated a nomination, and it is probable that Cyprian with his legal training recognised such a proceeding as both irregular and undesirable. The 'judgment of God' probably means no more than the smooth progress of the election and consecration without any untoward natural phenomenon.

The second question is fully discussed in Cyprian's treatise on the Unity of the Church. The essential points in his argument may be enumerated as follows:

(a) The source of unity in the Church is the unity of the Blessed Trinity.

(b) Church unity rests in the solidarity of the whole episcopal body. (It is a favourite expression of Cyprian's

that the bishops are the *glutinum* or glue that binds the Church together.)

(*c*) The solidarity of the episcopal body is represented by one bishop only in each locality.

(*d*) Where necessary the whole body of bishops decides together about debatable points.

(*e*) But the majority cannot compel the individual bishop to particular action in his own area.

(*f*) Of this unity Rome is (not the centre but) the symbol.

This is much the most complete theory with which the Church had yet been provided. Its most interesting feature is that while the unity of the Church rests upon the solidarity of the episcopate as a whole, each member of the episcopal body exercises the powers and functions of the whole. To use a modern illustration, the position is analogous to that of a husband and wife who have a common account at a bank, each having power to draw upon the whole amount. So each bishop has full and inalienable powers within his own see so long as he remains in the communion of the Church: each and every bishop can draw upon the whole treasury of episcopal power. The theory was based upon what Cyprian believed to be the facts of the original institution, when the government was laid upon one man, Peter, in order to emphasise the ideal unity, and then was conveyed in the same terms to the apostolic college as a whole. Significant in this respect is his use of the illustration from the Jewish hierarchy. Tertullian had compared bishop, priest, and deacon to the High Priest, priest, and Levite, but to Cyprian Christ is the High Priest, the bishops are the priests, and the presbyters are the Levites.

Within the limits of the unity thus expressed and guaranteed the operations of grace are closely confined. If the minister validly ordained breaks from the communion of the Great Church he loses all power to minister. 'The oblation cannot be consecrated where the Holy Spirit is not.' Nor will even the prayers of such a one avail to secure grace. There is indeed, says Cyprian, no grace outside the Church, and it is on that theory that Cyprian can with

remorseless logic deny the validity of heretical and schismatic baptism.

Yet we are not to think of Cyprian as a hard and narrow ecclesiastic. His great popularity with the laity and his earnest desire to associate them with himself in every official act preclude the thought that he loved to lord it over God's heritage. The consistent mildness of his tone in controversy, and his refusal to constrain those who differed from him form strong arguments in the same direction. Whatever overstatement there may have been arose from the effort of the legal mind to force into the stiff moulds of logic the abundant, free-flowing life of the Spirit.

CHAPTER XI

THE SECOND LONG PEACE

WE return to the general course of the history: we had reached the point where the edict of Gallienus (260) had begun a period of peace for the Church. During the second half of the century there was a more pronounced rest from persecution than there had been during the earlier half. This is not to say that there were not occasional executions, especially among the soldiery, as witness the martyrdom of Trophimus, a native of Antioch in Pisidia, c. 280. But the Church was now becoming too strong to be attacked by the weak emperors of the period. They had troubles enough and to spare on the frontiers and in Gaul.

This is borne out by the records of Aurelian (270–275), the greatest of the emperors of this half-century, and the only one of whose relations with the Church we know anything. He was a good soldier, and his proud title of *Restitutor Orbis* was well deserved. He was, however, low-born and ignorant, filled with debased superstition and of conspicuous cruelty even for a Roman general. He was a devoted worshipper of the sun and was not above human sacrifice. He was certainly willing to persecute, and before his cruelties brought about his assassination there was a rumour that he had published a persecuting edict. Yet there was no persecution in his reign, and on the one certain occasion when we know him to have been brought into immediate contact with the Church he was constrained to recognise its right to existence and to the possession of property.

I

This was in the matter of Paul of Samosata, the outstanding figure in the Church at the time, or at least the

most notorious. He was Bishop of Antioch (*c.* 260–270) and a popular preacher of the worst type, in great request among the ladies and allowing himself when preaching to be applauded by a professional *claque*. But more than bishop, he was the trusted chancellor of Zenobia, Queen of Palmyra. This lady was important enough to shed lustre upon her servant. It was she who had consolidated the defence of the frontier against the Persians, and she was aspiring to the conquest of Egypt when the Roman government found her too powerful. Aurelian then had to take her in hand. But at present Paul basked in her prosperity.

To a doubtful morality he added a still more doubtful Christology. His views represent a fully developed Adoptianist or Dynamic Monarchianism. According to him the Son did not exist before the Nativity: Jesus was merely a human being who was indwelt by the Logos. The Logos was not a person but a quality of God, corresponding to intelligence or reason in man. By this indwelling Jesus was made worthy to be adopted into the Divine. But still it was not right to sing hymns to Him: Paul is alleged to have preferred that they should be sung to himself.

Three synods met at Antioch to consider his position. His skill in debate delivered him in the first two, but the third deposed him and put Domnus in his place. However, it was impossible to carry out the sentence, so far as the temporalities of the see were concerned, while Paul's royal patroness was strong. But after her defeat by Aurelian in 273 appeal was made to the Emperor. It was then that Aurelian delivered his famous judgment: that the property should be surrendered to those with whom the bishops of Italy and Rome (his own residence) held intercourse.

This incident is of particular interest for three diverse reasons. In the first place it is to be noted that a dispute concerning Church property has been referred to the State and the State has been compelled to recognise a standard of orthodoxy in order to settle it. Secondly, this is the first time that a synod has deposed a bishop and appointed his successor without any apparent reference to the local church concerned, a point which is particularly significant in view

of the growing power of the comprovincials which we have noticed under Cyprian. Thirdly, at one of these synods the term *Homoousios*, 'of the same substance', was condemned, either because Paul had used it in a materialistic sense, or because it was held to imply Sabellian doctrine, or else out of mere dislike for the Hellenised Christianity of Alexandria.

After this decision Paul of Samosata disappears from history. Uncertainty shrouds the fate of one of his friends the priest-theologian Lucian of Antioch, who was afterwards martyred. His views of the nature of Christ were much the same as Paul's, and his teaching probably had a considerable influence on the still greater heresiarch, Arius.

II

The finest contemporary ecclesiastical scholar was not present at the council that condemned Paul, having pleaded the excuse of old age and sickness. This was Dionysius, Bishop of Alexandria, who had been a pupil of Origen and later head of the famous catechetical school. Dionysius like Cyprian had probably been a rhetorician before his conversion. It was his wide reading of both pagan and Christian literature that led him to embrace the faith, and he never abandoned, as did so many Christians of his day, the practice of reading unorthodox books. This enabled him to carry the attack into the enemy's country. When he became head of the school in 231 he wrote his treatise *On Nature*, in which he entered upon a systematic refutation of the Epicurean philosophy. After sixteen years' labour in teaching he became Bishop of Alexandria, and had the difficult task of preserving his church in the midst of persecution.

On the outbreak of the Decian assault he waited quietly four days in his own home while the secret-service agent despatched by the prefect searched everywhere for him. Then he fled, was captured, condemned and banished. It was hurriedly done, but a follower who escaped told what had happened to a party of rustics engaged in celebrating a wedding. 'They', says Dionysius, 'with one consent as if at a signal all arose and came running at great speed and

fell upon us with loud cries. When the soldiers who were guarding us took to flight straightway, they came upon us just as we were reclining on the bare bedsteads. I indeed, God knows, taking them at first to be bandits who had come for plunder and ravage, remained on the couch where I was, undressed save for my linen under-garment, and began to offer them the rest of my clothing which was at my side. But they told me to get up and go out as quickly as I could. And then I, understanding why they had come, cried out begging and praying them to leave us, and if they wished to do us a good turn, I besought them to forestall those who had carried us off and cut off my head themselves. And while I thus cried . . . they raised me by force. And when I let myself down on my back to the ground, they took me and led me out, dragging me by the arms and legs. . . . And they also helped to carry me out of the town in their arms, and then putting me on a bare-backed ass, led me away.' After this deliverance he was taken to a place of safety in the Libyan desert, where he remained till the persecution was over and he could return to Alexandria.

During the short interval of peace that followed, Dionysius took up a mediating position in the baptismal controversy between Cyprian and Stephen, which we have already passed under review. When persecution broke out once more under Valerian he was again tried and banished. But in his exile he managed not only to hold meetings and convert some of the heathen in his neighbourhood but also to exert such influence on his church in Alexandria as to keep the services going there also. On the publication of Gallienus' edict he returned to his city and worked there for another five years, dying at last in 265 before the first council called at Antioch to deal with Paul of Samosata, which he had been unable to attend, had finished its sittings.

Such writings of his as are left to us are mostly fragmentary. Mention has already been made of the treatise against the Epicureans. Another important book is the *Refutation and Defence*, an answer to his namesake the Bishop of Rome, who had written to him on some charges of heresy arising out of the attitude he had taken up in the

Sabellian controversy. Dionysius of Alexandria had to deal with both types of Monarchianism. Not only had he to concern himself with the Adoptianism of Paul of Samosata, but he was also much troubled by a revival of the Modalist Monarchianism of Sabellius in Cyrenaica. In his letters in connexion with the latter trouble he had dealt with the subject from the point of view of the characteristic Pluralistic Trinitarianism of Alexandria. So doing he had seemed to over-emphasise the distinction between the Persons of the Trinity, and in particular he had rejected the term *homoousios*, which seemed to him to make the Trinity a thing of mere names. But the Roman Church thought *homoousios* equivalent to Tertullian's *consubstantialis*, which they had made a key-word in their exposition of the Trinity. The fact is that those who engaged in theological discussion had not yet settled their terms, and consequently the Latin West was drifting into a misunderstanding of the Greek East which is well illustrated by the correspondence between the two Dionysii. However, the Alexandrian bishop had no difficulty in showing that, whatever the difference in terminology, his meaning was the same as that of his namesake. It is certain that he had no intention of denying the eternity of the Son, though there is no doubt that Christological thought in Alexandria was more coloured by the subordinationism of Origen than was that in Rome.

As an interpreter of scripture Dionysius took up a middle position between the excessive allegorism of his master and the hard literalism of his opponents. The fragment that remains to us on the authorship of the Apocalypse is a critical examination of the question in quite the modern spirit, including a comparison of its literary style with that of the Fourth Gospel.

Dionysius' letters show a man of winning character and a refreshing directness of speech. He has a nicety of taste and a moderation that were all too rare in his day. One quotation from his correspondence we may allow ourselves. It will fill out our knowledge of the persecutions by reminding us that the Christian slave and the household servant had not only to fear the public tribunal but also the bullying authority

of the family to which he belonged. 'Ischyrion acted as steward to one of the authorities at a wage. His employer bade him sacrifice, ill-treated him when he refused, and on his persistence drove him forth with insults. When he still stood his ground, he took a big stick and killed him by driving it through his vital parts.'

III

Before we leave the third century it may be well to notice the extent to which greater calm had given opportunity for the development of ecclesiastical organisation. It has been said that Cyprian's doctrine of the Church and ministry produced a greater change in contemporary Christian thought than any movement before the Reformation. The allegation will at least give point to a consideration of the actual position of the ministry in this period.

The most detailed figures come from Rome, which for the purposes of ecclesiastical administration was divided into seven 'regions' by Pope Fabian. The historian Eusebius quotes the following list of ministers for Rome: 46 presbyters, 7 deacons, 7 sub-deacons, 42 acolytes, and 52 readers, exorcists, and door-keepers. From this it appears that each deacon, or arch-deacon as he would now be designated, placed in charge of one of the 'regions', had a sub-deacon and six acolytes to assist him.

The deacon was thus the most important officer next to the bishop and in early writings is always mentioned in the closest connexion with the bishop. It was his duty to administer the Communion to the faithful, to carry alms to the poor, to arrange for the seating in church, to bid the prayers of the congregation, to act as the immediate ecclesiastical servant of the bishop and to be in all things the bishop's 'eye'. He was elected by the whole community but was ordained by the laying on of the bishop's hands alone. The reason given for the latter custom was that he was ordained not to the priesthood but to minister. It was perhaps rather natural that with so much power in his hands the deacon should desire greater honorific prominence, and there are traces of a struggle over precedence with the

presbyterate. Certainly he was given from the outset the prospect of elevation to higher rank after good service, and the diaconate did in point of fact provide many members of the episcopal body who went straight to their new office without passing through the priesthood. But by the beginning of the fourth century attempts were being made to restrain their ambitions. Their gradual decline in importance coincided with a corresponding rise on the part of the presbyterate.

The presbyters had the honourable status of a council round the bishop, this status being symbolised by their seats on either side of him at the celebration of the Eucharist. They had also the same rights in the celebration of the Eucharist, this being symbolised at their ordination by the fact that when the bishop laid his hands on them he was joined by the members of the presbyteral college (*contingentibus etiam presbyteris*). But their functions of celebrating the sacraments and giving absolution were often monopolised by the bishop. It is possible indeed that where there were a number of household churches in one city the presbyters may have celebrated the Eucharist in some of them, but they would do so strictly as the bishop's delegates, and later when worship was centralised in a separate church building they appear only as the somewhat shadowy retinue of their leader. It was only as the bishops of small country places (*chorepiscopoi*) became fewer and were finally withdrawn that individual presbyters began to replace them, and thus for the first time took charge of local communities.

Throughout the first three centuries no very clear line of demarcation was drawn between the ordinary life of the clergy and that of the laity. The clergy for the most part earned their livelihood at secular trades. But as they began to be paid for their clerical work they withdrew more and more from the pursuits of the laity until in the fourth century such withdrawal began to be represented as a matter of obligation. In the early days the line between clergy and laity was drawn below the three offices of bishop, priest, and deacon; but soon minor offices began to grow up in association

with the ministry and gradually their holders began to claim recognition as clergy. The most important of them was the subdeacon. There is no trace of him in the second century, but by the third century he was fully established in Rome. He received an official appointment but no ordination. His duties were to assist the deacon both in church services and in the 'serving of tables' in the 'region'. The office of the acolyte was also derived from that of the deacon. He seems to have sprung into existence at Rome and Carthage about the time of Cyprian, but he was unknown in the East until much later. He was originally appointed to help the deacon in his administrative work but was afterwards given functions in church. Older than both subdeacon and acolyte was the reader. Originally he stood together with the widow at the head of the minor officials, but he soon lost that prominence. His duty was to read the lessons in the early part of the liturgy. His qualifications were not only the power to read well, but also a moral life in accordance with the Scriptures read.

Widows as a class apart date from New Testament times. We know from the *Pastorals* that they were entered on an official roll. This gave them a definite appointment, but it was expressly provided that they should receive no ordination. They must be tested by a long period of fasting, prayer and good works before appointment. The *Pastorals* insist that they must be at least sixty years old. Tertullian agrees, but the *Didascalia* says fifty. The latter book gives considerable attention to the position of widows, who by this time seem to have stepped beyond their proper bounds. They are ordered not to usurp clerical functions such as that of baptising; they are not to gad about and gossip; and they are to do nothing without the bishop. If the *Pastorals* point to the existence of an office of widows which has the duty of instructing the young, that function has now disappeared, for we are told that 'it is not fitting for a widow to teach'. The widows' position is simply that of those entitled to receive alms, in return for which their one duty is to offer intercession. 'Let the widow care for nothing else but to pray for those who give and for the whole Church.'

Such other functions as the widows ever fulfilled were now performed by the deaconess. Under this term we are not to understand a female deacon, but a person whose chief value was that she could perform for women such ministrations as could not in the circumstances of the time be well committed to men. Thus in Syria, while it was not permitted to a woman to baptise, the deaconess was expected to anoint the body of the female catechumen at her baptism. Similarly it was she who took the Sacrament to sick women and visited them when heathen prejudice would not admit the deacon into the home. The office does not seem to have been a common one, but it is significant of the respect in which it came to be held that the deaconess was required to take the newly baptised woman and instruct her. The *Didascalia* presses for a fuller recognition of the office. It seems to have been a creation of the late third century. At first it received simple appointment, but later there was a definite ordination with the imposition of hands.

Appointment without ordination was accorded to Healers and Exorcists. An interesting question is sometimes raised concerning the relation of the confessors to the regular ministry. The answer is that just as the martyr who had not yet been received into the Church was reckoned to have been baptised in his own blood, so the confessor who had suffered actual sentence could be reckoned as presbyter or deacon, and that without ordination. If, however, he had not been imprisoned, he might be reckoned as eligible for the ministry, but ordination would be required. In either case if a confessor were elevated to the episcopate consecration would be necessary.

It was thus considered that steadfast endurance of persecution manifested a special gift of the Spirit. In the opinion of many that gift also brought the power of remitting the sins of the weaker brethren. As that was a ministerial function it was a natural conclusion that its possessors could perform other ministerial functions also. Cyprian, however, drew distinctions. Two confessors who, as he admitted, on this reasoning had qualified for the presbyterate, he nevertheless adjudged too young to be allowed to take

up that work. He therefore compromised in their case by giving them the pay of presbyters but refusing to appoint them to any office higher than that of reader. This was sufficient to show the absurdities to which the practice of accepting courageous witness in place of ordination might lead, and a stop was soon put to the anomaly.

CHAPTER XII

THE END OF PERSECUTION

I

THE long peace was at last broken by the Emperor Diocletian (284–305). But the breach was not made willingly, and it is indeed a tragedy that the final struggle between Church and Empire should have begun in this reign. Diocletian was an able general, chosen by his comrades to rule the Empire as the one man who could reorganise both State and army. The difficulty of preserving their enormous territories was pressing heavily upon the government. Some of the outlying conquests had been abandoned, and a withdrawal effected within the line of the Danube and Euphrates. This still left a frontier of six thousand miles to guard, and the thirty legions were proving too few for the task. Many barbarians had been brought in to swell their ranks and the soldiers were growing ever more turbulent. Upon the civilians lay the burden of maintaining the growing army, and the consequent taxation was a fruitful source of discontent.

Diocletian was not afraid to look facts in the face: he saw that drastic measures were called for and he did not hesitate to take them. Recognising that it was no longer the Senate but the army that ruled the Empire, he removed his court from Rome to Nicomedia, where he would be nearer the threatened frontiers. There he lived in more than Oriental state and endeavoured to keep up the Olympian style that fitted his divine title. Recognising with equal clearness that one man could not expect to direct the movements of the widely scattered armies, and that the greatest danger to himself lay in the rise of possible rivals, he anticipated them by appointing colleagues whose interests would best be served by keeping him secure. Maximian

was made a second but inferior Augustus with control of the West, while Diocletian himself retained charge of the East. Each of the two Augusti had a Caesar to help him, Constantius being appointed to the West and Galerius to the East. Under this system the Empire was efficiently administered and the corrosion of its borders was for a time stayed. Except perhaps on the part of Constantius there was no sympathy among the rulers for the Christians. Diocletian was a superstitious but quite serious pagan, who would have been willing from the first to aim at religious unity, had not his statecraft warned him of the difficulties in the way. In any case for the first thirteen years of his reign, from 284 to 297, there was continual trouble with the Persians which made any such effort out of the question. Even after the conclusion of peace there elapsed another six years before the change came.

During the first part of the reign the Church was increasing rapidly in importance. In some places, especially in Asia Minor, Christians seem to have been in the majority. In the imperial palace they were occupying positions of trust, and the Emperor's own wife, Prisca, was a catechumen. Eusebius speaks of spacious churches having been erected in all the cities, and in Nicomedia itself the most noteworthy building was the Christian basilica. All this of course brought upon the Church the jealousy of the pagans, and led to the formation of a strong anti-Christian party, headed by the Emperor's son-in-law, the Caesar Galerius. He removed from his own army all soldiers who refused to sacrifice and continually urged Diocletian to begin the work of persecution.

Mutterings of thunder were heard before the storm broke. An example of what might happen was given in the case of the Manichees, against whom Diocletian published an edict in 296, ordering the leaders to be burnt and their books to be destroyed, while their followers were to be beheaded or sent to the mines. The next year, while the Emperor was awaiting news of Galerius's expedition against the Persians, he consulted the omens and was horrified at receiving no reply. The sacrificing priests told him that the reason for

the failure was that certain Christians present had dared to make the sign of the cross. In a rage Diocletian ordered all those present to sacrifice and sent the same command to the army. But for the time he smothered his anger, and nothing more seems to have been heard of the matter. Six more years went by and Diocletian's health showed signs of breaking. He was less able to withstand the importunities of his son-in-law. At last on a visit to Nicomedia in 303 Galerius over-persuaded his infirm leader.

The edict announcing the persecution was published on February 23rd, the feast of the *Terminalia*. It ordered that 'the churches should be levelled with the ground and the scriptures destroyed with fire, that they of honourable rank should be degraded, and that they of the imperial household, if they stuck to their profession of Christianity, should be reduced to slavery'. This edict can hardly have satisfied Galerius; it was not sufficiently bloodthirsty. Its effort indeed was to destroy the Church without resorting to bloodshed. If there were no churches and no gospels it was hoped that Christianity would die of inanition. The first blow was struck in Nicomedia itself, where the great church was ransacked and destroyed by the pretorian guard. The edict nailed to the palace gate was torn down by a Christian of rank, who at once perished for his temerity. Tradition identifies him with our own S. George.

The persecution promised to be as successful as persecutions generally are at first. The Emperor might never have thought it necessary to proceed to more extreme measures had not his fears been aroused by the outbreak of two fires in the palace. The Christians were of course blamed for incendiarism and sterner edicts began to appear. The second aimed at the clergy, commanding them all to be seized. The prisons were now filled to overflowing, and the resultant difficulty was met by a third decree which offered freedom to prisoners on condition of sacrifice, but, failing sacrifice, condemned them to the torture. This, while offering prisoners one more chance, was a quite logical deepening of severity; and it had a certain success. Then came the crowning effort to finish off the whole business in a fourth and

final edict. Hitherto the Government had been aiming at the strategic points. Now came the frontal attack in the shape of a challenge to all Christian people, offering them the alternatives of sacrifice or death with confiscation of property. In this, however, the enemy over-reached himself; even the pagans could not bear to wallow in so vast a stream of blood. 'The policy was wrecked on the conscience and humanity of heathenism.' In the East Galerius continued the effort for another six years, but in the West it came to an end with the abdication of Diocletian, followed by that of his fellow-Augustus Maximian.

This double resignation wrought chaos in the government. Diocletian, cultivating his cabbages in Dalmatia, saw the fabric he had so carefully reared come crashing down. At one time there were no fewer than six Augusti. Happily we need not follow their fortunes here, but we must notice that one of them, Constantine, the son of Constantius, was proclaimed by the troops at York, and speedily began to absorb the power of the rest. For a time, however, Galerius was the dominant force in the Empire, and while civil war raged in the West the work of persecution went on in the East. Galerius gained no temporal advantage by his persistence. His foes increased in number and his frame was weakened by a terrible disease.

At last he was constrained to acknowledge defeat: from his death-bed in 311 he published an edict of toleration. The original persecution, he said, had not after all been his fault but had owed itself to the factiousness of the Christians; he now saw that he had made an oversight in not recognising that their God could not be worshipped by them in conjunction with other gods; the persecution had failed in its effort to bring them back to their ancestral faith and had only ended in their worshipping nothing; so they must have leave to worship as they will, only he hopes that for his clemency they will remember him in their prayers. Perhaps he hoped that by this means he might obtain for his tortured body the relief that his own gods had denied him. Baker, however, suggests that by making the churches into legal *collegia* Galerius hoped that he was turning them, like the

pagan institutions, into hereditary closed corporations, so that they might soon die into insignificance. In this, however, he was doomed to disappointment, for in a day of privileged classes the Christians alone kept their offices open to all, and so not only maintained their own strength but ultimately secured political freedom for everyone. Whatever the explanation, it is certain that the Christians secured the right not only to exist but also to run their own affairs. *Denuo sint Christiani et conventicula sua componant.*

In the meantime Constantine had been making rapid progress. One rival remained in the West, the usurper Maxentius. In 312 he was met and crushed at the Milvian Bridge. This battle marks an epoch, for it helped to make the first Christian Emperor and so affected the history of European civilisation down to the present time. It was during the night before this battle that Constantine is generally believed to have seen the cross of light in the sky with the words *In hoc signo vinces*. Hence came the *Labarum*, the famous standard of Constantine, a spearhead forming the cross with the *Chi Rho*, the initial Greek letters of the name Christ, enclosed in a circle.

A very different state of things prevailed in the East. Galerius' successor, Maximin Daza, ignored the edict of toleration; set himself to restore the prestige and organisation of paganism; developed a pagan hierarchy on the model of the Christian system; and backed up these measures by a severe persecution. Peter of Alexandria suffered martyrdom and Lucian, the scholarly but heretical priest of Antioch, was also martyred. In Armenia, which was the first kingdom officially to accept the Christian faith, the whole nation had to defend itself with the sword against the efforts made to compel it to worship idols. But Maximin was not long in the enjoyment of power. Attacked by his colleague Licinius and forced to flee, he poisoned himself to avoid capture.

Constantine and Licinius were now left to share the Empire between them. They met and concerted their policy at Milan in 313. It is usually said that on this occasion they issued under their joint names an edict of religious toleration. There is, however, no trace of this famous 'Edict of Milan'.

What probably happened is that the two Augusti agreed upon some statement of toleration on the lines of the instructions already issued by Constantine to the governors in his area, and that Licinius agreed to send out similar instructions to the governors in the East. 'Everyone who has a common desire to observe the Christian worship may now freely and unconditionally endeavour to do so without let or hindrance. . . . To others also freedom for their own worship is likewise left open and freely granted as suits the quiet of our times, that every man may have freedom in the worship he has chosen, for it is not our will that anything should be diminished from any dignity or religion.' All confiscated Christian property was to be restored to its owners whether private individuals or communities, 'provided always that those who return it without price shall expect compensation from our benevolence'. Thus toleration became a fixed principle with the imperial Government, and although, as we shall see, Licinius became a persecutor in the East, there was never again a serious persecution of Christians in the West.

II

We should be lacking in gratitude if we did not here acknowledge the debt owed by the Church to the two contemporary historians of the last great persecution. Lactantius was a pagan orator of sufficient fame to be invited by Diocletian to open a school of rhetoric in Nicomedia. There he was converted to Christianity and lost his post in the subsequent persecution. His enforced leisure was employed in the writing of an apologetic work, *The Divine Institutes*, which has earned for him the title, 'the Cicero of Christianity'. Another book, in which the heat of emotion has spoilt his style, is that on the *Deaths of Persecutors*. Here he is no longer the sober historian but the bitter partisan, comparing his enemies to the evil beasts of the Apocalypse, and showing a power of invective that reflects no credit on his charity. After the establishment of more peaceful relations between Church and State he was appointed by Constantine tutor to his son Crispus.   Lactanius

Eusebius of Caesarea, on the other hand, never loses the suavity of the scholar. He was a polished and ceremonious orator, whose panegyrics endeared him to Constantine, and he was a student whose learning was so great that he was suspected, like Aristotle, of having known everything there was to know in his day. He was the 'father' of ecclesiastical history with an estimable habit of incorporating his authorities in his text. This habit has placed all subsequent historians in his debt, for, the greater part of the early Christian writings having been lost in the persecutions, a number of authors are known to us only through the fragments that remain stored in the pages of Eusebius' *Ecclesiastical History*. His *Martyrs of Palestine*, while it does full justice to the heroes of the Christian faith, is much less venomous than the work of Lactantius: it makes some allowance for the other side and shows how often the profession of Christianity was aggravated in the eyes of pagan magistrates by the fanaticism of the conscientious objector. He also wrote a *Life of Constantine*, for whom he felt a true regard which was warmly reciprocated.

III. THE NEW POLICY

Constantine and Licinius ruled side by side for ten years. Then came a dramatic change. The character of Licinius deteriorated; he became a persecutor of the Christians and a pagan champion, his watch over the frontiers became inefficient, and he signally failed to keep the line of the Danube. The reason for some of this was no doubt jealousy of Constantine; it meant that the partners had become rivals. An opportunity for ending an intolerable situation occurred in 323. That year the barbarians broke across the Danube; and Constantine was obliged to rush to the aid of his colleague. The common danger passed, the two turned on each other, and at the battle of Chrysopolis Licinius was utterly defeated. Henceforth Constantine decided to rule alone. Under Diocletian the power of the Senate had been broken by the removal of the court to Nicomedia and the power of the army by the appointment of two Augusti and two Caesars. Now we have a monarchy with a mobile army as a striking force and an advisory

consistorium as a sort of Privy Council. Together with this new form of government we also have a new capital, a new policy and a new religion.

The late tetrarchy had possessed capitals of a somewhat inferior type: Nicomedia, Milan, Sirmium, and Treves. Constantine determined to have a capital worthy of a great monarchy. He would not go back to Rome; that was too far from the frontiers and the real centre of interest. Also paganism was there strongly entrenched in the ranks of the old aristocracy and especially in the Senate. He looked for a fresh site, for in such surroundings he would have his hands free to mould the new organisation and to arrange a new political and religious policy.

At first he thought of Troy, but he changed his mind in favour of Byzantium. Here was a town formed by nature to be the centre of a great empire; from its seven hills it commanded the approaches to both Europe and Asia; its narrow straits joined East and West and were as good for communication in peace as for protection in war. Gibbon in an inimitable passage describes the founding of the new city on the site of Byzantium.

The prospect of beauty, of safety, and of wealth, united in a single spot, was sufficient to justify the choice of Constantine. But, as some decent mixture of prodigy and fable has, in every age, been supposed to reflect a becoming majesty on the origin of great cities, the emperor was desirous of ascribing his resolution, not so much to the uncertain counsels of human policy, as to the infallible and eternal decrees of divine wisdom. In one of his laws he has been careful to instruct posterity that, in obedience to the commands of God, he laid the everlasting foundations of Constantinople; and, though he has not condescended to relate in what manner the celestial inspiration was communicated to his mind, the defect of his modest silence has been liberally supplied by the ingenuity of succeeding writers, who describe the nocturnal vision which appeared to the fancy of Constantine, as he slept within the walls of Byzantium. The tutelar genius of the city, a venerable matron sinking under the weight of years and infirmities, was suddenly transformed into a blooming maid, whom his own hands adorned with all the symbols of imperial greatness. The monarch awoke, interpreted

the auspicious omen, and obeyed, without hesitation, the will of heaven. The day which gave birth to a city or colony was celebrated by the Romans with such ceremonies as had been ordained by a generous superstition; and, though Constantine might omit some rites which savoured too strongly of their Pagan origin, yet he was anxious to leave a deep impression of hope and respect on the minds of the spectators. On foot, with a lance in his hand, the emperor himself led the solemn procession; and directed the line which was traced as the boundary of the destined capital; till the growing circumference was observed with astonishment by the assistants, who, at length, ventured to observe that he had already exceeded the most ample measure of a great city. 'I shall still advance', replied Constantine, 'till HE, the invisible guide who marches before me, thinks proper to stop.'

Of this new capital the original church of S. Sophia was the centre and its public places were adorned with artistic splendours from the loot of many pagan cities.

With regard to the new policy we must observe that Constantine's task was first to restore and then to preserve the unity of his Empire. There were already two lines of cleavage, first that of religion, about one-tenth of the total population being at this time Christian; and second that of organisation, there being now a deep furrow driven between East and West. The difficulty was complicated by the fact that these two divisions crossed each other. Christians were far more numerous in the East than in the West, whereas Constantine in the West had favoured Christians while Licinius in the East had favoured pagans.

It is probable that Constantine set out with a deliberate intention to favour the Church, but even if that were so, it was necessary to placate the pagans. Consequently the policy agreed upon at Milan was a recognition of the complete parity of religions. But as the reign progressed Constantine supported the Christians more and more, and one can only conclude that his aim was to make of Christianity the cement that was to bind together the whole Empire. It seems possible, in spite of Piganiol, to trace this change of policy in the development of the Constantinian legislation. Until 323, when he got rid of Licinius, Constantine was

satisfied with laws that made for an equality between Christianity and paganism, but after that his legislation shows a distinct preference for Christianity.

The laws aiming at equality fall into two divisions as they seek to repress the exuberance of paganism or to raise the status of Christianity. The first class while regulating paganism nevertheless admitted its legality. Thus the feast of the *Quinquennalia* was celebrated with the usual pagan rites and ceremonies, but Christians were not to be forced into attendance at them. Again in 319 Constantine forbade private soothsaying, which might be used to the detriment of officials, but he gave express permission for open and public soothsaying. For a similar reason black magic was forbidden, but white magic, which was intended for the most part to promote the fruitfulness of the family and of the field, was allowed.

The second class of laws, intended to raise Christianity to an equality with paganism, included an enactment giving the same immunity from municipal duty to Christian clergy as was already enjoyed by pagan priests. This appears to have caused so great an influx into the clerical order that seven years later we find Constantine forbidding men of curial rank to be ordained. Again the manumission of slaves was allowed to be performed in the churches just as it was already performed in the temples, and the Church was given the same power to receive legacies as was already possessed by the pagan organisations. But perhaps the most significant evidence of this policy is to be found in the decree of 321 regulating Sunday observance. That ordinance puts the Lord's Day on the same level of observance as the pagan festivals and marks it by the cessation of work. It is noteworthy, however, that the day is described by no Christian appellation but simply as *dies venerabilis solis*, and no pagan could well object to that.

Of the laws that show the clearest desire to favour the Church we must note especially the measure, mentioned by Eusebius in his *Life of Constantine*, putting a stop to official sacrifices. The purpose of this was that Christians might be able to accept office as magistrates. There was of course

as yet no effort to make Christianity the established religion—that did not come until the reign of Theodosius—but the alliance between Church and State was cemented by the appropriation of part of the tax on corn to the needs of the Church, this probably implying the transference of some of the dues that were already paid to the pagan priests. At the same time taxes on celibacy were abolished, a measure which strongly assisted the rise of monasticism. Also it is to be noted that the bishops were given the right to act as judges where both parties to a suit agreed to accept their verdict; and in some cases it seems that their judgment was given the force of law when only one party wished it. Further evidence of partiality to the Church is to be found in the fact that Jews were forbidden to persecute any of their nation who became Christians.

A considerable amount of the social legislation of Constantine shows a desire to approximate to Christian standards. As early as 315 the crucifixion of slaves was abolished; slaves were not to be prevented from attaining their liberty when the usual conditions were satisfied; and the families of slaves were not to be dispersed when their ownership changed hands. Savage punishments were inflicted for failure to observe the moral law, and the practice of concubinage was prohibited to married men. Children began to enjoy some measure of protection: they could still be sold at birth and exposure was not forbidden, but the practice was relieved of some of its horror by the declared willingness of the State to rear foundlings. The kidnapping of children was henceforth to be heavily penalised. The punishment of criminals was made a little more merciful, and a stop was put to the branding on the face and scourging of debtors. Even the animals were better used: drivers in the postal service were told not to beat their horses unmercifully. It was also forbidden to commandeer beasts used in field labour for transport purposes.

About Constantine's personal religion the most divers views have been, and still are, held. It is doubtful whether he was a genuine Christian who whole-heartedly accepted the faith and teaching of the Church; or whether he was

really a syncretist whose desire was to establish a universal deistic religion; or whether he was an astute statesman who believed he could find in Christianity the social and moral force that would bring unity to his empire. The evidence is conflicting. Duchesne, who accepts the first possibility, points out that in the fourth century there was no such thing as a free-thinker, that Christianity was certainly favoured in Constantine's family, that his sister had the Christian name Anastasia, and that his mother Helena was believed to be the discoverer of the true cross. Müller and Piganiol, who take the second possibility, point out that by heredity Constantine was bound to the worship of Jove and Hercules, but that after he began to achieve fame he showed a marked veneration for the sun, which seems to have represented to him the unity behind the many different forms of religious belief. Certainly he dropped the title of *Invictus* and replaced it with that of *Victor*, and he also, like his immediate successors, retained both the name and office of *Pontifex Maximus*. The many scholars who adopt the third possibility point to the ambiguous character of many of Constantine's acts. The famous vision of the cross of light and the regulation with regard to Sunday are both capable of a pagan as well as a Christian interpretation. His postponement of baptism until he was on his death-bed might lead to the same conclusion, had it not been a sufficiently common practice. His handling of ecclesiastical problems shows that his greatest anxiety was to maintain peace and unity. He encouraged the Church to act as 'an informal parliamentary system': her organisation, covering the whole empire, was built up on civil lines and in her synods she offered an opportunity of free debate to replace the old method of deputation to government. There was undoubtedly enough to make encouragement of Christianity the best policy.

It is possible that the three suggestions are not mutually exclusive. If the formidable array of letters adduced by Baynes can be regarded as genuine, there is left no doubt that Constantine regarded himself as a genuine Christian. He even speaks of himself as 'the bishop of those without',

and uses such flattering terms of the episcopal office that Piganiol thinks he ultimately became the tool of the bishops whom he had enriched. At the same time his acceptance of Christianity need not have been altogether exclusive: he may have regarded Christianity as the highest expression of the monotheistic faith towards which he himself had been feeling his way, and he may well have been disinclined to kick down the ladder by which he had ultimately climbed to security. Certainly policy would dictate an effort at toleration during the early part of his rule and growing favour to the Church in proportion as Christianity gained dominance over its rivals. His was probably one of those cases in which policy and conviction coincide. It is sometimes said that the murder of his son Crispus and of his wife Fausta are ugly facts in the way of accepting Constantine as a genuine Christian. But it is possible that the end of Crispus was really made necessary by the severity of the laws against immorality which Constantine himself had promulgated, and the death of Fausta is shrouded in so much mystery that we can draw no certain conclusion from it.

The doubt that hangs over Constantine's personal religion has its counterpart in the various estimates of the effect of his reign upon the Church. The ease with which Christianity could now be practised brought many unworthy elements into the Church and helped to lower its standard. Walter Hilton says, 'So many fish were brought into Peter's net that it was well nigh to breaking', and Dean Inge has gone so far as to say, 'After Constantine there is not much that is not humiliating.' Whether the latter verdict is justified the following pages will show, but it is certain that in some respects at least his reign inaugurated a great forward movement in Christianity, a movement in which he himself assisted not only by his legislation but also by his building projects and other schemes for ennobling the worship of the Church. It is now that we get the real birth of Christian architecture, now that monasticism begins, now that Christians are able to exert their influence on the social life of the day. One may regret the loss of warlike virtues when battles are over, but that is a poor reason for belittling peace.

CHAPTER XIII

THE RIVALS OF CHRISTIANITY

BEFORE we enter upon the history of ecclesiastical affairs during the reign of Constantine it will be well once more to look round the world-arena and see what opponents Christianity had to face. The disappearance of persecution and the cessation of all obligation to Caesar-worship made the fundamental issues all the clearer. We shall find that the Church had serious rivals to its claims as an institution, as an intellectual system, and as a school of morals. For an example of the first we shall take the Mystery Cults, of the second Neo-platonism, and of the third Manicheism.

I

The first centuries of the Christian era had seen a considerable interchange between East and West. The prevailing Caesar-worship had carried to the East the gospel of all-conquering might, and the East had brought to the West a revival of the power of the old gods together with a professional priesthood, whose chief business was to secure a guarantee of immortality for the individual. This contribution of the East was made through the Mystery Cults, the origin of which lies far back beyond the reach of history but seems to have rested in a strong belief in a relation between human life, with its manifold aspirations, and the yearly dying and rising again of nature. The recognition of this real or fancied relation emerged into a cult in Thrace during the sixth century B.C., based on the myth of Dionysus and the Titans. In the frenzied ceremonies of this cult the raw flesh of a bull was eaten by the worshippers and they believed themselves united with the deity whom it embodied or represented. Later an intellectual rationale of faith was

given by the Orphic teachers, with the result that a number of cults sprang up associated with different myths but all having the same end in view. They were popular and non-philosophical, but they offered to the average individual an opportunity of escape from the allotted destiny which held him imprisoned. In the period with which we are concerned these cults appear in four main types.

The best known were the Eleusinian Mysteries, which derived their name from Eleusis, twelve miles from Athens. The myth upon which they were based was that of Demeter and her daughter Persephone, who was carried off to the underworld by Pluto but was allowed to return to earth for a period each year with the Spring. The applicant for admission to the cult-brotherhood was prepared by being kept fasting in a dark room. He was then given a specially concocted drink, was exposed to a bright light in which he saw the images of the gods, and was ready to believe he was so far identified with the divinity as to be able like her to overcome death. This cult lasted until A.D. 395, when it disappeared in the sack of the temple of Eleusis by Alaric.

Another of these cults came from Phrygia and was held in honour of the goddess Cybele. To it initiation seems to have been given by a kind of baptism in the blood of a bull, known as the *Taurobolium*, a ceremony which was sometimes borrowed by other cults. A third was the cult of the Egyptian goddess Isis. It is in connexion with this that we learn the syncretistic nature of these religions, for in the best description of it that we have, to be found in Apuleius' *Golden Ass*, we are told that Isis identified herself with most if not all of the principal female deities of the time. The fourth of the cults is that of Mithras, an old Aryan deity who had come from India and Persia through Asia Minor and had been warmly welcomed, especially by the soldiery, in the West. He was there identified with *Sol Invictus*, the sun who always conquered darkness and renewed his strength every morning. This cult included the *Taurobolium*, which it had borrowed from the Mysteries of Cybele, and in it sacramental meals were so important that Justin was constrained

to explain them by saying that the demons had imitated the Christian Eucharist.

These cults were strong rivals of the Church on the institutional side. In their easy tolerance they were quite unlike Christianity, but they resembled it closely in so far as they were both individualist and universalist. The old nationalist and aristocratic sentiment was beginning to disappear, and the two units of society were now the individual and humanity as a whole. In these cults all barriers were broken down: women were admitted as well as men, slaves as well as the free-born. In a period of doubt and disorganisation they offered a guarantee of salvation and immortality. By their secrecy and their elaborate ceremonies they appealed to the love of esoteric knowledge in those who had no power to follow philosophic reasoning. It is often alleged that Christianity borrowed from them some of its most distinctive features, such as belief in a Saviour God and the use of sacraments. While that is manifestly untrue, it is very likely that Christian leaders often worked out their own systems against the background of the Mysteries and in forms of thought that were common to both. The similarity between the terminology of the early Christian writings and that of the Mysteries shows how great was at once the danger and the triumph of the Church. Christianity beat the mysteries on their own ground. It had the advantage of being based not on a myth but on a historic Person. It appealed equally to the individual and to the whole human race. It knew no barriers and it offered to unite all men with God. And it was immeasurably superior in its moral values.

II

On the intellectual side the greatest rival of Christianity at this time was Neoplatonism. The best exponent of this philosophical system was Plotinus (205–270), who like Origen had been a pupil of Ammonius Saccas at Alexandria. After eleven years with him he had joined the Emperor Gordian on his expedition to Persia, and on his return spent the rest of his life in Rome. So great was his credit in high quarters that Gallienus is said to have offered to build him a

philosopher's city in the Campagna on the model of Plato's *Republic*. His views are set forth in the *Enneads*, which are really his lecture notes edited by his pupil Porphyry. He sets himself to attack the three enemies of the good life, namely materialism, scepticism and dualism. In reply to these he sets up the thesis that reality is spiritual, knowable and single. In his system there are two Trinities, that of God, which consists of the absolute, the mind or spirit (*Nous*), and the soul; and that of man, which consists of *nous*, soul and body. Man has contact with the universe by means of the senses, the discursive reason, and spiritual intuition. The senses and the material world that they perceive are viewed by Plotinus as possessing an inherent imperfection. Even the discursive reason can only know reality in a secondary way. Consequently Plotinus dismisses science, and contends that the only sure way of transcending evil and attaining to the knowledge of God is by spiritual intuition, which to him is equivalent to ecstatic communion. Since the Absolute is beyond all distinctions, even that between the knower and the known, progress towards God is described as 'the flight of the alone to the Alone'. This system triumphed over all other methods of intellectual discipline in our period and found itself face to face with Christianity as its only rival in the sphere of philosophical thought.

Porphyry (233–300) was a pupil of Plotinus at Rome and combined the teaching of his master with an asceticism that demanded abstinence from all flesh food. He was a determined enemy of Christianity and made a shrewd attack on the record of Christian miracles. For all that his books were published by Constantine, and the Arians were often known by the name of Porphyrians. His views led him to a very pessimistic estimate of this present life, and it was only with difficulty that he was restrained from suicide as the best means of fulfilling his ambitions. With his pupil Iamblichus, who died about 330, the school began to degenerate into theurgy and magic. The 'ideas' of Plato were by him turned into gods and demons who were believed to be amenable to manipulation by magical arts. The last great teacher of the

school was Proclus (410–485). With him the triads of Plotinus became emanations from pure being not unlike the aeons of the Gnostics.

It is easy to see what influence this school of thought must have had upon Christian leaders. It was from it that they learnt what was involved in a metaphysical sense by calling God a Spirit. They were also helped to free themselves from their primitive eschatology and to get rid of that crude anthropomorphism which made even Tertullian believe that God had a material body. Nevertheless Christianity had the advantage, and that in three respects. It knew that the distinctions in the Divine Being, which the Neoplatonists themselves recognised, must be within and not outside the innermost core of the Divine Unity. Again Christianity did not appeal, like Neoplatonism, to the learned and philosophically minded only, but taught that even the humblest had access to God. And thirdly it knew that in the human life of Jesus the Godhead was in contact with the world: therefore the ultimate nature of God could not be arrived at by a process of abstraction but only by a positive affirmation of all that was best and highest in human experience.

III. MANICHEISM

The chief rival to Christianity in the field of ethics was the teaching of Manes, which has been variously described as a modification of old Babylonian religion, a hybrid Zoroastrianism, a variety of Gnostic speculation, and a Christian heresy. Manes was born about A.D. 215 of Persian parents, and seems to have been brought up as something like an Ebionite Gnostic. He became a great ascetic who had already attracted a few disciples by the time he was twenty-five, but he did not begin his public teaching until two years later on the day of the crowning of Sapor, March 20, 242. He did thirty years' missionary work, and achieved a great reputation, especially in India and China. At home, however, religious leaders were not so pleased with his activities, and a few years after his return the jealousy of the Magi caused him to be flayed alive.

His system was both a philosophy and a religion, pro-

viding a 'true *gnosis*' with regard to the constitution of the natural world as a necessary step towards the elimination of moral evil. In typical Eastern fashion it presented itself as a strongly defined dualism between light and darkness, the light being identified with moral goodness and the darkness with moral evil. But it is noticeable in this case that the good was not wholly synonymous with spirit nor evil with matter. In the cosmogony with which Manes justified this dualistic view it was shown how in the beginning light and darkness had been entirely separate. In the light dwelt God and from the darkness proceeded Satan. The latter attacked God's realm of light, but was opposed by the Primal Man whom God had formed for its defence. The man was armed with the wind, the light and the fire; Satan with the smoke, the cloud, the consuming flame and the scorching blast. In the fray Satan prevailed, and the man had to be rescued by the heavenly powers, but, as was perhaps natural, the panoply of the two combatants had become inextricably inter-mingled. Out of the mixture the heavenly powers made the present world, which, as Dr. Burkitt says, is neither light nor darkness but a smudge; and that explains how it happens that all things, animate as well as inanimate, contain some portions of light. The present scheme of existence, however, provides an opportunity for the escape of these fragments of light to their heavenly home. Various prophets have appeared from time to time to help in this process of liberation. The succession has been maintained by Adam, Noah, Buddha, Zoroaster, Jesus, and last and most important of all by Manes himself, the Paraclete. What precisely Manes meant by the assumption of the name Paraclete is not clear; perhaps he had picked it up without any very definite idea of its meaning from some Christian sect such as the Montanists.

The actual cult of Manicheism consisted in a rigid asceticism, which in some measure was expected of all classes, while a higher standard was expected from the Elect than from mere Hearers. None was allowed to slaughter animals, because that would be to destroy some portions of light, but the Hearers were permitted to eat flesh food when it had been slain by others. The higher class might

not even pluck fruit or gather vegetables, but had to subsist on food supplied by their commoner brethren. Nor could the Elect hold property or marry, because this would have been to create fresh prisons for the light. The members seem to have joined together for prayers and hymns, but there were no temples, altars or images. The things most strongly forbidden were idolatry and magic. The sect seems to have been carefully organised with headquarters at Babylon and a graded hierarchy. There were even reflexions of the Christian sacraments in the *signacula oris, manuum, sinus*. The first of these 'seals' put restriction on food and speech, the second on outward actions and the third on sexual desires.

The very fact that Manicheism appeared in Rome as a Persian sect was sufficient to ensure for it there a cordial hatred. It was condemned, as we have seen, in 296 by Diocletian, who ordered its books to be burnt. Yet it made headway even among Christians, particularly among the monks of Egypt; and during the fourth century it spread throughout the Empire. It is difficult to see why, with its rejection of a true Incarnation, it had any attraction for Christians, but that many fell away to it is evident from the repressive measures undertaken by the Christian emperors. The greatest of all its converts was Augustine, who was a Hearer for nine years, but at last found in it a stepping-stone towards Christianity. It lasted on through the Dark Ages, becoming a name of terror to medieval Europe. The Albigenses suffered from their association with it in the popular imagination. In the East it probably disappeared during the Mongol invasion of the thirteenth century, but in the West the fear of it was still strong enough to bring discredit on the Knights Templars in the fourteenth. Its effects last on to-day in the fear of claiming all truly natural life as good. But Christianity has always triumphed over it by asserting that evil, however powerful, is subject to the over-ruling providence of the one good God who is the supreme Governor of the universe.

CHAPTER XIV

ECCLESIASTICAL TROUBLES

THE most serious foes of Christianity at this time were not the rival systems to which we have just given consideration but those of her own household. When the pressure of persecution was removed it was found to have left some serious problems for solution, and if Constantine had hoped to use the Church as the cement by which to bind together his Empire, he was to find that the cement was showing signs of cracking before he had the chance to use it. In Rome the Pope Marcellinus had had the temerity to die in his bed, and as this was not the kind of thing that was expected of a bishop in time of persecution, it resulted in an annoying schism. In Alexandria a difficult situation had arisen over the action of Meletius in venturing to perform ordinations in that city while its own bishop was taking refuge from the attentions of the soldiery. But quite the most serious of these troubles arose in Africa, in the provinces of Numidia and Mauretania, where in the shape of Donatism there appeared what Bright called 'perhaps the ugliest phenomenon in ancient Church history'.

I

It all sprang from the doubts cast on the position of Mensurius, Bishop of Carthage. He was accused of being a *traditor*, that is one who in the persecution had handed over sacred books to the government officials. He defended himself by saying that the only books he had handed over were composed by heretics, and although the soldiers had been quite content with them it was no crime to get rid of books which the Church would be glad to be without. But he had also aroused dislike by following the example of Cyprian in not being too easy with confessors who received

overmuch adulation from their admiring brethren. He had even said that some of the confessors had provoked the police to imprison them, hoping thus to wipe out the memory of a somewhat sordid past.

In the attitude he thus adopted he had been joined by his archdeacon Caecilian, who on his death succeeded him as bishop. This promotion aroused the anger not only of other expectant presbyters but also of the wealthy lady Lucilla, to whose devotion to the bone of an alleged martyr Caecilian had taken grave exception. The moderates made the mistake of hastening forward his consecration, not waiting for the attendance of the other bishops of the province. This gave special annoyance to the bishops of Numidia, who found the business concluded before their arrival. But worst of all the counts against Caecilian was the fact that one of his consecrators, and indeed the chief officiant at the service, was Felix of Aptunga, who was himself alleged to be a *traditor*. Lucilla now persuaded the opposition party to take a definite step. A meeting of seventy bishops was held, as a result of which Lucilla's own chaplain, Majorinus, was consecrated as a rival Bishop of Carthage.

The schism thus started was duly reported to Constantine. He accepted Caecilian, to whom the majority clung, as the rightful bishop, and when in 313 arrangements were made at Milan for giving protection to the Christian Church, the followers of Majorinus were expressly excluded from this clemency. The schismatics protested against such treatment, and asked the Emperor to show his well-known justice by allowing their case to be examined by neutral bishops from Gaul.

In this controversy it is important to remember that there were two different sets of questions at issue. The first were topical, relating solely to the situation at the moment. It had to be decided on the one hand whether Felix of Aptunga was or was not a *traditor*, and on the other whether, supposing that he were a *traditor*, that fact would invalidate the consecration of Caecilian.

But behind these immediate questions there lay others of deep and indeed fundamental principle. Does the

unworthiness of a minister affect the validity of an ordinance? If a sacrament is celebrated by a person of doubtful character, is its value therefore destroyed? This is perhaps the most important question in sacramental theology. The second deals with the nature of the Church. Are only good people to be recognised as members of the divine society, or does it include the imperfect as well? Is the Church a museum for saints or a school for sinners?

This is the first time that the issue had come up in this form. Such precedents as there were did not all point the same way. In the old controversy over heretical baptism Cyprian and the African Church had taken the line that sin destroyed the office of the minister and so invalidated his sacraments, whereas Rome and the West generally had held that only a sentence of deposition could deprive an ecclesiastic of his *charisma*. Again some of the Donatists were no doubt seriously perturbed by the thought that the Church seemed to be conforming to the standard of the world, and they were genuinely anxious to preserve its high ideals. It is probable that for this reason they claimed for themselves the proud title of the 'communion of saints', a title which the Great Church speedily claimed as more appropriate to herself.

It is noteworthy that no one wished to take refuge in the thought of an invisible Church. The Church was the visible organisation and no other was thought of. Also it is possible that the dispute was complicated by racial jealousies among the Roman and Phoenician sections of the population. Further between proconsular Africa with Carthage as its metropolitical see and the province of Numidia there may have been disputes on questions of boundaries. But with these we need not now concern ourselves.

The attitude of Constantine was a mixture of indifference on the questions raised and infinite patience in endeavouring to bring the disputants to an agreement. Within seven years there were five investigations. The first was the council held at Rome (313) in response to the request of the Donatists for Constantine's intervention. At the Emperor's request the Pope together with the Gallic bishops of Autun,

Cologne and Arles was to meet representatives of both sides in the Lateran. But the Pope prevented this from being a mere imperial commission, and turned it into some sort of ecclesiastical council, by adding fifteen Italian bishops to the gathering. The assault was led by Donatus, the Bishop of Casae Nigrae, but his witnesses could prove no case against Caecilian. The attack was then turned upon himself and he was excommunicated.

The second investigation arose out of fresh disturbances at Carthage. A new hearing had been demanded by the Donatists on the ground that the case of Felix of Aptunga had not been examined. The proconsul Aelianus held an enquiry in 314, whereupon a clerk confessed that he had been guilty of forging the incriminating letter which was being produced to prove Felix a *traditor*; and the Donatist case again collapsed.

In the same year a far more important council was held to deal with this and other subjects at Arles. The Emperor was determined both to bind the Christians together and to unite them in common service to the State. He did all he could to make the meeting effective. He offered free transport to the bishops who needed it and even made it possible for three bishops to be present from Britain. As the main result of the council Caecilian was confirmed in the possession of his see and the Donatists were again condemned. But much other important business was done and a number of canons were passed. The Roman view of the validity of heretical baptism was upheld as against Cyprian's. Ordination was to be regarded as valid even if the bishop who performed it was a *traditor*. Henceforth at least three bishops were to be present at and to share in the consecration of another bishop. The clergy were not to be allowed to follow the profession of gladiator, circus charioteer or actor. On the other hand Christians might now accept office as magistrates since the supreme magistrate was himself a Christian. Any soldiers who refused service as incompatible with Christianity were threatened with excommunication. Further, lending on usury was forbidden; the innocent party to a divorce was denied the right of remarriage. Finally, Easter was to be

kept on the same day by all churches, the date to be announced from Rome.

In spite of the prestige which attached to this council the Donatists were still unsatisfied, and they appealed once again to Constantine in person. In 316 he declared against them and determined to try what severity could do. He caused their churches to be confiscated and put in the charge of the imperial treasury. He wished to put the leaders to death, but commuted their sentence to one of exile. Then relenting still further he recalled them about 320. At this time Donatus the Great was their leader, but whether this is the same person as the Donatus who had argued their case at Rome is not clear. The *reductio ad absurdum* of the whole dispute came at the fifth investigation in 320 at Algiers, when it was conclusively proved before the consular official that the leading Donatists had themselves been *traditores*.

The later history of Donatism showed the usual power of a religious pretext to gather round it many subsidiary motives. The theological movement soon took on a social colour. It became a rising of the poorer section of the population against the landowners, and perhaps also of the native section against the dominance of the Romans. About the beginning of the next reign the Donatists began a series of efforts to redress their own wrongs by forceful measures. Bands of *Circumcelliones* or wanderers among huts appeared, armed with stout clubs which they called Israels, and their war-cry *Laus Deo* became a terror to the respectable classes. Constans, son of Constantine, tried alternate policies of stern repression and bribery. But even his advances were met with the retort *Quid imperatori cum ecclesia?* 'What has the Emperor to do with the Church?' This declaration of independence might have won much more sympathy if it had not been in obvious conflict with the Donatists' early appeals to Constantine. It now led to a more determined effort at repression, and after many of the sectaries had been driven from the country and the rest temporarily silenced, peace was announced at a council held at Carthage in 348.

It will be seen that this controversy had far more than a

local significance. It gave the opportunity for the working out of some vital theological questions. The proper relation of the State to the Church, the true holiness of the Church apart from the holiness of its individual members, the correct determination of the validity of sacraments, and the indelibility of orders, were all matters the consideration of which was advanced a stage as a result of this schism. And on the purely practical side it gave an opportunity for the development of the conciliar method of dealing with ecclesiastical difficulties which was to reach such a height of importance in the universal upheaval caused by the next great controversy.

II

If Constantine had found the unifying power of Christianity fail him in the West he was almost immediately to find it failing him also in the East, and that in consequence of a controversy the significance of which he was much less capable of understanding. It arose in Alexandria, which, as we have noticed, was the meeting-place of philosophy and Christianity. There the great philosophical difficulties were sure to be most keenly felt. The fundamental question how to connect the One and the Many had been answered in different ways by Philo, the Gnostics and the Neoplatonists. The Christians had answered it with their doctrine of Father, Son and Spirit; and the special contribution of Alexandrian theologians had been what we have already described as a pluralistic Trinitarianism, an interpretation of the Divine Nature in which the distinction between the Three was somewhat sharply marked.

It happened that one of the best-known presbyters in the city, named Arius, had emphasised this characteristic Alexandrian teaching in such a way as to make it almost appear that there were three gods. A complaint was made against the Bishop, Alexander, because he did not immediately condemn such false doctrine. Alexander felt obliged then to take action. In a charge to his clergy in 318 he tried to explain the true nature of the Trinity and to check the evil consequences of a too pronounced pluralism. In this

charge he made the Son equal to the Father and explained the relation between them by using the word *homoousios*, 'of the same substance'. This was to run counter to the Origenistic subordinationism which was so popular in Alexandria and also to use a term against which strong objection had been brought by his own predecessor Dionysius. He was promptly accused of Sabellianism, and Arius saw the chance of winning a great victory.

Arius was not sorry for the opportunity. He had had a somewhat chequered career, having been involved in the schismatic ordinations of Bishop Meletius. For that he had been suspended, but later he had been restored and was now in charge of the suburb Baucalis. This was a particularly important charge, for it was there that were situated the granaries from which corn was shipped to Rome. There was much to commend Arius for such a position: he was a person of commanding presence, tall, grave, and with a great reputation for asceticism. He had been a friend of confessors and a pupil of the martyr Lucian of Antioch. Indeed it is sometimes thought that he had imbibed a kind of Adoptianism from this Lucian, who, it will be remembered, was a friend of Paul of Samosata. Certainly the Adoptianist Christology was not unlike the view taken by Arius, but it should be borne in mind that his interests were really Trinitarian, and that he was standing as a champion not of the characteristic teaching of Antioch but of that of Alexandria. It may be said, however, that in point of fact Arius combined an Alexandrian view of God with an Antiochene view of Christ.

There need be no doubt that Arius was genuinely anxious to preserve the unity of the Godhead against the surrounding polytheism. But he tried to do this by supposing that the Christian tradition could be explained as belief in one Supreme God with two inferior deities. According to him the unity of God excluded not only all distinctions within the Divine Nature, but also all contact with the external world. Therefore to make creation possible an intermediate Being was necessary. That Being Arius found in the Logos.

His doctrine of the Logos was as follows: in the first

place the Word was the minister of creation and therefore He was more than man, and inasmuch as He was the creator of all other beings He could rightly be called God. In the second place, however, He was the Son and therefore He was less than the Father. And since He was begotten He was in some sense a creature and was certainly not eternal. He was formed out of things that did not exist, and although He was formed before time itself began, yet there must have been once when He was not. Thirdly He was obviously subject to pain and change, but by the exercise of His own will He remained good. The Father, knowing from all beginning that this would be so, had adopted Him proleptically as His Son. This doctrine was sometimes put in the form of a syllogism:

> Christ is the Logos incarnate,
> Christ is capable of change and suffering,
> Therefore the Logos is capable of change and not equal to God.

It will be recognised that this intermediate Being of Arius is really modelled on the pattern of the old Greek heroes. He is neither truly human nor truly divine. He hovers between earth and heaven touching neither. As has been well said, he is an incarnation of what is not God in what is not man. Consequently he could not be a truly effective agent of either revelation or redemption.

Arius' doctrine of the Spirit is much less developed, but He is held to bear the same relation to the Son as the Son bears to the Father. He is the first-created of the Logos in the same way as the Logos is the first-created of the Father. Thus Arius' doctrine of the Trinity really presents us with the philosophy of the day in a Christian dress. It is a teaching more closely paralleled by the heathen triads than by the truly Christian doctrine of the Trinity.

Arius was a born propagandist. He put his abstruse theological speculations into the form of catchy rhymes, on the model of the *Thalia* or marriage songs, which were sung about the streets, and even, it has been said, by the fish-porters on the quays. These verses he strengthened by some useful quotations from the Scriptures. 'The Lord

created me in the beginning of His way, before His works of old' (Prov. viii 22, LXX). 'God hath made that same Jesus . . . both Lord and Christ' (Acts ii 36). 'Being made so much better than the angels,' 'The apostle and high priest of our profession, Christ Jesus, who was faithful to Him that appointed Him' (Heb. i 4; iii 1, 2). His teaching on these texts appeared attractive to many. To the learned no doubt it seemed to save the prestige of philosophy; to converts from paganism it seemed to preserve monotheism; even to the devout it would seem to save the literal meaning of many scriptural passages. But it was in plain conflict with usual Christian doctrine.

A private interview between Alexander and Arius having failed to compose their differences, two clerical meetings endeavoured to settle the question, but without success. It 321 a synod was summoned and was attended by the bishops of Egypt and Libya. By this synod Arius was condemned and excommunicated. He thereupon left Alexandria and travelled East, where he was well received by Eusebius of Caesarea and later by Eusebius of Nicomedia. News of this growing difference of opinion and its rapid spread through the East was brought to the imperial court, but Constantine took no action until after he had defeated Licinius. Then in 323 he intervened for the sake of unity, and sent his friend Hosius, the Bishop of Cordova, with a letter asking Alexander and Arius to put a stop to their disputes, which after all were about nothing but words. This failing to produce the desired effect, a synod was held at Alexandria in the presence of Hosius. Arius was again condemned.

Our knowledge of the next steps depends on the genuineness of two newly discovered documents. If, as is probable, we should accept them, then a synod was held at Antioch in 324. This did not settle the question between Alexander and Arius, but excommunicated Eusebius of Caesarea, who had stood out as the champion of Arius and failed adequately to defend his own orthodoxy. The first of our two documents purports to be the synodal letter announcing this fact. The larger issues were left to be settled at a council which was to

be summoned at Ancyra. This was the see of Marcellus who was known to be a fervent opponent of Arianism. It looks as if it was intended to finish off the question there, and then to present the Emperor with a *fait accompli*. Our second document is a letter from Constantine himself ordering the council to meet, not at Ancyra but at Nicaea. This town was in Bithynia not far from the imperial residence at Nicomedia. Constantine thus gained the initiative. He put a stop to the holding of a merely Eastern synod, and replaced it by an oecumenical council in which might be heard the judgment of the whole Christian world. Thus peace, he hoped, might at length be secured.

CHAPTER XV

THE PROGRESS OF ARIANISM

THE date for the assembling of the Council of Nicaea was May 20, 325, and it lasted into August. It was attended by about 300 bishops; Eustathius gives the number as 270, while popular prejudice preferred the number 318, but that was probably arrived at through the mystical connexions of the number of the armed servants of Abraham (Gen. xiv 14). In spite of the Emperor's effort to make the Council as representative as possible, most of the attendant bishops were from the East. Many of them were still bearing marks of the sufferings inflicted upon them during the persecutions. Sylvester, the Bishop of Rome, was not present, but he was represented by two legates. With some of the combatants we have already met, while others now come before our notice for the first time.

I

The one of whom we already know most is Eusebius of Caesarea. He had been adding to his immense stores of learning by reading in the library of Pamphilus, the friend of Origen. This association had no doubt helped to influence him in the direction that was to be taken by Arius. Pamphilus perished in the persecution of Diocletian, but during his imprisonment he and Eusebius had collaborated in writing a *Defence of Origen*, a work which Eusebius had finished alone after his friend's martyrdom. What had been Eusebius' own fortunes during the persecution is not at all clear. He was accused of having offered sacrifice, but in all probability the soldiers had forced him to go through the gestures of burning incense to Caesar's genius, thus saving his life but destroying his credit with a section of the faithful. He had then travelled in Egypt where he saw many other martyrdoms

and gathered material for another book. When the trouble was over he was made Bishop of Caesarea. On the outbreak of the Arian controversy he had written to remonstrate with Alexander, but in spite of his interest in this dispute he found time to finish his *Ecclesiastical History* before the Council of Nicaea met. It has been a matter of discussion whether his theological views should be described as liberal or conservative. It is probable that he disliked exclusive formulae, and that he had the scholar's disinclination to give official definition to speculative theories. But if the evidence we have already adduced is as reliable as we believe it to be, then it is clear that he had not been able to deliver himself from the charge of heresy, and that he was already under a cloud when the Council assembled. It is certain in any case that he had spoken of the Son as a secondary God.

His namesake Eusebius of Nicomedia was even more definitely committed to Arian views. This man was essentially a courtier prelate. He had supported Licinius even when that Emperor was a confessed opponent of the Church, and he had been a great friend of his wife Constantia, the sister of Constantine. When Arius was driven from Alexandria Eusebius had offered him a ready shelter, and by this action enabled a local dispute to embroil the whole of Christendom, although Duchesne is going too far in saying that 'if Eusebius had minded his own business Arianism would have remained a purely Alexandrian question'.

The person who was to become the most famous opponent of the Arians was Athanasius, of whom it has been said that if ever a man was divinely raised up to deal with an emergency it was he. The best evidence of that is his longevity (*c.* 297–373), which enabled him to see the controversy through from the beginning until all was over but the recording of the decision. At the time of the Council he was not yet thirty, while Arius was forty years older. Athanasius was a Greek of Alexandria. There as a boy he had attracted by his earnestness the notice of Alexander, the Bishop, who took him into his household. Thus he had the opportunity not only of obtaining a good education but also of meeting the best thinkers of the time. He had a close acquaintance

with many of the martyr heroes, and he also knew some of the leaders of that new type of Christian discipline, monasticism. The greatest exponent of this ascetic Christianity was Antony. Of him Athanasius wrote a biography, and his unworldly example he tried to imitate as closely as possible in his own life. Thus he gained for himself the title of an ascetic and also won the adherence of the Egyptian monks to his views.

Athanasius was evidently a man of considerable personal courage. As a witness to this we may cite his action when a police boat was chasing him on the Nile. In the gathering gloom the officers called out, 'Have you seen Athanasius?' and Athanasius himself answered, 'Yes, you are not far from him now,' and they raced on while he escaped at his leisure. His main interest was not in philosophical speculation but in soteriology. His little book *De Incarnatione* was written before he was twenty-one, that is to say while he was still in the household of Alexander and when the Arian controversy had not yet begun. Nevertheless it is an answer to what was afterwards the minor premiss of the Arian syllogism. Its main position is that the Logos must be truly God or we cannot be saved. The method of that salvation he states in characteristic fashion: 'God became man in order that we might become divine.'

The most imposing of Athanasius' friends was Eustathius, the Bishop of Antioch. This prelate had been a confessor in the Diocletian persecution, and had been Bishop of Beroea (Aleppo in Syria) before he was translated to Antioch. He was a great opponent of the subordinationism of Origen, which had been propagated by Lucian and Eusebius of Caesarea. Theodoret tells us that he had the seat of honour at the Emperor's right hand in the Council, but Sozomen contradicts this. In any case he had great claims on the Emperor's favour, and in this respect, as in that of theology, he was a rival of the two Eusebii.

II

On the first day of the Council the gathering was held in the large hall of the imperial palace. After the Emperor's

impressive entrance a congratulatory address was given in his honour, probably by Eustathius. The Emperor replied briefly in Latin, and then publicly burnt a number of letters that the bishops had written to him incriminating each other. His small knowledge of Greek made it impossible for him to preside at the meetings of the Council. Who did preside is not clear. Certainly it was not the papal legates; it was probably Hosius of Cordova, Eustathius and Alexander being associated with him. After the first day the meetings were held in the church, but with the doors open, because there were laymen present and even pagan professors. As the *Acta* of the Council have not been preserved for us, we have to rely for our information upon the accounts of eye-witnesses and historians.

There seems to have been considerable preliminary examination of Arius, but the first definite business was the production of an Arian statement of faith by Eusebius of Nicomedia. This was at once rejected and torn in pieces. The next attempt was made by Eusebius of Caesarea, who put forward his own creed, either because he had to prove his orthodoxy, or because he hoped it might become a basis of conciliation. As soon as this creed was recited it was noticed that the Arians, whose bishops numbered twenty-two, were winking and nodding to each other. This meant that they would be prepared to accept this statement of faith, which in point of fact was completely silent on the points at issue. It contented itself with describing the Logos as 'the first-born of every creature' and 'born before all ages', vague phrases which could easily be interpreted in an Arian sense. The rest of the bishops realised that, as it stood, Eusebius's creed was thoroughly unsatisfactory. We have it on the authority of Eusebius himself that they thereupon decided to make it clearer by the addition of certain clauses. They substituted the word Son for Logos, and they added to the definition of the Son the phrases 'of the substance of the Father' and 'of one substance with the Father' (the famous *homoousios*). This gave a positive definition of the faith which preserved at once the unity of the Godhead and the distinctions within it, and so completely excluded

Arianism. But in order to make assurance doubly sure they added a series of negative clauses to the end of the creed in the shape of anathemas against those who used certain well-known Arian phrases. The creed with its double defence against false teaching having thus been completed they decided to ask all the assembled bishops to sign. This was a new use for creeds, and it was the first time that bishops had had such a test of orthodoxy imposed upon them. Who actually proposed it in this form is not known, but probably it was either Hosius or the Emperor himself prompted by Hosius.

THE CREED OF NICEA

We believe in one God, the Father almighty, maker of all things both visible and invisible;

And in one Lord, Jesus Christ, the Son of God, only begotten of the Father, that is of the substance of the Father, God of God, Light of Light, very God of very God, Begotten not made, of one substance with the Father; Through whom all things were made, both the things in heaven and the things on earth;

Who for us men and for our salvation came down, and was made flesh, and was made man,

He suffered,

And rose again the third day,

Ascended into heaven,

Is coming to judge quick and dead;

And in the Holy Ghost.

But those who say, There was once when He was not, or He was not before He was begotten, or He was made out of nothing, or affirm that the Son of God is of a different hypostasis or substance, or is a creature, or is subject to change or alteration, these the catholic and apostolic Church of God anathematises.

All the bishops except two signed the creed. The Eusebii agreed under protest, being over-ruled by the influence of the court. The two recusants were the Libyan bishops, Theonas and Secundus. Together with Arius they were sent into exile. Shortly after the adjournment Eusebius of

Nicomedia followed them into banishment, either because he withdrew his acceptance of the creed or because, like Theognis the Bishop of Nicea, he refused to agree to the anathemas. Thus the Council ended in a signal triumph for Alexander and his friends. Two years later the conversion of Arius was announced and the excommunicated bishops were received back into the fellowship of the Church. Arianism was not openly professed for another thirty years.

But the Arian heresy was not the only business with which the first oecumenical council dealt. The opportunity was taken to settle various questions of ecclesiastical organisation. Church administration usually followed the lines of civil development. It had been one of the reforms of Diocletian to add to the number of provinces and to group them in various 'dioceses', each in charge of a 'vicar' responsible to himself. The precise connotation of the terms is different in our day, the 'diocese' being now a section of the 'province'. It is easy, however, to see in this civil organisation the model of the Church's metropolitical authority, what we now call dioceses having been grouped together in a province and placed under the bishop of the most important town.

There were two instances, however, in which the rights of such metropolitans were transcended by those of still greater ecclesiastics, namely Rome and Alexandria. The sixth canon of Nicea orders that as the bishops of central and southern Italy are directly subject to Rome, so the bishops of Egypt should remain under the immediate jurisdiction of Alexandria. The rights of Antioch are also specially mentioned; and Bright sees in this canon the recognition of 'three virtual patriarchates'. It is interesting to note that in the seventh canon Jerusalem merely takes precedence of the bishops under the jurisdiction of Caesarea. A further point of interest is the complete absence of reference to any universal rights of the Bishop of Rome.

During the Council the question of Easter once more came up for discussion. Hitherto the festival had been kept by many without regard to the day of the week. It was now declared that it must always be observed on a Sunday. Further, if the 14th Nisan, the day of the Jewish Passover,

fell on a Sunday, Easter Day was not to be observed until the following Sunday. In order to avoid any difference between East and West it was left to the Bishop of Alexandria (the home of the best astronomy of the period) to decide the precise date each year and to communicate it to the Bishop of Rome, both bishops then promulgating it to the dioceses. This at least is the assertion of Cyril of Alexandria and Leo, although some doubt has recently been cast upon it.

Another matter dealt with was the Meletian schism, which was still troubling the peace of the Church of Alexandria. It was ordered that Meletius should no longer be permitted to ordain, and that the ordinations already performed by him should be 'confirmed by a more sacred ordination'. Even so those originally ordained by him were to work only under the authority of those ordained by the regular bishops of Alexandria. Meletius himself, though prohibited from performing the functions, was allowed to retain the rank and title of bishop.

It was ordered that in future three bishops should be present and share in the consecration of a bishop. Further canons regulated the conditions on which alone excommunication was to be imposed, and ordered that two provincial synods were to be held yearly. A matter of discipline with which the Council dealt was that of the *subintroductae* or spiritual sisters whom some of the clergy were accustomed to keep in their houses. Although it was no doubt often found possible to maintain a purely spiritual relationship in these cases, they were sometimes the cause of scandal, and the Council wisely ordered that the custom should cease.

III

To return now to the course of the Arian controversy. It has often been pointed out that with the Council of Nicea Christianity had entered upon a new stage in its development. It was now officially linked with Hellenic philosophy. Metaphysics had been brought in to assist religious faith, and in an authoritative formula it had been found necessary to employ a terminology coined in paganism. This may be an exaggeration, but it is an exaggeration of a truth. The

traditional faith had been compelled to express itself in rational terms, and the period of definition had inevitably begun. Further, the Nicene victory had been a little too speedy; there had been no time for a wide general discussion. The Council had judged the question; it still remained for the Church to judge the Council. Some hesitation and even reaction were inevitable. But such reaction seemed likely to be of a conservative type: it would express itself in a dislike of the new tests.

Some sign of this may be detected already in the letter sent by Eusebius of Caesarea to his diocese endeavouring to explain his attitude at the Council. Duchesne calls it a 'pitiful and insincere' letter, and so perhaps it was. But Eusebius was in a difficult situation. It was not merely that his sympathy for Arius was well known and that he had to explain why he had signed an anti-Arian formula, but the greatest scholar in the Church had to show why the Council had not accepted his creed as it stood. At first he speaks of the Council having approved his creed, with the addition of the one word 'consubstantial'. Later, however, he says that the addition of this word 'gave rise to the following formulary', an expression so ambiguous that Müller thinks the creed used by the Council as a basis was not that of Eusebius at all but a Jerusalem creed.

Worse still for the prestige of the Council was the fact that the settlement reached had been imposed on the assembled bishops largely by pressure from outside. It has been suggested that if the Emperor had not taken so strong a line the differences would ultimately have composed themselves. Constantine indeed seems to have begun to think that he had made a mistake in exiling recalcitrants. That may be the reason why, as we have seen, a kind of amnesty was declared in 327. It was perhaps natural that the returning exiles should wish to turn the tables against their opponents. It was far too dangerous yet to attack the creed, but something could be done to undermine the credit of individuals. And unfortunately some of Athanasius' friends were only too open to attack.

The first to suffer was Eustathius of Antioch. He was the

most active literary opponent of the Arians. They dared not attack his orthodoxy, but they brought against him a charge of immorality, and when that failed they levelled against him the far more serious charge of having defamed the Emperor's mother Helena. She had been a supporter of Lucian, and Eustathius was doing all he could to uproot every trace of Lucian's teaching. But he need not have said in public that Helena had once been a maid at an inn, which implied a good deal more than it said. For this he was deposed in 330 and sent into exile, where he died. This had serious consequences for the Church of Antioch. The friends of Eustathius refused to accept the ministrations of his official successors, and continued to hold their own meetings under the presbyter Paulinus. This led to a schism of which we shall hear more later.

The second person to be attacked was Marcellus of Ancyra. Here was one whose orthodoxy could be brought into question. He was so opposed to anything like 'pluralism' that he taught that the Logos was one with God in the same way that reason is one with man. Further he asserted that this Logos was not the Son of God from all eternity but only became Son at the Incarnation. This seemed to many hardly distinguishable from Sabellianism, but it actually occurred in a treatise against the Arians which he had had the temerity to present to the Emperor. The result was deposition and exile.

This cleared the way to Athanasius himself. He had been present at Nicea as deacon and assessor to his Bishop. The year after the Council he had succeeded his friend and patron as Bishop of Alexandria. He was still young and impetuous, and stirred up enemies by his drastic method of dealing with the Meletians. Several charges were brought against him; first that he had taxed the Egyptians in order to provide himself with linen vestments, and second that he had given a purse of gold to the rebel Philumenos. Then there came the story of the broken chalice: he had sent an underling to stop the ministrations of an insubordinate priest, and the man had obeyed his instructions so literally as to interfere in the course of the Mysteries and to break

the chalice containing the consecrated wine. To this Athanasius replied that in that village there was no church; that it was not a Sunday; that there was therefore no Eucharist and consequently no chalice. Even more picturesque was the charge that he had murdered Arsenius and cut off his hand for magical uses; to which Athanasius replied by producing Arsenius alive in court with both hands intact. However, his enemies were still strong enough to accuse him before a council, which was held at Tyre in 335, when the bishops were on their way to the dedication of the church of the Holy Sepulchre at Jerusalem. By this council he was condemned. He repaired to the Emperor in person at Constantinople, but there he was met with a charge that he had caused delay in the despatch of the corn ships from Alexandria to Rome. For this he was sent into his first exile (336).

Once Athanasius and his friends were out of the way, the next step was to begin a series of attacks on the Nicene doctrine. The difficulty about this was that the Arianisers had really no clear-cut views of their own, as was shown by the fact that they put forward no fewer than seventeen creeds in the twenty years between 340 and 360. They seemed to have become a mere political party with the aim of destroying Athanasius but with no fixed theological position. In some respects matters were made easier for them by the death of Arius in 336, which removed their most suspected leader, and by that of Constantine, who had supported the Nicene party, in the following year.

The government of the Empire was now divided among Constantine's three sons. Constantine II ruled the West, Constans the centre, and Constantius the East. Of these Constantine was orthodox and recalled Athanasius in 338, and Constans also was sympathetic to the Nicene faith. Constantius, on the other hand, was entirely under Arian influence. He made Eusebius of Nicomedia Bishop of Constantinople in 339, and exiled Athanasius for the second time in the same year. This latter step was ultimately of some advantage to the orthodox, for Athanasius went to Rome, where his friendship with Pope Julius did much to bring

the West and East closer together in alliance for the defence of Nicene teaching. But for the time the changes in the government told in favour of the Arianisers. Dislike of the term *homoousios* now had a chance to find expression. Some hated it because it was unscriptural, some because it had been once condemned, and some because it seemed to savour of materialistic notions. Three determined efforts were made to overthrow it.

The first was in 341 when a council met at Antioch on the occasion of the dedication of the Golden Church which had been founded by Constantine I. The bishops began by frankly abandoning the position of Arius. 'He was but a presbyter, how could we bishops be suspected of submitting to his guidance?' Then they made various temporising efforts, and put forward four creeds, none of which was of much importance. The one valuable thing they did, a step which was to affect the whole subsequent history of Europe, was to consecrate Ulfilas as Bishop of the Goths.

The next attempt occurred two years later in 343, when by arrangement between Constantius and Constans a council was held at Sardica (the modern Sophia). The Western bishops favoured Nicea and the Eastern were opposed to it. The result was a split, each side separating off and holding a little council of its own. The Westerns, left to themselves, reaffirmed the creed of Nicea. But, what was more important for later history, they agreed among themselves that if any bishop felt aggrieved by any action taken against him on the part of a superior he should have the right to appeal to the Bishop of Rome. This was the beginning of the appellate jurisdiction of the Roman see. The canon in which it was embodied was so important that it was often referred to by the Roman Church as a canon of the great Council of Nicea itself.

The third attempt took place in the following year, 344, at Antioch. On this occasion some show was made of cutting off extremes from both wings. Photinus of Sirmium, a pupil of Marcellus of Ancyra, was condemned, and a few Arian phrases were ruled out; and then a conciliatory creed called the Macrostich was put forth.

After this there was a suspension of hostilities. Comparative peace reigned for the next ten years, and Athanasius returned from exile in 346. If the first stage of the controversy had ended in a victory for the *homoousios*, the second stage ended in a draw.

A third stage, which was to mark the victory of Arianism, was made possible by fresh changes in the political situation. Constantine II died in 340, and the western portion of the Empire was added to that of Constans. In 350 occurred the revolt of Magnentius, who, after the assassination of Constans, usurped the rule of the West and centre. He still, however, had to reckon with the ruler of the East. In 353 he was thoroughly defeated and committed suicide. The whole of the Empire was thus once more united under the rule of one man, and that man was Constantius, an avowed opponent of Nicea. All his influence was exerted on the Arian side. The only difficulty was to find a formula upon which everyone could be made to agree.

By this time the Arian sympathisers had divided themselves into three main groups, and each group in turn gained the upper hand. In the first flush of victory it was the extreme Arians who took advantage of the situation. Their formula was that the Son was *unlike* the Father, whence they were called the Anomoeans. At the Council of Arles in 353 the Emperor coerced the assembled bishops into accepting this formula, and he repeated this process later at the Council of Milan (355). The aged Hosius of Cordova was compelled to agree. Liberius, the Bishop of Rome, at first refused, but when sentence of exile was passed upon him he too agreed—a terrible fall for the bishop of the first see in Christendom. Then, it is said, there remained not a single bishop in possession of his see who had not taken up a position against the *homoousios*. Athanasius himself was exiled for the third time (356–362), and the infamous George of Cappadocia was intruded into his see. But in his enforced retirement Athanasius was not idle. He wrote his *Orations*, the *Apology to Constantius*, the *Apology for Flight*, and his *History of the Arians*. The Arians signalised their victory by putting forth a manifesto known as the

Blasphemy of Sirmium (357), in which there was contained a prohibition of the use of the words 'essence', 'of the same essence' (*homoousios*), and 'of like essence' (*homoiousios*).

But this was too much for the conscience even of the Arians themselves. The coalition that had brought about so devastating a result fell to pieces as soon as its object seemed achieved. This was made clear at the Synod of Ancyra in 358. Some less extreme formula was obviously necessary or it would be difficult to maintain that Christ was divine in any sense. Consequently the synod condemned the conclusions of Sirmium because they excluded the formula *homoiousios*, 'of like essence'. This was the formula of the Semi-Arian party, and with its affirmation they came into power. Unfortunately for themselves they used their influence to secure the exile of the Anomoean leaders. In the nature of things the extreme Arians soon began to return, and to work for the destruction of their opponents. A third party with a new formula was necessary.

This was found in the Homoeans who wished to drop all talk of 'essence' and affirmed simply that the Son was *like* the Father (*homoios*). This became the key phrase of another creed of Sirmium, known as the Dated Creed, which was revised by a synod held at Nice. At Ariminum in 359 the government again put forth its authority and forced this Homoean creed upon the whole Church. This situation was confirmed at Constantinople in the following year when the great church of S. Sophia was dedicated. It is of the situation thus created that Jerome used his famous epigram, 'The whole world groaned in amazement at finding itself Arian.' Now indeed Athanasius might have been pardoned if he had thought that he stood alone against the world. But the expression *Athanasius contra mundum* was never more than a rhetorical phrase. There were many knees that had not yet bowed to Baal, and an event was soon to occur which would show how weak was the grasp of Arianism upon the Church. The following year in Paris the troops mutinied against orders sent them by Constantius, and proclaimed as Emperor their leader Julian. Julian had no choice but

to march against his rival. Constantius set out to meet the peril but died before contact between the two armies could be made. Julian thus became sole ruler of the Empire, and a new stage in the history of Arianism had begun.

CHAPTER XVI

JULIAN AND THE CAPPADOCIAN THEOLOGIANS

I

THE man who became Emperor in such dramatic circumstances had had a singular career. At the age of six he had been saved together with his brother Gallus, aged thirteen, from the efforts of Constantius to rid himself of all possible rivals for the imperial authority. The instruments of his rescue had been the two Arianising bishops Eusebius of Nicomedia and Mark of Arethusa. Consequently, when the existence of the boys was revealed and they were confined in the fortress of Macellum, they were brought up under Arian influences. Julian himself, who was of a religious turn of mind, became a Reader.

Later Constantius found himself in need of assistance, and in 351 he promoted Gallus to the rank of Caesar. The youth thereupon contrived to get Julian restored to his proper rank and liberty. But Gallus was a failure; and he was soon murdered, probably by the orders of Constantius. Julian was sent to the university of Athens, where he spent the happiest years of his life, and was a fellow-student of two of the theologians with whom we shall be concerned later in this chapter, Basil of Caesarea and Gregory of Nazianzum. Later he was recalled to the court and was married to Helena, the sister of Constantius. But his greatest friend was the Empress Eusebia, who gave him a library as a wedding present, and protected him for the rest of her life. At the age of twenty-four he was made Caesar and became governor of Gaul. Curiously enough he showed himself an able general. The German tribes were very troublesome at the time, but Julian effectively checked them by his victory at Strassburg in 357. He was a self-conscious soldier: he took Alexander as his model, and wrote an

account of his own wars after the pattern of Julius Caesar. His success and his popularity with the troops aroused the jealousy of Constantius, who took steps to separate Julian from his army. He summoned the flower of Julian's legions to join himself in his campaign against the Persians. They, however, realising the meaning of this command, refused to obey it, and, with what result we have already seen, proclaimed Julian Augustus.

Julian now threw off the profession of Christianity. He had already been initiated into the Eleusinian Mysteries and received the *Taurobolium*. It was therefore clear when he started on his epic march that the issue lay between Christianity and paganism. As far as the moral character of the two rivals was concerned, there can be no doubt that the comparison was in favour of the pagan. Self-conscious as ever, Julian determined to give an example to the world of a philosopher upon the throne. He now modelled himself upon the pattern of Marcus Aurelius. He began by cleansing the palace of the throng of menials and sycophants who had swarmed round his predecessor. He showed himself a glutton for work, supervising the whole administration of the Empire by day, and by night snatching as many hours as possible from sleep for the study of philosophy. But this was not to endure. The danger on the Persian frontier called for a new expedition. Crossing the Tigris, he divided his army into two parts to sweep the country. He himself declined the siege of Ctesiphon, and, misled by treacherous guides, burnt behind him the boats that had served for a bridge, and penetrated deeper into the interior. The country, wasted by the inhabitants, gave no support to his troops, and he was forced to retreat. His other army made slower progress and failed to effect a junction with him. He was held up outside Nisibis, and there he was killed by a chance spear.

There can be no doubt that Julian was a deeply religious man and that he had a real devotion to philosophy. His love of learning was such that he wept at leaving Athens. His bravery and ability are beyond question. He had a great sense of duty, and his disinterested toil for his country recalls the best traditions of Roman history. It has been

pointed out that he would have been a distinguished man even if he had never worn the purple. Yet there were curious streaks in his character which made it impossible for him to achieve real greatness. He had an odd sort of affectation, which to-day we associate with the *Quartier Latin*, cultivating slovenliness in order to avoid the reproach of foppery. His gauche manners caused amusement at court, and the general public was astonished at his beard.

It is an interesting question why at this time of day he should have taken so retrograde a step as to support an effete paganism. One must remember that the cause of paganism did not yet seem to be altogether lost. Christianity had been tolerated for no more than fifty years, and the majority of the people had not yet accepted it. Further, like most aesthetes, Julian was excessively credulous, and found his love of the miraculous and the magical better satisfied in paganism than in Christianity. Also his literary aspirations were better supported by the glories of the old pagan classics than by the new Christian writings. Moreover, the type of Christianity with which he had been brought in contact was that of the logic-chopping Arians and of his murderous uncle Constantius. His hatred of the latter was sufficient of itself to turn him against the religion that Constantius could profess.

Something of this can be seen in Julian's writings. His first book was entitled *The Caesars*. In this the various emperors are called before the gods for judgment. The career of each one is passed under review, and in the end the palm is awarded to the philosopher-emperor Marcus Aurelius. His second book is the *Misopogon* or Hater of the Beard. This is a singularly undignified retaliation upon the Antiochenes, who when he visited their city had poured unmeasured scorn upon his beard. It has been aptly described as 'a singular monument of the resentment, the wit, the humanity and the indiscretion of Julian'. And lastly there is the *Contra Christianos*, which is not a very original book, but is based largely upon the *True Word* of Celsus. Its argument is threefold: Christianity gives a false view of God in the anthropomorphism of the creation story (Plato's

cosmogony is held to be better than that of Genesis); secondly
Christianity is both novel and plebeian, for it sets people
against the old ancestral standards of their race and is
consequently fit only for the brutish and uneducated;
finally an incarnation is unworthy of the nature of God,
for the highest God would be deprived of His majesty in
thus entering into the indignities of human flesh, but in
point of fact the Incarnation never happened, for Christ
was merely a dead man whose worship was inaugurated by
the evangelist John.

Julian made a deliberate attempt to revive the fortunes
of paganism. He was himself a Neoplatonist of the school of
Iamblichus. In this school, as we have already remarked, the
old Platonism had been corrupted by the practice of magic
and theurgy. It was held that if the First Cause manifests
itself in the natural order, it can be controlled by the manipulation of the material universe. Magic is such manipulation
at one's own discretion.

On the foundation of this philosophy Julian set himself to
build up a kind of pagan catholicism, a sort of pagan universal church which should be capable of vying in every
department with the Christian Church. Julian himself was
at the head of it, for the emperors had not yet dropped the
title of *Pontifex Maximus*. Julian turned the title once again
into a reality, and enjoyed the work. He officiated at the
sacrifices; he tried to imitate the Christian charitable
institutions and ecclesiastical organisation; he even endeavoured to set up pagan nunneries on the model of the
Christian convents. It was not his fault if he was the only
man in the Empire who was still capable of taking paganism
seriously. If he had not tried to link his revival with an
emphasis on morality, he might have succeeded better, but
people were not to be made moral by philosophy. Nor was
a failing creed to be bolstered up by openly imitating the
best points of its victorious rival.

But the reason for Julian's failure is also to be attributed
in great measure to his own character. Good and able as
he was, he cannot be relieved of the charge of being a crank
and a faddist, and once that was realised it was hopeless to

expect the sober bulk of the people to follow him. Julian himself seems to have felt before the end the hopelessness of his task, and even if the cry *Vicisti Galilaee* is apocryphal, it represents a substantial truth.

The effect of Julian's reign upon the Church was quite different from that which he expected. His original claim was that he tolerated all religions alike. But this toleration was such as to press hardly upon the Church. All pagan temples and lands that had been confiscated were to be returned to the original owners, a measure which in view of the decreased numbers of pagans needed some modification. A more spiteful measure was the command forbidding Christian teachers to give instruction in the pagan classics. This was done on the ground that they could not believe what they were teaching, but its effect was to withdraw from their pupils the groundwork of a literary education. So anxious was Julian to embarrass the Church that he even promoted the restoration of the Jewish temple at Jerusalem. This project, however, was frustrated by a mysterious outburst of fire in the foundations, which so terrified the workmen that they were unwilling to proceed. A more crafty measure was the recall of the exiled bishops. It was expected that this would result in a series of fresh quarrels which would inevitably discredit the Christian society. The only success achieved, however, was in Africa, where the Donatists took the opportunity to seize some of the Catholic churches and set to work to rid them of their alleged defilement by white-washing the walls and scraping the altars. Elsewhere the bishops who had before been estranged began now to close their ranks against the common foe.

This was most clearly seen in Alexandria. Athanasius returned in 362, and in the same year summoned a council which did much to effect a *rapprochement*. At this council the terms for the reception of Arians were settled: the leaders were to be put to penance but the rank and file would be accepted on the mere repetition of the Nicene Creed. Also the misunderstanding which had arisen over the meaning of the term *hypostasis* was cleared up. In the West this word had been taken in its etymological sense as equivalent to the

Latin *substantia*, meaning 'nature', whereas in the East it had come to have the meaning of 'person'. As the whole Trinitarian doctrine rested on the distinction between nature and person it is obvious how much confusion such a misunderstanding could cause. It was agreed henceforth to accept the word in its technical sense of 'person', thus making it equivalent to the Latin *persona*. Further, notice was taken of the new difficulty that was arising about the Person of Christ. In reaction against Arian belittling of the Divine Nature of Christ, some of the Nicene party had begun to belittle His humanity. The council sought to redress the balance by asserting in emphatic terms that Christ was possessed of a real human soul. Difficulties had also arisen with regard to the Holy Spirit. Some who rejected the rest of Arianism nevertheless described the Holy Spirit in Arian fashion as a creature. The council affirmed His divinity, and Athanasius was of opinion that the creed ought to be completed by declaring Him to be 'of one substance with the Father' as had already been asserted of the Son. Together with arrangements for putting an end to the Meletian schism at Antioch, this completes the excellent work done by this Council of Alexandria.

Julian thus found that his policy of toleration was not working out well. Had he lived he would probably have gone on to persecute. He certainly took no steps to punish the mob who shamelessly ill-treated his old protector Mark of Arethusa. He dismissed all Christians from his bodyguard, deprived the clergy of their privileges, and made them repay the grants given them by the State. Athanasius was once again banished, and departed into his fourth exile in 362. But this growing harshness was not an unrelieved disadvantage to the Church. The Christians who suffered most from it were the various sections of the Arian party. The courtier Homoeans lost their imperial protector, and the philosopher Anomoeans found that philosophy was for the time being the cherished privilege of the pagan world. Both classes were thus deprived of their special advantages, and when they had to rely only on the merits of their case they could not compete with the Nicenes. This was discerned by most of

the Semi-arians or Homoiousians, and there consequently took place a considerable reconciliation between the followers of the *homoousios* and those of the *homoiousios*. They had been ready enough to fight over the iota when that seemed to make all the difference in belief about the relation of Christ to the Godhead, but when they found they were both trying to say the same thing they managed to smooth away the difference in terminology. The reign of the Apostate was thus an actual gain to the Church in so far as it forced the combatants into a position in which that discovery could be made.

II

Julian's immediate successor Jovian favoured the Nicenes, but his reign was short, and when Valentinian succeeded him it was to revert to the division of the Empire. Valentinian himself reigned in the West and supported the orthodox, but he gave the East to Valens, who was a strong upholder of the Homoeans. While Valentinian was anxious to leave the Church alone to settle her own affairs, so long as she maintained public order, Valens threw the whole weight of his influence on the side of the party he favoured. But his effort to compel the Church of the East to embrace Arianism was thwarted by the Cappadocian theologians. Of these the chief was Basil of Caesarea (329–379).

This great hero of the Eastern Church was the son of Christians of wealth and position. He was first educated at Constantinople, where he was a pupil of Libanius, the best pagan teacher of the day. Thence he went to the University of Athens, where he met Julian. A studious youth, he was saved from the practical jokes of his fellow-freshmen by the protection of Gregory of Nazianzum. After finishing his course at Athens he visited the hermits in the Egyptian desert, and being attracted towards asceticism went on to visit the solitaries in Palestine and Mesopotamia. This brought him into contact with the Semi-arians through Eustathius of Sebaste, who, though of Arian sympathies, was the greatest contemporary preacher of asceticism. The double result of this experience was that Basil learnt both

how to win over the Semi-arians to orthodoxy and also how to improve on ascetic methods so far as to introduce a new type of asceticism into Asia Minor. This was the Coenobitic system which had the advantage of encouraging the Christian social virtues among those who practised it. Basil had admired the hermits, but he had shrewdly asked, 'If you continue to live alone, whose feet will you wash?'

Basil became Bishop of Caesarea in 370. This was a very important post carrying with it the position of exarch of Pontus and involving the oversight of Cappadocia. Since this area was a stronghold of Arianism it meant that an orthodox bishop would be able to exert Nicene influence at a strategic point. Athanasius realized the critical nature of the appointment, and felt that now it was made he could put off the harness he had worn so long and die in peace, which he actually did in 373. As bishop, Basil displayed organising ability of no mean order. He set himself to administer charity on such a scale that his hospitals, workshops and settlements soon took on the proportions of a good-sized town. He seemed to be the only man in the East who could successfully oppose the Emperor. He retained his see while Valens was persecuting the orthodox bishops, and when the Emperor journeyed to the East in 371 there was an extraordinary scene in which Valens was completely overawed by the ecclesiastic. But Basil was less successful when in 372 he sent a commission to set in order the affairs of the Church in Armenia.

Apart from this Basil seemed to have friends everywhere, and this enabled him to mediate between East and West on the subject of the term *hypostasis*. In conjunction with Ambrose of Milan he brought over to the Nicene party many malcontents of the Semi-arian party. He was a voluminous theological writer and helped to advance the development of the doctrine of the Trinity. In this respect he pointed out the difference between an absolute and a numerical unity. From the point of view of mere numbers, he said, God was no more one than three, because all numbers imply an opposition to other numbers, whereas in the nature of God there are no relations which involve

contradictions. He also used his literary ability in aid of the Church's worship. There is an universal Eastern tradition that he composed a liturgy, but the present *Liturgy of S. Basil* has been so interpolated in the course of the centuries that it is impossible now to distinguish his contribution from the rest. *

Basil had a younger brother, Gregory, by whom he was called master, but by whom as a theologian he was excelled. This Gregory was the most philosophical of the Cappadocians. He was not much interested in affairs, although at Basil's wish he became Bishop of Nyssa, but he exercised a powerful influence on the thought of the time. He was an admirer of the speculations of Origen, and his views on the Trinity are stated in his book *Quod non sint tres Dei*. The term God, he said, is indicative of essence, not declaratory of persons. The relation of the first Person to the other two is not a relation between genus and species, because the divine substance exists from all beginning in three *hypostases*. Thus the correct formula by which to describe the Trinity is 'God in three Persons'. The term Godhead really implies activity (*energeia*) or operation, and the unity of the three Persons is seen in the fact that all operate together in whatever is done. In spite therefore of the emphasis on the distinctness of the permanent *hypostases* the doctrine of Gregory of Nyssa is not tritheism but typical 'pluralism'. *

The third of the Cappadocians, Gregory of Nazianzum (329–389), was the son of the Bishop of that place. Basil was his close friend at Athens, and when Basil became Bishop of Caesarea he consecrated Gregory as Bishop of Sasima. In so doing he sacrificed the comfort of his friend to the exigencies of the ecclesiastical situation. Sasima was a wretched little posting town in the Taurus, but it was situated at a strategic point between East and West, and it was important to have there a champion of the Nicene faith. In 378 Gregory was sent on a mission to Constantinople, which since the time of Eusebius of Nicomedia had been a stronghold of Arianism. Gregory's business was to try to convert the people there to orthodoxy. His strong weapon was his power as a preacher. He took possession of a private house, where he delivered discourses on doctrinal subjects.

He soon realised that the first necessity was to inculcate some idea of reverence and worship, both of which had nearly disappeared under the corrosive influence of hair-splitting controversy. In this he was so successful that his house soon became the Church of the Resurrection. To it came Jerome, at first to listen and then to applaud.

* The most important of Gregory's discourses were published as the *Five Orations*. The first declared that devotion, not controversy, is the right method in religion. The second sought to show that God is incomprehensible in any merely human terms. The third and fourth elaborated the position that God is always Father and the Word always Son. And the fifth dealt with the doctrine of the Holy Spirit, declaring that since the Spirit has a substantive and not merely contingent existence He is both God and eternal. The importance of this position is that it maintains the distinctness of the persons without separating them from each other. The Godhead is seen to be not a barren numerical unity but a living richness in itself. Unity and not identity is the catchword, *unitas* rather than *unum*. Thus Gregory became the greatest theologian and orator in the Eastern Church of his day. We shall see later how for a moment he became Bishop of Constantinople.

It will be noticed that these Cappadocians all based their teaching on the Neoplatonist philosophy. Thus like Origen and most of the Alexandrians before Alexander they were pluralists in their view of the nature of God. Harnack believed that in their anxiety to reconcile the Semi-arians to the Nicene faith they originated a new orthodoxy, and that they only got the term *homoousios* accepted by explaining it in the sense of *homoiousios*. Really, however, all that they did was to revive the Origenist tradition and to popularise the formula, one *ousia* (nature or substance) and three *hypostases* (persons). They saw, as it has been said, that what the second and third Persons of the Blessed Trinity derive from the first is not their substance but that which makes Them persons. Thus these theologians give us the thought of Alexandria carried to its logical conclusion.

While the Cappadocians were thus working for unity

in the East, several notable theologians were performing a similar benevolent function in the West. Of these we now draw attention to one, Hilary of Poitiers. Hilary was the son of pagan parents and was converted to Christianity in manhood. By this time he was married and the proud possessor of a daughter. About 353, when still a layman, he was elected Bishop of Poitiers. Two years afterwards he received a complimentary visit from Martin of Tours, and started out on an active campaign against the Arians in Gaul. For this orthodox zeal he was banished by Constantius to Phrygia about 356. This visit to the East was of great importance both for his own education and for the establishment of sympathy between East and West. He employed his enforced leisure in learning Greek and in pursuing his studies in the Eastern Fathers. He also at this time composed the *De Synodis* and the *De Trinitate*. In these works he pointed out that just as the term *homoousios* was capable of a Sabellian interpretation so the term *homoiousios* was capable of an orthodox interpretation.

In 359 the two Councils of Seleucia in the East and Ariminum in the West synchronised. Hilary was able to attend the Council of Seleucia and there he did good work in explaining to the Eastern bishops the true state of things in Gaul, but he was so shocked by what he deemed the irreverent language of the Anomoeans that he left the Council. He obtained an interview with Constantius and was allowed to return to Gaul. Here his knowledge of the controversy enabled him to disentangle the Semi-arians from their alliance with the extreme Arians, and to win over many of the former to the Nicene position by showing that what they meant by the term *homoiousios* was precisely what the Nicenes meant by *homoousios*. In this effort he showed himself a model of conciliation. He did not excommunicate the bishops who had signed the Ariminum decrees, but gathered together assemblies of Gallic bishops for mutual explanation. He spent the years 362–364 in doing similar work in Italy, but a complaint lodged against him by the Arian bishop, Auxentius of Milan, caused Valentinian to drive him back to Poitiers, and there he died in 368.

Hilary is interesting theologically, because he gave currency to the idea of the coinherence (*circumincessio*, *perichoresis*) of the Persons in the Trinity. The term is already to be found in the Macrostich creed of Antioch in 344. The theory, as found in Hilary, is that the three hypostases are inherent in each other. As Christ in the Fourth Gospel, speaking of His own relation to the Father, could say 'I in Thee and Thou in Me', so it can be said that the Spirit is in both the Father and the Son, for He is the Spirit of both. The Cappadocians, like all pluralists, found it difficult to know how to place the Holy Spirit, but Hilary is one of those who carry the doctrine of the Trinity a step nearer its conclusion by realising that the Holy Spirit is necessary to make the relation of unity between the Persons possible. It is seen that this relation is itself a Person, and that the Godhead, in the innermost core of His Being, is not abstract but concrete. So through all the difficulties and troubles of the period, we may believe, some real advance was made in the knowledge of God.

CHAPTER XVII

THE GOTHS AND THE CHURCH

I N the meantime the menace on the frontiers of the Empire was growing ever more grave. Since this was to have a profound effect upon ecclesiastical affairs it may be worth while to trace its origin and development.

I

During the reign of Alexander Severus the Goths had appeared on the shores of the Black Sea. They had come down from Scandinavia and had spent some time on the German Baltic coast before splitting into two sections, the Visigoths of the West and the Ostrogoths of the East, with the river Dneister as the boundary between them. It is then that we find them moving further south, and by 238 we hear of them actually crossing the Danube and plundering lower Moesia. In 251 they crossed the Danube again and penetrated to Thrace and Macedonia. It was now that Decius tried to check their advance, with the tragic result that we have already seen. In the confusion that followed their victory they were offered subsidies to keep them quiet, but from time to time they broke out in raids which covered practically the whole coast of Asia Minor. Between 268 and 270 they were driven back by Claudius, who defeated them in a decisive engagement at Naissus (Nish). There followed a century of quiet except for some minor outbreaks under Constantine. The line of the Danube was taken as the acknowledged boundary of Gothic territory.

During the latter part of this period, however, the Romans were occupied with other threats to their frontiers besides those of the Goths. There were the German tribes, especially the Alemanni, who were subdued by Julian, but broke out again in 365 and had to be dealt with by Valentinian. In

Britain also Valentinian had his troubles. Between 366 and 370 he sent his general Theodosius, who with much skill and bravery subdued the Picts and Scots after they had enjoyed a period of successful rebellion. During the three following years the same general was conducting campaigns in North Africa, where he managed to subdue a revolt of the Gaetuli. He himself, however, was accused on a trumped-up charge of treachery, and was beheaded.

By this time there had arisen new trouble from the Goths. They were being pressed by the Huns, a Mongolian tribe from the north-east of the Caspian, who having terrified China had now turned to the south and west. They destroyed the kingdom of the Ostrogoths, and the great Gothic king Hermanric died by his own hand rather than witness the dissolution of his vast empire. In their extremity the Goths turned to the Romans, and asked leave to settle in Thrace. It was easier to grant that request, and to give them a subsidy, than to go to war with them. Unfortunately, however, the Roman administration turned out to be thoroughly bad. The Goths in their new home grew dissatisfied and broke out into open rebellion. Valens, who was now Emperor in the East, called for the aid of his Western colleague, Gratian, but instead of waiting for it he attacked at Adrianople (378). A humiliating defeat was inflicted on the Roman arms, and Valens himself was killed. This result was due to the mobility of the Gothic troops under Fritigern, and it led to important changes in Roman military tactics, their boasted infantry being now largely abandoned in favour of cavalry. Gratian appointed a new general, Theodosius, to assist him against the Goths and made him Emperor with command of the East in 379. The two peoples were already considerably intermingled, but the Goths now began to flood the Empire. Gradually Theodosius began to come to terms with them, a process made easier by the death of their two renowned leaders, Fritigern and Athanaric. Peace was formally declared in 382, and four years later Theodosius admitted no fewer than forty thousand Goths into the imperial service. Naturally all institutions not firmly grounded began to change their character. It has

been said that only two things survived, the Empire itself which was rooted in history and the Nicene faith which was rooted in Christ.

II

Christians had not been idle all this time: many efforts had been made to bring the knowledge of the gospel within reach of these barbarians. Catholic missionaries had been at work among the Goths from the time that they reached the Black Sea. The Ostrogoths in the Crimea had been evangelised by orthodox teachers, and we have mention of churches at Kertch and Sebastopol. Further missionary work was done by Christian captives whom the Goths took back with them from their raiding expeditions. Ambrose in his *De Officiis* mentions the vast crowd of Christians held by the barbarians in 378; it was on their ransom that much of the Church's charity was spent. That they would not necessarily be without Christian ministrations in their captivity we can guess from the fact that already in the lists of the bishops present at the Council of Nicea we find the name of a certain Theophilus, Bishop of Gothia. But the orthodox were not the only ones to show themselves forward in this work. We have information that monasteries were founded in Gothic territory by heretics called Audians. They were a sect inaugurated by a certain Audius, and their main peculiarities were a dislike of the Paschal arrangements made at Nicea and an inclination to a strongly anthropomorphic view of God. Had not God said 'Let us make man in our image'? then what form could He bear other than that of man? Owing to their incalcitrance they were exiled from their home in Mesopotamia to Syria in the last years of Constantine, and they had pushed their travels further afield until at last they had come within the territory of the Goths.

But far the most important effort at the conversion of the Goths was that made by another unorthodox Christian, the great Ulfilas. This renowned missionary was himself a member of a family that had been taken captive from Cappadocia in the reign of Valerian. He was brought up

as a Christian, and at the age of thirty had become a Reader. He was evidently considered a person of some importance, for in the reign of Constantine he was sent to Constantinople as an envoy or hostage for the Gothic king. While there he came under strong Arianising influence, and was made much of by Eusebius of Nicomedia. At the Council of Antioch he was made Bishop of the Goths (341).

The advantage of having such a man at the head of the Christian mission was that he was familiar with the three tongues, Latin, Greek and Gothic. Hitherto Gothic had found expression as a literary language only in the barbarous runic script. This had raised an additional barrier between those who used it and the culture of the Graeco-Roman world. Ulfilas felt that the best and most permanent means of building up his people in the tradition of a Christian civilisation would be to create for them a new Christian literature. He began with the formation of an alphabet, and then translated the Scriptures into Gothic. He thus put into their hands all the canonical writings except the books of Kings: those he would not translate, because, as he said, his people knew enough of fighting already. So Ulfilas became the father of all Teutonic literature; and in the efforts of this noble-hearted missionary we see the beginnings of one of the main sources of the Christian civilisation of Europe.

Such a scheme was too successful for the immediate peace of its inaugurators. In 348 all preachers of the Christian faith were turned out of Gothic territory. Ulfilas and his friends took refuge on Roman soil. This no doubt left them free to minister to the many barbarians who were now found intermingled with the civilised peoples of the Empire. But it also had the effect of infusing some measure of spirituality into Arian circles. Ulfilas himself was present at the Homoean council held at Constantinople in 360. He was even able to enter into negotiations with the severely orthodox Emperor Theodosius. In 381 the latter summoned him to Constantinople, and it was there that he crowned his efforts to gain internal peace for the Church by persuading the Emperor to summon a new and universal council for the

settlement of all outstanding questions of faith and organisation. This is not to suggest that he proved false either to his friends or to his own convictions. Feeling that his health was failing and that he would not live to give expression to his views at the council, he wrote out a statement of his belief, which was still definitely Arian. After the composition of this testament he died.

The expulsion of Ulfilas from Gothic territory did not mean the end of all missionary effort. Acholias, the Bishop of Thessalonica, put himself in charge of the work, and encouraged those who had been converted to remain steadfast in their faith. They needed courage, for they now had to undergo a period of persecution, which was particularly severe during the troubles with Valens (367-369). But the spread of Christianity was soon to be furthered by a quarrel which occurred between the two Gothic leaders, Athanaric and Fritigern. The latter with all his people made terms with the Romans and accepted the Christian faith. Athanaric visited his wrath upon the Christians who remained under his rule. To this time belong two of the most famous Gothic martyrs, S. Sabas, who perished in 372, and S. Nicetas, who gained his crown in 378. But the victory of Christianity was virtually won. The residence of a vast number of Goths in Thrace hastened its achievement. That the type of Christianity was Arian rather than Nicene was due to the work of Ulfilas and also to the fact that at that time Arianism was the official religion of the Emperors. Arianism became the national religion of the Goths, and thus it gained new strength just at the moment when its hold on the Empire was beginning to relax.

It has been said that 'the Nicene faith won its victory in the confusion of the greatest disaster that had ever yet befallen Rome'. Before his tragic death Valens had realised his mistake in persecuting the followers of Athanasius. He had arranged to recall the exiled bishops, and his design was carried out by his successor Gratian. The new Emperor did his utmost to insist on theological peace. He allowed no open quarrelling and granted toleration to all but the most extreme parties on either side, the Anomoeans and the

Photinians. At the same time he took a bold step in order to assure the Christian Church of his full sympathy and support. He abandoned the title and insignia of *Pontifex Maximus*, and ordered the removal of the Altar of Victory from the Senate. It was on this altar that members of the Senate were accustomed to throw a few grains of incense as they took their place in the house, and its removal put an end to the traditional 'parliamentary prayers'.

Still further steps were taken by Gratian's colleague Theodosius. During a serious illness he received orthodox baptism, and after this he sternly repressed all heresy. To such length did he carry this policy that he even refused an official funeral to Ulfilas. He turned the Arianising Bishop Demophilus out of Constantinople, ordered all churches to be placed in the hands of the Nicene clergy, and, as a test of membership of the Great Church, insisted on communion with the bishops of Rome and Alexandria. It seemed to him necessary for the safety of the Empire that if Gothic Christians were Arian, true Roman citizens must confess the Nicene faith. Thus it is in a sense true that 'Arianism was put down, as it had been set up, by the civil power'. Nevertheless in the midst of all the terror and confusion of those times Christianity had succeeded in making its way into the hearts of the people, and now for the first time it became possible to make Christianity in very truth the established religion of the Empire. In recent years it had been tolerated and even favoured, but now at last it was incorporated with the State to the exclusion of other religions. The sign and seal of this incorporation is to be found in the Council of Constantinople.

III

Very curious events had been happening in that city. We have told how Gregory of Nazianzum had begun his mission there, and how his Church of the Resurrection had become a force in the religious life of the capital. When the Emperor Theodosius was ruling, it was clear that he had much more sympathy with Gregory than with the bishop of the city, Demophilus, who was of Arianising sympathies.

When he had emerged from the Gothic conflict the Emperor had time to deal with Demophilus, and offered him the alternative of acceptance of the Nicene faith or exile. To his honour Demophilus chose exile; and then it became a matter of speculation whether he would be succeeded by Gregory. This was a possibility that was viewed with much anxiety by Peter, the Bishop of Alexandria. He was holding somewhat precariously to his position as second bishop after Rome. He shared with his brother bishop of Rome the right of deciding the date of Easter for the whole Christian world. By Theodosius he had been named together with the Bishop of Rome as the practical adjudicator of the rights of intercommunion. But if there should be a strong orthodox bishop in the second capital of the Empire it was more than likely that his own position would be forfeited. He resolved to take steps.

He found a ready instrument to his hand in the person of a certain Maximus, who having been a Cynic philosopher had now turned Christian. This man he despatched to Constantinople to work himself into the affections of the guileless Gregory. When the process was sufficiently advanced, a number of Egyptian prelates travelled from Alexandria in the corn-ships bound for Constantinople. Arrived at their destination they proceeded in the dead of night to consecrate Maximus as bishop of the city. But the service was long, and they were not able to complete it before the faithful began to enter the church at dawn, and interrupted the proceedings. It was now inevitable that Gregory should become Bishop of Constantinople. Much as he disliked the prospect, he allowed himself amidst the greatest excitement to be taken to the church. The weather was inclement, but at the very moment of his solemn enthronement the sun broke through the clouds, and the divine judgment endorsed the action of the multitude. That action was also acceptable to Theodosius, who vindicated it by excluding all heretics from the city, and placing their churches under the jurisdiction of the new bishop. It was in this atmosphere that the council assembled in 381.

In spite of the attempt at oecumenicity only 150 bishops

were present. The poverty of the attendance was due to the absence of the Western bishops and of the Egyptians, who did not receive their invitations in time. The greatest of the Easterns, Basil, was already dead, but most of the bishops present were of his party. Their most important action was to register a decision against Arianism and to reaffirm the Nicene faith. But out of this reaffirmation an interesting question arises. In what precise creed did the council express its faith? The later Council of Chalcedon and the historian Epiphanius both attribute to Constantinople the creed which is now generally used at the Eucharist, and which in the Book of Common Prayer is called the Nicene Creed.[1] In modern times, however, it has commonly been held that our creed shows too many dissimilarities from that of Nicea to be justly called by that name. It has been pointed out that our creed has many affinities with that of Jerusalem, and it has been suggested that it may well have been put forward by the Bishop of Jerusalem in order to defend his own orthodoxy before the council. An alternative suggestion is that it may have been the creed used at the baptism and consecration of Nectarius, which, as we shall see presently, took place during the council. In either case the fact that the assembled bishops accepted it as orthodox would sufficiently explain its attribution to the council. But recently Dr. Badcock has contended that all this supposition is unnecessary. According to him our creed is a true lineal descendant of the official creed of Nicea. And there is this at least to be said for the view that the council believed themselves to be reaffirming the actual creed of Nicea, that it is unlikely that after sixty years of struggle on behalf of a particular creed they would in the very moment of victory abandon that creed to take up another. But whether the creed they actually used was the original creed of Nicea or such an enlargement as we now use can probably never be determined. Since, however, the doubt has been raised it has become the custom to refer to our creed not as the Nicene Creed but as the Niceno-Constantinopolitan Creed.

[1] Of course, with the exception of the famous *filioque* clause. For a careful consideration of the whole question see Kelly, *Early Christian Church* (Longmans 1950).

The second heresy disposed of was that of Macedonianism. Macedonius had been Bishop of Constantinople from 352 to 362. His name is associated with a particular doctrine of the Holy Spirit, although in point of fact he seems to have had no connexion with it. The view to which his name has been given was really an extension of the Arian teaching with regard to the Logos in order to make it cover the case of the Spirit. According to it the Spirit cannot be held to be consubstantial with the Supreme Godhead, because He is a creature. It should be noticed that the personality of the Spirit was not brought into question. But the best that the Macedonians could think of Him was that He was a kind of superior angel. For this reason they were often called *Pneumatomachoi*, fighters against the Spirit. This matter had already been discussed at Alexandria in 362, and Athanasius, as we have seen, had suggested that the Nicene Creed might be completed by the addition of a declaration of the consubstantiality of the Spirit, since the *homoousios* applied as much to Him as to the Son. The suggestion was made in a letter to the Emperor Jovian, but it was never carried out: there is still no word in the creed as to the consubstantiality of the Holy Spirit. But the doctrine implied in the term had been proclaimed by five synods under Pope Damasus, and Basil had contended that it was his own doctrine in his treatise *De Spiritu Sancto*. This doctrine was now vindicated by the Council of Constantinople.

It is possible that the increased attention given to the doctrine of the Spirit was responsible for an interesting liturgical development. In the Eucharist it was the custom to pray for the descent of the Spirit upon the elements of bread and wine. This acquired a special significance in the East. The change by which these elements became the Body and Blood of Christ was held to be due not to the recitation of the original words of institution (which was the usual Western theory) but to the prayer for the descent of the Spirit.

The third heresy to occupy the attention of the council was that of Apollinarianism. Apollinarius was the last of

the great Hellenic students to tackle the question of Christology. The doubt about the nature of the Trinity which had been brought to the front by Arius had inevitably concentrated itself upon the person of Christ. And since the position taken up by the Arians had favoured the Antiochene view, with its emphasis upon the subordination and the human nature of the Son, it was certain that there would be a reaction to the Alexandrian view, which laid the greater stress on the divine nature. Apollinarius pushed this reaction to an impossible extreme.

This teacher had had an interesting career. His father had come from Alexandria and had been a master in the schools of Berytus and Laodicea. It was in the latter town that the son was born about 315. With his father he enjoyed to the full the S. Luke's summer of Greek thought. It was no scandal at that time for Christians to sit at the feet of pagan lecturers. There were, however, even then some lengths to which one could not go; and when it was known that father and son in the course of some literary exercises had actually joined in singing a hymn to Bacchus, public feeling was strong enough to insist upon their temporary excommunication. Nevertheless they did not lose the friendship of Athanasius, and the younger Apollinarius was permitted to lecture in Laodicea and in Antioch. When Julian ordered all Christians to cease giving instruction in the classics, the Apollinarii saw the harm that would be done to the general education of their people and immediately set themselves to fill the gap by re-writing some of the Old Testament in the conventional forms of Greek literature. In 361 the younger Apollinarius was made Bishop of Laodicea, and by 362 his peculiar Christology seemed sufficiently important to receive attention at the Council of Alexandria. In 373 it had created a definite sect; in 377 as the result of an appeal by Basil it was condemned in Rome; and in 379 it was again condemned by a synod at Antioch.

In the development of his Christology Apollinarius started from the assumption that Christ was only one person and that His personality had its source in the Logos. From this he proceeded to draw two conclusions: first that

since the Logos was certainly not subject to change (thus giving the lie direct to the Arians), Christ could have had no human will; and second that since man is divided into body and soul and the personality resides in the soul, therefore in Christ the human soul must have been replaced by the Logos. In the second of these conclusions Apollinarius had entered upon the field of psychology. It is sometimes disputed whether he really did start from such a crude dichotomy of human nature into body and soul. Even if he did, it is certain that he soon passed beyond it to the trichotomist view that man is divided into body, soul and spirit. In this stage he believed that the seat of the personality is the spirit, and that being so he declared that in Christ the place of the spirit or *nous* must have been taken by the Logos. In either case the conclusion was roughly the same and the objection taken to it by the Church was the same. If Apollinarius' view was correct, then the Incarnation was incomplete, for the highest element in man's nature was not assumed by the Logos; thus it would not be possible to say that Christ was perfect God and perfect man. This conclusion was not only inadmissible from the point of view of doctrine, it would also have the direst practical consequences, for what the Logus did not assume, that He could not redeem. If we remember that the characteristic Eastern view of the method of salvation was that it proceeds by way of a spiritual alchemy in which our humanity is gradually transformed into something which is divine, we shall see how inevitable was this objection. For if Christ had not assumed the whole of our humanity He could not come into complete contact with the whole of our nature and there would remain something in us which was not changed. This untouched Achilles' heel would make impossible our transmutation to immortality. It was thus quite out of the question for the Church to make terms with such a Christology, however glad she may have been of Apollinarius' help in extinguishing the dying embers of Arianism. Quarrels among the Apollinarians helped to discredit their teaching, and the assistance of the Emperor Theodosius completed the triumph of orthodoxy.

Another question with which the council was concerned was that of the Meletian schism at Antioch. It will be remembered that when the ultra-Athanasian Eustathius of Antioch had been deposed, a series of Arian bishops had been appointed in his place, but the orthodox had refused their ministrations and had continued to meet under the presbyter Paulinus. A new situation was created when in 361 the newly appointed Bishop Meletius abandoned the Arian creed, and accepted that of Nicea. The Council of Alexandria had thereupon suggested that the orthodox should now reconcile themselves with Meletius, but this had been made less easy by Lucifer of Calaris, who had stepped in and consecrated Paulinus as bishop. An arrangement was concluded that on the death of one of the two rivals the other should succeed to the entire episcopal jurisdiction within the see. Meletius had never been acknowledged as the rightful bishop by Rome, but he presided at the Council of Constantinople and at the enthronement of Gregory. Soon after this he died, and was reckoned by the Roman see among the saints. According to the arrangement already concluded Paulinus should have now been recognised as Bishop of Antioch by all parties. But the Meletian party, thinking that acquiescence in this solution would seem to give a victory to Western influences, refused to honour their compact, and appointed as their bishop a certain Flavian, a presbyter who had solemnly promised never to accept such an honour even if it were offered him. This so horrified Gregory that as a protest he promptly resigned the see of Constantinople to which he had been so recently translated. Nectarius, an unbaptised layman, was appointed to fill the vacancy, and as soon as he was baptised and consecrated he became president of the council.

One other step taken by the council demands our attention. It is important as carrying a stage further the development of the patriarchal organisation. A canon ordered that henceforth the Bishop of Constantinople should take the next place in honour after the Bishop of Rome. The reason given was that since Constantinople was the new Rome it should naturally come next after the old Rome. This did not mean

that the jurisdiction of the see of Constantinople was changed; for such purposes it still remained within the exarchate of Heraclea. But the canon did give it the second position in Christendom from the point of view of precedence. The object of this was to checkmate the ambitions of Alexandria. At the same time Antioch began to decline in importance. Now that the danger to the Empire had shifted from the Persian to the Danubian front, Antioch was no longer the most necessary headquarters for the army, and its deterioration in secular importance involved its diminishing ecclesiastical significance. These changes in the East inevitably heightened the prestige of Rome in the West and indeed throughout the whole of the Christian world.

CHAPTER XVIII

MONASTICISM AND THE FALL OF PAGANISM

FROM the time of Constantine to that of Theodosius there had been a great growth in the power of the episcopate. It has been suggested that towards the close of his reign Constantine was delivering himself more and more into the hands of the bishops. However this may be, it is certain that in enlisting the influence of the chief officers of the Church for political ends the government was in fact making them into great State officials. We shall in future see some striking examples of the power they exercised in secular affairs. But at the very period of this rise it was to some extent balanced in ecclesiastical affairs by the growth of a new religious movement among the laity. This was the ascetic movement which we know as monasticism.

I

The word is derived from the Greek *monos*, alone. As we use it, the term is applied to all those who live apart from the world, whether as solitaries or in communities. The origin of the custom is not wholly Christian. There were Egyptian monks of Serapis, and there were members of Orphic societies who led a strongly ascetic life, and there was a highly developed monasticism in Buddhist circles. Among the Jews there were some, like the Essenes and Therapeutae, who followed the same ideals. Philo says that in addition to these there were many Jews in Alexandria who left their homes to live in cottages apart. It is all the more interesting to notice that it was in Alexandria that the Christian monastic movement began.

The important element in this asceticism was the entire abstinence from sexual intercourse. All Alexandrians held it as their highest ambition to attain to a true *gnosis*, or

knowledge of reality, and it was believed that celibacy would further that quest. That the celibate life was a better life than that of the family was believed to be evident from our Lord's words about those who made themselves eunuchs for the kingdom of heaven's sake and those who left all to follow Him. S. Paul's somewhat grudging recognition of the married state seemed to point to the same conclusion. Chrysostom indeed believed that the monastic life was simply a reproduction of the life lived by the primitive Christian community in Jerusalem. This was not to say that ordinary Christians had no right to live in the world, but simply that there was a higher as well as a lower standard of Christian living. The recognition of two standards offered no difficulty, for it had been present in Christian teaching ever since the publication of the *Didache*.

Those who sought to live by the higher standard at first made their effort in their own homes, but presently they moved out into huts and gradually found their way into the deserts, where they lived alone in separate dwellings or in caves. No doubt many were moved to do this out of concern for the rapid deterioration of the Church's standard after peace was brought by Constantine. But also some of those who missed the old heroism that had been called forth by the persecutions found a new opportunity for the display of courage in their loneliness. The waste places of the earth were the last strongholds of the demons. Those who went out to meet them there were not fleeing in cowardice from a world that had grown too hard for them, but were volunteering for service in the front line of the Church's warfare against the forces of evil, and they needed to the full the ascetism, the special training of the athlete and soldier, to fit them for the task. No doubt motives were mixed, as they always are, and it has been suggested, though without much evidence, that social conditions also helped the growth of this movement. It is possible that a certain percentage of the early followers of this way were Copts who were trying thus to find a refuge from their Greek and Roman lords.

The system developed in three stages. The first was the eremitical, the stage of the 'solitary' proper. The earliest

Christian hermit of whom we have any knowledge is Paul of Thebes. He is said to have retired to a grotto on the Egyptian coast of the Red Sea during the Decian persecution. But how far he is a merely legendary character cannot be determined. He is said to have been visited by one whose historicity has recently been re-established, namely the famous Anthony, who appears to have lived from 251 to 356. Anthony was a Copt, with little learning but much given to contemplation. After having been converted by hearing the gospel story of the Rich Young Man he spent fifteen years in ascetic practices in a hut near his own home, and then departed in 285 to take up his abode in a rock tomb in the Thebaid. By this time monasticism must have already advanced some way in Alexandria, for we hear that before his departure Anthony deposited his sister in a convent. Many stories are told of his mental struggles, of his exhaustion almost to the point of death, and his retirement to still more desolate loneliness. From this retirement he returned to encourage the Alexandrians in the persecution engineered by Maximin in 311, and again in their struggles with Arianism in 352. His friendship with Athanasius did much to gain for the bishop the firm support of the ascetics.

Other enthusiasts of this type were soon to be found not only in Egypt but also in Syria and Mesopotamia. In the latter region they were at first banded together as 'Sons of the Covenant', but this communal life was only meant in their case to be a preliminary training for the more lonely existence of the hermit. It was perhaps to be expected that in such circumstances there would arise much competition in austerity, each solitary striving to outdo the others in self-torture. While the Egyptian asceticism was mostly what one might call natural, such as the deprivation of food and sleep, further East the Oriental love of suffering led to much unnatural asceticism. There were saints who ate nothing but grass; others who lived in trees; and still others who raised themselves above the common herd on pillars. Hilarion of Gaza (c. 300–360) is said to have been the first to introduce this kind of ascetic Christianity to Palestine;

and Simeon Stylites (385–459) is the most famous of the pillar saints. The latter must not be dismissed with a sneer. He had lived alone in a cave until his growing reputation drew upon him the unsought attention of the multitude, and it was to escape the crowd that he mounted his pillar. From this eminence he was wont to preach to hosts of semi-barbarians, and they were converted, if we may believe the legend, in their thousands. On such an audience the respectable methods of a moderate Christianity might have had no effect whatever.

The second stage was that of the semi-eremitical type. Those who belonged to it lived together in a *Laura* or open street. This custom arose out of the fact that a famous hermit would find himself surrounded by a group of devotees who settled near him and endeavoured to imitate his method of life. In this system there were many single cells, close together but preferably out of ear-shot, or else two or three ascetics would live together in a single cell, the whole forming a kind of colony. The members met together only for worship on Saturday and Sunday. There was no common rule of life or established authority; nor was there any regularised work. All had the same ideal, which was that of contemplation, but within that ideal each did what was right in his own eyes. This method was practised by great numbers in Lower Egypt. It seems to have been started by Anthony for the followers who wished to copy his asceticism. The man who developed it was Ammonius, who round about the time of the Council of Nicea became the head of six hundred monks in the Nitrian desert. Six miles away Macarius became the head of a similar organisation at Scete.

The next stage was the coenobitic phase, that of the monastery proper. The originator of this type was Pachomius (*c.* 290–345), who according to Weingarten had learned monastic practice as a monk of Serapis. In any case he had had a military training. Released from the army, he spent twelve years with the hermit Palaemon. After this he started a scheme of his own, founding a monastery at Tabennisi, an island of the Upper Nile. The peculiarity of Pachomius'

system was that the ascetics lived under a common roof and were placed under a common authority. This involved an addition to the elements of the ascetic life. Hitherto the requirements had been poverty and chastity; to these was now added obedience. But the system of Pachomius went further than that: he saw that a common life must necessarily involve some organisation; people living in community under one roof with one table could not live simply as individuals. Here his military training was useful. He made manual labour an effective part of the monks' everyday existence, and he divided them out into cloisters on the basis of their handicrafts, the produce of their toil being sold in Alexandria for the supply of their common needs. Individualism, however, was by no means suppressed. Within the limits of the common system there was still room for much private experiment, and this still resulted in competitive austerities. It did not seem so ridiculous as it does to us. The ascetic was essentially the Christian athlete, and if competition is not the soul of athleticism it seems at least to be a necessary accompaniment. During the growing luxury of the age of Constantine these monks increased greatly in numbers. Pachomius founded no less than eight monasteries with thirty or forty monks in each. By him or by his sister there were also founded a number of cloisters for nuns.

This coenobitic system entered upon its best line of development under the influence of the Cappadocian theologians. We have seen how keen was the interest of Basil of Caesarea in the Egyptian and Palestinian solitaries. About the year 360 he even tried an experiment in that way of life himself. But he saw its deficiencies, and when he came into a position of authority he set about the establishment of a new coenobitic type, the main elements of which are set forth in his longer and shorter rules and may be summarised as follows:

(a) The suppression of anchorites. They were assembled into monasteries where the life was fully organised with common roof, common table, common worship, and fixed hours for meals.

(*b*) The removal of monastic establishments from the deserts to the neighbourhood of cities.

(*c*) The firm restriction of austerities. Work, thought Basil, was more important than self-inflicted suffering. Even worship must not be so prolonged as to become a grave strain. Consequently Basil reduced the hours of prayer to eight a day.

(*d*) The pursuit of learning. The introduction of scholarship into the cloister was to have its effect upon the history of theological thought in the immediate future. Later it was to have a more profound effect in the West, where the learned monk was to become one of the most conspicuous figures in the medieval world.

The introduction of monasticism into the West followed upon the visit of Athanasius to Rome in 339, when he was accompanied by two Egyptian monks. These examples of a new type of piety aroused great interest, which was further stimulated by the translation of Athanasius' *Life of Anthony* into Latin. A mixed community of coenobites and semi-solitary ascetics was founded on the Aventine Hill, protected by Pope Damasus and for a time controlled by Jerome. Martin of Tours introduced the system into Gaul. He first made trial of the hermit's life, and then founded, about 360, a monastery at Ligugé near Poitiers, which was afterwards removed to Marmoutier (*Martini monasterium*) just outside Tours. The monks lived in little caves on the face of the cliff overhanging the Loire, and the site is still preserved to show in most vivid fashion what were the conditions in which the early monks passed their lives. In 410 a monastery which was to become very famous was founded at Lérins by Honoratus, and five years later Cassian founded two monasteries, one for each sex, near Marseilles. Cassian drew up the first monastic code for Gaul in his *Institutes* and *Collations*, which reveal a system standing midway between the old Eastern type and the later Western. On the whole it may be said that Egyptian influence remained strong in Western monasticism until the time of Benedict.

In Wales and Ireland monasticism may have been an

indigenous growth; at all events it shows strikingly individual features. There the monasteries were organised on
a basis parallel to that of the tribes. The ecclesiastical
organisation was interlaced with it to such an extent that
the abbot of a monastery might have several bishops
among the monks who were subject to his rule. In its loose-
ness of formal rule and its encouragement of individual
austerity Celtic monasticism had much in common with
the early Egyptian type. It is significant in this respect
that contact with the East was maintained by Ireland long
after it had been lost elsewhere in the West.

The rapid growth and wide extent of monasticism show
that it met a felt need in the life of the Church. The fact
that at its inception it was so largely a lay movement gave
it a certain independence of the bishops, which it has never
entirely lost. Sometimes, it is true, the influence of the monks
was a strong support to bishops who were sorely troubled
by the inroads of heresy or persecution. At other times the
monks were a very insubordinate element in the life of the
Church, and during the prolonged theological controversies
they were occasionally a terror to the churches near which
they abode. From the first, efforts were made to bring them
under control. It is disputed whether Athanasius did or
did not ordain Pachomius to the presbyterate, but there
can be no doubt that he won by this or some other means
the adherence of the monks. In 451 the great Council of
Chalcedon, in order to insure their good behaviour, placed
all communities of monks under the rule of the bishops.

II

The growth of monasticism was coincident with the
downfall of paganism: it is in the fourth and fifth centuries
that we see Christianity become triumphant over the forces
against which for the first three centuries it had waged so
heroic and so unequal a struggle. Harnack says that the
Church first became Catholic when it defeated polytheism,
nature worship, and the dualistic philosophy of religion.
The implication is that it defeated them only by incorporating a good deal of them into its own system. There can

be no doubt that in details of administration and worship, as well as in the rationalised statements of faith, many elements of contemporary culture were employed. How indeed could it have been otherwise? No one blames modern missionaries for using as far as possible the best elements of the culture already found among their converts. It does not necessarily mean that in so doing they abandon the original standards of Christian faith and practice.

In the period with which we are now dealing it is a significant fact that paganism tried to rekindle its dying fires by borrowing from Christianity. This was pre-eminently the case under Julian, but he only succeeded in bringing paganism into ridicule. When he died he was succeeded by officers of the army who had thrown up their commissions rather than yield to the Emperor's pagan proclivities. Jovian, who actually succeeded him, was one of these, and he was a baptised Christian, the first Emperor who was a fully professed Christian at the time of his accession. Jovian's opinions were orthodox, but he refused to persecute those who differed from him. Nevertheless during his reign a number of pagan temples were closed in deference to public feeling. Valentinian continued the policy of freedom for all, but together with Valens he tried to prune away the less reputable elements of paganism. In particular he forbade the nocturnal celebration of the Mystery Cults, making a sole exception in the case of the Eleusinian Mysteries, which were too strongly established to be interfered with at the moment.

A considerable step forward was taken by Gratian. He not only dropped the title of *Pontifex Maximus*, which since the time of Augustus had constituted the Emperor the head of the State religion, but also, when at his succession the Senate presented him with the usual priestly robe, refused on conscientious grounds to accept the gift. He took an even more important step in sweeping away the great Roman colleges with their religious establishments. These had been maintained by the State, and their destruction meant that paganism was no longer 'on the rates'. A dramatic witness to the defeat of paganism was the order that the

Altar of Victory be removed from the Senate (382). This was not obeyed without a protest. The presence of the altar dated from the time of Augustus; Constantine had removed it and Julian had restored it. The pagan senators still claimed to be in the majority, and they found an advocate in the famous orator Symmachus. The speech in which he defended the use of the altar created such an impression that after the death of Gratian Valentinian II had to meet it point by point. For this task he made use of the ability and reputation of Ambrose of Milan, and Ambrose is generally agreed to have carried off the honours of debate.

It was the Emperor Theodosius who finally put down official paganism. He closed the temples for worship but allowed their use as museums and for other public purposes. There was no persecution of individuals, and even Symmachus was permitted to remain unmolested. In Rome itself, the greatest stronghold of official paganism, the temples were not handed over to the Christians, and it was not until 612 that the famous Pantheon became a Christian church. In spite of the absence of coercion no fewer than six hundred of the ancient patrician families of Rome were converted to Christianity. This turnover had a marked effect on the Church in the capital city, even bringing about liturgical changes. Greek seems now to have been abandoned in Christian worship, and it is from this period that we date the beginning of the Latin canon of the Mass.

A very different story comes from Alexandria. There the downfall of paganism was accompanied by wild scenes. The Bishop Theophilus, preparing a church for Christian use in 385, dug into the foundations and discovered a number of unseemly relics left by the pagans who had once worshipped there. These relics he caused to be carried in derision through the streets of the city. A riot ensued, and the pagan priests with their followers took refuge in the temple of Serapis, whence they made sorties, capturing a number of Christians whom they tortured and killed. It was only by the intervention of the imperial troops that the temple fortress was finally subdued.

Similarly in North Syria Marcellus, the Bishop of Apamea, showed himself zealous in the destruction of pagan temples. But his zeal brought about his own undoing. Finding a temple strongly protected, he marched against it with a force of soldiers and gladiators. In the midst of the conflict the pagans discovered him praying for the success of his troops, and they took him prisoner and burnt him alive.

It was in the country districts that paganism lingered longest, whence the name (*paganus* = countryman). There is reason indeed to believe that in the East the remoter districts were never completely converted and were still to some extent pagan when the Mohammedan invasion swept all before it. In the West, particularly in Gaul, we have many stories of the conflict between individual bishops and the forces of paganism. Indeed it is probable that many of the legends of contests between Christian heroes and dragons reflect the conditions of this period, the dragon being symbolical of paganism. It is in such an environment that we must set the life-story of Martin of Tours (316–396).

Martin was born at Sabaria in West Hungary, the son of a pagan soldier. He early acquired a taste for the Christian religion, and ran away to a church at the age of ten in order to be received as a catechumen. Five years later he entered the army, and served in it until the famous incident near Amiens in 334, when he shared his cloak with a beggar. After this he was baptised, and got his discharge from the army two years afterwards. He lived for a time as an ascetic near Poitiers and converted his mother to Christianity. He also entered upon a warm defence of the Nicene faith and of his bishop Hilary, who was now being sent into exile for his adherence to it. He settled for a time in Milan, but was there badly treated by the Arian Bishop Auxentius. On Hilary's return he joined him at Poitiers and, as we have seen, founded the first Gallic monastery at Ligugé. On Hilary's death Martin continued his ascetic life until in 372 he was invited to become Bishop of Tours. He refused, but the people inveigled him into a visit to a sick person,

captured him on the way, and carried him off to consecration. The neighbouring bishops, who as yet knew little
of monasticism, disliked the idea of having this unkempt
monk as a colleague, but in spite of them Martin managed
to combine his episcopal office with the practice of asceticism,
and moved his monastery to the banks of the Loire opposite
his cathedral at the site now called Marmoutier. He entered
with zeal into the chief concern of the contemporary
episcopate, which was the elimination of paganism. His life,
written by his friend, the converted nobleman Sulpicius
Severus, tells how successful he was in winning the Gaulish
peasants from their devotion to idols. In this his personal
bravery was a great factor. On one occasion, it is said, he
induced the waverers to set aside their superstitious fears
by allowing himself to be tied to a sacred tree while it was
being felled.

Martin was also involved in the controversy that arose
over a new heresy called Priscillianism. This was a compound
of Gnostic speculation with a pronounced asceticism. It
had been brought from Egypt to Spain by a certain Marcus
in 370. In Spain Marcus won over the rich layman Priscillian,
who in his turn converted several bishops. The new opinions
were condemned at a council held at Saragossa in 380. The
local bishops loved luxury and hated asceticism; and so
two of them, Ithacius and Idacius, turned the charge against
Priscillian into one of Manicheism. The usurper Maximus
was persuaded to take proceedings against him, but Martin,
who was then at Milan, induced him to promise that there
should be no bloodshed. Pressed on, however, by the bishops
the Emperor at last gave way, and Priscillian with six of
his followers was executed. This constituted the first execution of Christians by Christians for heresy. In their
horror at this deed Martin and Ambrose of Milan excluded
Ithacius and his party from their communion. Later, however,
Maximus was about to execute two counts whose loyalty
had been suspected, but offered to give them their lives at
Martin's request if he would receive back Ithacius and his
friends into communion. Martin yielded, but ever after
believed that his power of working miracles had been

withdrawn as a punishment for his complaisance, and in consequence he would never again attend a meeting of his brother bishops.

Martin's greatest contemporary was Ambrose of Milan (340–397). This very remarkable prelate was the son of a Christian noble, and was trained in the service of the government, achieving the position of consular officer of Aemilia Liguria, with headquarters at Milan, by the age of thirty-four. A vacancy arose in the see of Milan, and during the debate on the election a child's voice started the cry 'Ambrose for bishop'. Although only a catechumen Ambrose was elected by popular acclamation (374). He began by distributing his wealth to the poor and then set himself to complete his theological education. With him we come to the period of great ecclesiastics who could subdue even the court to their will. At this time the most powerful political personage was Justina, the widow of Valentinian I. She was a staunch Arian, and in 385 made a determined effort to obtain one of the Milan churches for Arian worship. She was checked by the resolute attitude of Ambrose, but the next year she tried again. Ambrose filled the disputed church with a vast crowd of the faithful in order to prevent the soldiery from taking forcible possession. His effort to stay the nervous fears of the congregation during the all-night vigil is said to have led to the custom of antiphonal chanting. But a definite principle was enunciated during the struggle. The Emperor, said Ambrose, was within the Church but not over it.

With Gratian Ambrose was on much better terms and acted as his spiritual guide. He had great influence too with the usurper Maximus, whom he induced to leave Valentinian II in charge of Italy, Africa and Western Illyricum, thus avoiding much bloodshed. Ambrose also gained a great ascendancy over Theodosius. He induced him to remit the punishment of a bishop who in an excess of zeal had been guilty of the destruction of a Jewish synagogue. Again in 390, when Theodosius had put to death seven thousand of the inhabitants of Thessalonica as an act of reprisal after the mob in that city had done to death their

military governor, Ambrose actually made the Emperor perform public penance for his deed.

It was hardly to be expected that Ambrose could become an original theologian. Nevertheless his influence in this sphere was immense. Although he never met Athanasius he was a great supporter of the Nicene faith, and did much to ensure the triumph of the *homoousios* in the West. His greatest book is his *De Officiis Ministrorum*, modelled closely upon Cicero, by the means of which he began that close association between the ethics of Stoicism and Christianity which was to last throughout the Middle Ages. This may be said to have involved the Latinisation of Christian ethics. The Latinisation of sacramental theology is also largely due to Ambrose, and it is now the custom to trace through him that realistic and quasi-physical interpretation of the Eucharist which is supposed to offer a sharp contrast to the more mystical doctrine of the East. In other departments of theological thought the same tendency may be traced to Ambrose, and some scholars now believe him to have been the actual author of the so-called Athanasian Creed. But perhaps the greatest work that he did for theology was in his sermons. He was a great orator. Augustine, then a teacher of rhetoric, came to hear him, and, admiring his thought no less than his style, was led by him to the verge of conversion.

Of Ambrose's contribution to the defeat of paganism little remains to be said. He was not one of those who had to meet the old religion in its country fastnesses, but he was called, as already narrated, into the higher flights of the controversy. It was to Ambrose that Valentinian turned for help and vindication against Symmachus. And Ambrose carried with him the conviction not only of the Emperor but also of the majority of the people in his defeat of the greatest pagan orator of his day.

It should also be added that Ambrose was one of the great hymn-writers of the Early Church. Twelve hymns are usually ascribed to him, of which four are regarded as certain. The doctrinal quality and religious value of the latter may be tested in the English Hymnal (14, 49). Two

at least of the hymns for the Canonical Hours may be his, that for Sext 'O God of truth, O Lord of might', and that for None 'O God, Creation's secret force'. One hymn ascribed to him, 'O Strength and Stay upholding all creation', has achieved fame in its English translation.

NOTE

It may assist the student at this point to have before him a table of the Emperors of both East and West, with their respective dates:

WEST	EAST
Valentinian I, 364–375	Valens, 364–378
Gratian, 375–383	Theodosius I, 379–395
Maximus (usurper), 383–388	
Valentinian II, 383–392	
Honorius, 395–423	Arcadius, 395–408
Valentinian III, 424–450	Theodosius II, 408–450
Maximus, 455	Pulcheria and
Majorian, 457–461	Marcian, 450–457
Liberius Severus, 461–465, and other phantom emperors until the last, Romulus Augustulus, is forced to abdicate, 476	Leo I, 457–474
	Zeno, 474–491
	Anastasius, 491–520

CHAPTER XIX

DIVERGENCE BETWEEN EAST AND WEST

THE difference between the theologians and administrators of the Church in the East and those of the Church in the West, of which a hint has already been given, began to make itself more definitely felt in the fifth century. It can be discerned especially in the Origenistic controversy in which one of the protagonists was the learned Jerome, and it can be recognised also in certain actions and events that formed a background to the life of Chrysostom.

I

Origen had been held in high honour as a scholar and theologian from the time of his death until the end of the fourth century. Athanasius had reckoned him as orthodox, and Basil held him in such veneration that he collected and published an anthology from his writings under the title of the *Philocalia*. But after this certain difficulties were felt about his speculative theories. His pronounced allegorism began to jar on people who were becoming more and more accustomed to a slavish literalism. His doctrine of the pre-existence of the soul seemed to have no certain warrant in Scripture. His subordinationism was less and less acceptable to the devout, who had fought against the extreme expression of it in Arianism and were now determined to secure the fullest reverence for the divinity of Christ. The defeat of paganism and the long struggles against heresy made theologians very unsympathetic towards his universalism, which had been so wide as to allow a place for the ultimate salvation even of the devil. With the growth of Western influence in theology more emphasis was being placed on the purely redemptive aspect of religion and less on that philosophical side of it which had been so

dear to Origen. But more than all this was the dislike that now began to be felt for the spiritualising effect of his teaching. Origen had taught a spiritual doctrine of the resurrection; he had refused to believe in the resuscitation of the material body and had taught that the body with which we are clothed after the resurrection will be immaterial. And this doctrine of the resurrection had been closely paralleled by his view of God. Origen had eschewed all anthropomorphism and had taught that, since God had no body, parts or passions, His being must be entirely spiritual. Opposition to this teaching came to a head in a controversy in which the great scholar Jerome was closely concerned. But before we can understand its importance in the life of this contradictory person we must trace his career to the point when he became involved in it.

Jerome was born at Stridon near Aquileia about 346. His parents were Catholics, but in the course of his studies at Rome Jerome learnt to live riotously. Before he was twenty, however, he was converted to a practical Christianity, and showed the change in his manner of life by taking up the habit of visiting the martyrs' tombs on Sunday afternoons, and allowing himself to be baptised. After a visit to Gaul he began his writing of Christian literature with a commentary on Obadiah. He joined a group of friends, including Rufinus, in living an ascetic life at Aquileia. When the little community was broken up, Jerome, leaving behind his family but taking with him his library, departed to Antioch. There he fell into a fever and had a vision which changed the course of his life and ambitions. Hitherto, he was persuaded, he had been not a Christian but a Ciceronian. To remedy this misdirection of his studies he retired into the desert to live the life of a hermit. The habit of study was strong upon him and he took the opportunity of learning Hebrew from a Christian Jew. He was driven out of his retirement by the local monks because of the bitterness arising out of the Meletian schism at Antioch. To this city he returned in 379 and was ordained to the priesthood by the eminently orthodox Paulinus; but it was contrary to his own wishes, and he is said never to

have performed priestly functions. He was in Constantinople in 381 studying under Gregory, but it is curious that he never even mentions the Council of Constantinople. For the next four years he was in Rome, where he revised the Latin translation of the New Testament, and began those studies of the Greek version of the Old Testament in comparison with the original Hebrew which led ultimately to the composition of the Vulgate. It is noteworthy that at this period he defended the clouded reputation of Origen. Here also he met Paula and Eustochium, together with other patrician ladies whom he encouraged in the practice of asceticism. He was now mentioned as a possible successor to Pope Damasus, but he had an unhappy knack of scurrility that made him unpopular, and he was not elected. His successful rival Siricius had no sympathy with him, and so in 385 he left Rome to return to Antioch.

Paula and Eustochium went with him, and in their company he visited Alexandria and the Egyptian monks. When he returned to Palestine it was to settle in Bethlehem. There he controlled a monastery and a hospice, while his old friend Rufinus had a similar institution not far away on the Mount of Olives. Paula conducted a convent for women, and the inmates of her establishment met for worship with those of Jerome's on Sundays. In these circumstances Jerome had sufficient opportunity to carry on his studies in Hebrew and Chaldee, and to write many letters which still give us vivid glimpses of the life of the period. Some disturbance, however, was caused by an invasion of the Huns, which occurring in 395 considerably delayed the publication of the Vulgate. Worse disturbance to this idyllic life was caused by Jerome's own controversial temper. Of the disputes in which he became involved five demand our attention.

The first was with a certain Jovinian, who having once been a monk had now abandoned that life and had taken to writing against those who spoke too highly of celibacy. Jerome refuted him so successfully that he left no room for marriage at all. His friends thought it wise first to curtail and then to suppress his books on this subject.

The second dispute was with one Vigilantius, who took up much the same attitude as Jovinian. Having been first brought up at an inn, Vigilantius had then received a good education and had travelled much in the East. He was, however, repelled by the excessive asceticism that he discovered there, and he wrote against some of the abuses of his time. He said that the honour paid to the tombs of the martyrs passed the bounds of propriety, and maintained that the miracles attributed to them were false. He affirmed also that the hermit's life was simply cowardice, and contended that all who sought the office of presbyter should be married before ordination. In replying to him Jerome was at his worst. He saw nothing but blasphemy in his suggestions. He further accused Vigilantius of stealing his precious manuscripts when on a visit to him at Bethlehem.

A controversy in which he engaged with Augustine was not allowed to proceed to such an extreme. The difference arose out of Jerome's interpretation of Galatians ii. He affirmed that Peter had only *pretended* to accept the Mosaic ordinances just in order to give Paul a chance of showing up their absurdity. Augustine was undoubtedly right in exposing the ridiculous nature of this exegesis, but he was on less secure ground when he tried to persuade Jerome to abandon the use of the Hebrew text in his translation of the Old Testament because of the damage that it might do to the faith of the simple. What would people think, asked Augustine, if they found that Jonah had slept under a gourd and not, as the earlier version had said, under ivy?

The fourth controversy was with the Pelagians, but as it will engage our attention later we will omit it for the moment in order to consider at some length the trouble that arose over the teaching of Origen. This can best be discussed in three stages, the first including events as they occurred in Palestine, the second the events at Rome, and the third those in Egypt.

The acute differences that had arisen over the speculations of Origen, with the mention of which we began this chapter, were felt with especial keenness among the monks of Egypt, where they caused a division between the

ascetics of Nitria and those of the Thebaid. The former were frankly Origenist, accepting the Hellenistic disparagement of the body and believing in the resurrection of an immaterial body only. The monks of the Thebaid, on the other hand, who were for the most part Copts and followed the rule of Pachomius, were of strongly anthropomorphist views. It was when he had lived as a monk among the former section that Jerome's neighbour, John of Jerusalem, had imbibed Origenist views. His brother bishop, Epiphanius of Salamis, was of the opposite opinion, and by him, when he visited Jerusalem, John was invited to repudiate Origenism before the assembled congregation in his own cathedral. John of course refused and a heresy hunt was started against him. Epiphanius managed to elicit the sympathy of Jerome's community at Bethlehem. Further, in order to make the congregation at Bethlehem independent of John's ministrations, Epiphanius actually ordained Jerome's brother Paulinianus to the priesthood. John on his side obtained the help of Rufinus' community on the Mount of Olives, and tried to get the government to assist him by ejecting Jerome and his friends from their homes in Bethlehem. It was only the irruption of the Huns that prevented the latter proposal from being put into effect. The timely delay gave an opportunity for the mediation of Theophilus of Alexandria. Rufinus and Jerome were publicly reconciled at the Church of the Holy Sepulchre in 397, and Bishop John regularised the ministrations of Paulinianus at Bethlehem.

The second stage of the trouble opened in Rome with the return of Rufinus, who translated into Latin Origen's *De Principiis*. In his own preface to the book Rufinus gave an honourable mention to Jerome. But this alarmed Jerome, who was told by his friends that his reputation for orthodoxy was at stake. Jerome therefore sent to Rufinus what he believed to be a more exact rendering of Origen's work together with a friendly covering letter. But the friends of Jerome through whom the communication was sent were base enough to suppress the letter. Rufinus in order to claim as much support as possible pointed out that Jerome himself was originally an Origenist. It cost Jerome three books

of *Apology against Rufinus* to refute the charge. Jerome had the support of the new Pope Anastasius, who was strongly anti-Origenist. Rufinus, thus defeated, retired to do literary work in 410, the year that Rome fell before the arms of * Alaric.

But in the meantime a third stage of the conflict had opened in Egypt. Theophilus of Alexandria (385–412) in a pastoral letter of 399 had asserted the incorporeality of the Godhead. But later in order to curb the power of the Nitrian monks, who were becoming a source of annoyance to him, he changed sides. Enlisting on his behalf the sympathy of the anthropomorphists, he got the Nitrian Origenists condemned at a synod held in Alexandria (400) and drove them forcibly from their retreats. As a result of this violent action four of them, known as the Tall Brothers, fled to Constantinople to seek the help of Chrysostom. This was to stir up the long-standing rivalry between the two great sees of Constantinople and Alexandria, and Theophilus himself repaired to Constantinople in order to use the new controversy as a convenient weapon against Chrysostom.

II

Chrysostom had already had a somewhat chequered career. He was born in 347, the son of the general Secundus. His teacher was Libanius the famous Sophist. After his education was complete he practised as an advocate at Antioch. There he was much affected by the asceticism of Basil of Caesarea, and also by his intercourse with the ascetic Meletius, once Arian and now orthodox Bishop of Antioch, by whom he was not only baptised but also ordained Reader. He would have liked to live the life of a hermit, had not his mother persuaded him not to leave her but to pursue ascetic practices in his own home. He influenced his friends in the same direction, and even persuaded Theodore of Mopsuestia, of whom we shall hear later, to break off his engagement to marry. A narrow escape from being discovered in possession of a book of magic, which he had only picked up by accident, produced on him such

an impression as to convince him that he ought to devote himself entirely to the ascetic life. After ruining his health by his austerities he returned to Antioch, and was ordained deacon in 381 and priest five years later.

It was now that he gained his great reputation as a preacher and his nickname of the 'golden-mouthed'. For sixteen years he preached each Saturday and Sunday, with additional sermons on Saints' Days and during Lent. His most famous addresses were the *Homilies on the Statues*. The mob in the city had taken down the statues of the Emperor and his family and dragged them with insults th ough the streets. When the deed had been done, the whole city was afflicted with terror at the thought of the vengeance that Theodosius might wreak upon them. It was while they were waiting for the news of the Emperor's decision that the Homilies were preached, and Chrysostom used the opportunity to turn the terrified population from the fear of man to that of God.

In 398 John Chrysostom was made Bishop of Constantinople, much against his own will and even more against the will of Theophilus of Alexandria who was forced to consecrate him. In his person a confirmed ascetic succeeded to the somewhat luxurious Nectarius. The people liked both his devotion and his eloquence. The clergy, however, disliked his discipline. He set himself to reform them and especially to discourage their habit of keeping *subintroductae* in their houses, a custom that still survived in spite of the prohibition of Nicea. He competed with the remaining Arians by reviving the nocturnal services enlivened with antiphonal chanting. He did valuable mission work among the Goths who were now very plentiful in Constantinople, and he even found time to send evangelists to the Scythians who were wandering along the banks of the Danube.

He was, however, hardly the right person to deal with political personages. At first he got on well enough with Eudoxia, the powerful wife of the weak and shifty Emperor Arcadius. But he earned her enmity when she fell out with the favourite Eutropius, by giving him sanctuary in one of the churches, although Eutropius himself had been the

author of a law prohibiting such sanctuary. Also Chrysostom felt himself compelled to protect the people against the growing power of Gainas the Goth, who had usurped administrative authority in the city. After Eutropius and Gainas had both been finally disposed of, Chrysostom remained the only obstacle between Eudoxia and complete ascendancy over her husband. The feud between them deepened when, in spite of her, Chrysostom exercised metropolitical authority at Ephesus and deposed six bishops for simony. On his return he referred publicly to the Empress as Jezebel.

Her opportunity came when the Tall Brothers arrived in Constantinople, followed hard by Theophilus. Chrysostom gave shelter to the monks, and Theophilus found a ready helper in Eudoxia. With her aid an assembly, known as the Synod of the Oak, from the quarter in which it was held, was summoned in 403, and Chrysostom was called upon to answer for his actions. It was a 'packed' gathering and by it the bishop was exiled. A timely earthquake terrified the superstitious Empress and she allowed Chrysostom to be recalled. Her resentment smouldered, and burst into flame again when the Bishop objected to the dedication of her statue outside a church where he happened to be preaching. He regarded the ceremony, taking place at such a moment, as a demonstration against himself. 'Once more', he exclaimed, 'Herodias is dancing, once more she demands John's head on a charger.' He was seized as he was about to baptise three thousand catechumens on Easter Eve, 404, and was exiled to Cucusus, a village in the Taurus. There he spent what have been described as the three most glorious years of his life, controlling from his exile practically all the ecclesiastical affairs of the East. An end was put to this by an order to move him further afield. The soldiers were promised a reward if he failed to survive, and, their harshness proving successful, he died in 407.

III

This affair resulted in still further emphasising the growing difference between East and West. At this time

Innocent I, one of the greatest of the Popes, was ruling at Rome. He was not approached in the matter of Chrysostom until 404, and then first Theophilus and afterwards Chrysostom sent him a version of what had occurred. Innocent thereupon asked for a new council and got the support of Honorius, who was now Emperor in the West. The messengers of both Emperor and Pope were roughly handled in Athens and the council was refused. Innocent, left to form his own judgment on the matter, excommunicated Chrysostom's opponents, and sent him letters of comfort. The dispute continued after Chrysostom's death, his enemies refusing to allow his name to be entered on the diptychs for honourable mention in the Eucharist. Innocent refused to yield to this act of malice towards a great and good bishop, and quarrelled with the three most important sees of the East, Constantinople, Antioch and Alexandria, rather than see such injustice done.

Thus divergence was exhibited on a point of honour. It was to be seen also in a characteristic difference in point of view. All this time the West had been building up a compact and legal system of belief and practice which was to outlast the Empire and subdue the barbarians. The only issue which disturbed it was the great moral question involved in Pelagianism, which we shall have later to consider. The East on the other hand was not worried about moral questions at all, but was still busy working out its theology on the basis of philosophy. Paradoxical as it may seem, this made possible a certain sympathy with pagan thought which would have been very unlikely in the West. A remarkable instance of this is to be found in the life of Synesius of Cyrene.

Synesius was born in 370 of a noble family, and was brought up as a pagan. He studied philosophy at Alexandria under the woman teacher Hypatia. After his return to Cyrene he was sent on an embassy by the combined communities of the Pentapolis to seek from the Emperor Arcadius a reduction in taxation. While at the court he delivered a daring oration on Kingship (399). This was in effect a manifesto of the anti-German party, exhorting the Emperor

to rely on the older elements in the State and to free himself from Gothic influence. The embassy over, Synesius returned to his books and his country life. Cyrene was at this time a pastoral province often overrun by barbarians. The government officials, although appointed personally by the Emperor, were too supine to protect their charge. In their stead it fell to the Christian clergy to raise troops and attend to the civil needs of their people. Although the populace had no voice in the appointment of high government officials, they could at least choose their bishop. Consequently when a vacancy occurred in the see, Synesius, in spite of the fact that he was still a pagan, was invited by them to accept the office. At first he refused on the ground of conscientious scruples. He held, he said, unorthodox views on the resurrection, and even if he could bring himself to give up his pack of hounds he would certainly not surrender his wife. All the same Theophilus of Alexandria, when the matter was referred to him, overruled the objections and persuaded him to accept. Once consecrated, Synesius proved an excellent bishop and used his new ecclesiastical powers with great effect. In order to reduce Andronicus, the governor of the province, to some sense of justice, he excommunicated him and ordered that none should meet him or eat with him until he had reformed. Synesius was not only a man of affairs but also a man of letters. It is significant of his complex character that his last letter was addressed to Hypatia and his last poem to Christ.

A third point in which the divergence between East and West may be most clearly seen is that of administration. After the death of Theodosius the division of the Empire into an eastern and a western half, each with its own Augustus, was resumed under his sons Honorius and Arcadius. But there was a real difference in the position of the Church in the two parts of the Empire. In the West the very absence of the Emperor from Rome threw into strong relief the prestige of the Pope, and even made it necessary for him to exercise much political influence which would never have fallen to his lot if he had been overshadowed by the ruler of the

State. The Bishop of Rome was thus already the undisputed head of a great organisation over which the Emperor had very little control. In the East, however, a very different state of things prevailed.

There had been much rivalry among the three great sees as to which should take the lead, and Constantinople, which appeared to the others an upstart see, had succeeded in getting that position assigned to herself officially at the council of 381. But it was at Constantinople that the power and authority of the Eastern Emperor was most strongly felt. We have seen how Theodosius took Church affairs into his own hands and how Eudoxia was able to circumvent Chrysostom at every turn. It must be admitted that the succession of bishops at Constantinople shows us very few capable administrators; even when there is a good man like Gregory or Chrysostom he is much more saint and scholar than statesman. Thus there came about in the East a state of things in which the Emperor himself was the effectual head of the Church, a system which a later day was to recognise as Caesaro-papalism. This was to have a particularly bad effect on the churches lying along the outskirts of the Empire, for the more their own national characteristics developed the less were they willing to follow the lead of a Church that was under the heel of the Emperor.

But there was one special reason why the Pope was left free from interference at this time, while he perfected the ecclesiastical system of Rome. The main danger point of barbarian invasion was no longer the line of the Danube but Italy itself. The civil and military authorities were far too busy with their attempts to keep the enemy out of Italy to be able to give themselves to the details of Church affairs. The Huns were pressing upon the rear of the Teutonic tribes and driving them over the boundaries.

Alaric, the Gothic general in Illyricum, besieged Aquileia, but in 402 he was defeated at the battle of Pollentia by Stilicho, a German general in the Roman army, and was forced to retreat. Four years later 200,000 barbarians descended from the Alps and advanced as far as Florence. Stilicho, however, was again a match for them, and beat

them back. But at the end of that year the Vandals broke through all along the line of the Rhine. And now the Romans lost their leader, for Stilicho was murdered in 408. In the absence of his old adversary Alaric again marched on Rome, and at last captured it in 410. It was a merciful fact that the invaders were Christian. The Arian Goths were far more gentle than other conquerors might have been. Augustine, in his *City of God*, points out that even pagans sought a refuge in Christian churches and did not seek in vain. There followed a period of great confusion until peace was restored by the general Constantius in 417. During the course of these events the Church gained in prestige while other institutions lost. Later the Church, as the one vital and effective institution left, was to take the lead in dealing with the barbarians. Thus in the West it came about that the Church began to overshadow the State, while in the East the State overshadowed the Church.

It must be admitted that the Church in the East had to some extent brought this trouble upon itself by accepting the civil government's help in the control of ecclesiastical affairs. Constantine had set the example of using the Church as an instrument in secular government. This meant that he had first induced the bishops to devise one creed and then tried to force it on the whole empire. Theodosius actually established Catholic Orthodoxy by the same means. Naturally it was in Constantinople, the effective seat of government, that the Emperor's influence was most strongly felt. Perhaps its most tragic result was that it ultimately led to the break up of the eastern empire.

CHAPTER XX

NESTORIANISM AND PELAGIANISM

THE characteristic difference between East and West can be seen once again in the religious controversies which each had to face during the early years of the fifth century. Both were concerned with what was at bottom the same difficulty. The question as to the true capacity of the nature of man was bound to come up for discussion sooner or later, and it so happened that it arose simultaneously in West and East, but in the former it presented itself as a practical moral problem, while in the latter it came to the front in the effort to settle the problem as to the precise nature of the manhood in Christ.

I

In the East there had been a strong reaction against the teaching of Apollinarius because it had mutilated the manhood of the Saviour. The Alexandrian school, which had given rise to that essentially 'pneumatic' view of Christ's person, had consequently suffered something of an eclipse. It was now the turn of the Antiochene school, with its habit of beginning from the side of the human nature, to put forward its effort to solve the problem. The first to make this attempt was Diodore, who was head of the catechetical school at Antioch and afterwards Bishop of Tarsus (378–394). He was a supporter of the Nicene faith, and had even been instrumental in procuring the expulsion from Antioch of Aetius the famous Anomoean. He was himself exiled for his anti-Arian opinions, but was recalled on the death of Valens and was present at the Council of Constantinople, at which Apollinarianism was condemned. In opposition to Apollinarius, Diodore taught that the Son of God is to be distinguished from the Son of David.

The latter was simply the temple for the indwelling of the Word or Logos. Thus God the Word ought not to be called Mary's son. If one asks how the Logos dwelt in Christ, the answer is, 'Much as He dwelt in the prophets', only in their case the indwelling was partial and temporary, while in His it was entire and eternal.

A pupil of Diodore was Theodore of Mopsuestia (c. 350–428), who in Antioch was a friend of Chrysostom. He was best known as a commentator on the Biblical writings, following the usual Antiochene method of literal exegesis. One valuable principle enunciated by him was that there could be no true allegory which did not depend first upon a fact of history. He discriminated among the various books already held sacred, excluding from his own canon of the Old Testament Job and Canticles, and the Catholic Epistles from the New Testament. He took up the cudgels against Apollinarius, and in doing so laid tremendous emphasis upon the reality of the human nature of our Lord. It is probable that the Nestorian controversy is due to him more than to any other teacher. It is often doubted whether Nestorius himself was a Nestorian, but there can be no doubt that Theodore was a Nestorian before Nestorius. Although his teaching was not expressly condemned until the controversy of the Three Chapters in 553, he certainly asserted the peccability of Christ. In endeavouring to determine how the Logos was united with the manhood in the Saviour, he points out that three methods of union were possible, either assumption of the manhood by the Logos, or the cohesion (*sunapheia*) of the two natures, or the indwelling (*enoikesis*) of the Logos in the manhood. The last method was the one that seemed most likely to Theodore. He asserted that this indwelling was not in essential nature (*ousia*), nor merely in operation (*energeia*) but in good will (*eudokia*). This implies of course two separate persons who could exercise good will towards each other, and it implies also that the union between them could be no more than a moral union. The analogies used to illustrate such a union, such as that of marriage and that of the relation between soul and body, were somewhat conflicting; but

Theodore penetrated to the heart of the difficulty, although he did not solve it, when he refused to assert the impersonality of the human nature of Christ. To him Christ was a man who became God rather than God who became man. Consequently Mary could be called *Theotokos* (Mother of God) only in a secondary sense.

The populariser of these views was Nestorius, a famous preacher and abbot at Antioch who was appointed by Theodosius II to be Bishop of Constantinople in 428, the year of Theodore's death. He set himself, as soon as he reached his diocese, to a determined heresy hunt. His chaplain emulated him, and preached a sermon in which he expressly denied the right of the Virgin Mary to the title *Theotokos*. Nestorius in support preached a course of sermons the gist of which was that what is born of flesh can be no more than flesh. The imperial court accepted these views but the rest of Constantinople objected. Nestorius had a forcible way of dealing with opponents; a deputation of monks who came to protest against his teaching was thrown into prison.

The controversy now began to assume grave proportions. On Lady Day, 429, a great panegyric was preached on the Mother of God, and Nestorius exercised his right of reply. What was his precise teaching became a matter of dispute, but we can rely for the final expression of his faith upon the *Bazaar of Heracleides*, an apology published by him after his downfall. There Nestorius asserts that he did not repudiate the title *Theotokos* but only objected to it as liable to give rise to misunderstanding. He would have preferred the title Mother of Christ. In his doctrine concerning the two natures Nestorius uses the term *prosopon* (person) of each, but he postulates a certain give and take between them which enables him to speak also of one resultant *prosopon*. 'I separate the natures, but unite the worship.' In spite of this explanation the position still remains unsatisfactory. There are really two persons and the union between them is moral rather than essential.

The most strenuous opposition proceeded, as was natural, from Alexandria. There Cyril had succeeded Theophilus

as bishop, and it is an interesting speculation whether in the subsequent disputes he was animated more by the old ecclesiastical rivalry between his see and that of Constantinople or by the theological rivalry between his see and that of Antioch. He intervened in the controversy in 429, issuing an encyclical to the monks of Egypt in which he asked the plain question, 'Is Mary's Son God or not?' This he followed up with two letters to Nestorius. But Nestorius had already stirred up fresh trouble for himself by giving hospitality to the Pelagian exiles, thus arousing the animosity of Pope Coelestine. Cyril pursued his tactical advantage further by writing to the Emperor in order to detach him from the side of Nestorius.

The keynote of the Cyrilline Christology is expressed in the phrase 'God as man'. The incarnate Christ, while being one Person only, undergoes both human and divine experiences in virtue of His two natures. These are held in unity by the *communicatio idiomatum*, that is, the capacity of each nature for sharing in the experiences of the other. The Logos, however, did not take on a human personality, but rather humanity itself. That which supplies the personal element in the Christ is the Logos. The assumption of humanity by the Logos had taken place in the womb of the Blessed Virgin. Therefore that which was born of her is God and she is properly entitled to be called the Mother of God.

Ranged on the side of Cyril was now Coelestine of Rome. He had had communications received from Nestorius translated into Latin so that he might understand them, and he had also received letters from Cyril. He called a council at Rome in 430, condemned Nestorius, and arranged for Cyril to act as his proxy in carrying out the excommunication of Nestorius, if the latter did not repent within ten days. Cyril made the mistake of going beyond his terms of reference. Having got Nestorius condemned at a council in Alexandria, he added on his own authority to the synodal letter addressed to Nestorius twelve anathemas, to which he demanded Nestorius' assent. This letter arrived at Constantinople on December 5th, but in November Theo-

dosius II and Valentinian III had ordered a general council to meet at Ephesus by Pentecost, thus preventing Coelestine and Cyril from settling the question out of court.

II

When the Council of Ephesus first assembled there were 158 bishops present. Africa was represented by one deacon only, the great Augustine having died six months before the letter of invitation arrived. These bishops were all opponents of Nestorianism and had no difficulty in agreeing to the condemnation of Nestorius, who had himself refused to attend the council. The reason for this easy victory was that John of Antioch together with Theodoret of Cyrus and forty other bishops of the opposite faction delayed on the road and did not arrive at Ephesus until after the council had taken action. On hearing what had happened John and his supporters held a council of their own. They made a good tactical move in not defending Nestorius directly but in levelling their attack against Cyril's Twelve Anathemas. The result was that they excommunicated Cyril and his supporters until such time as they should repudiate the anathemas.

Both parties now tried to get the support of the Emperor. The court officials, however, were afraid that undue influence might be brought to bear upon their ruler, and saw to it that very little news filtered through to him. The bishops were reduced to all kinds of shifts in order to get their messages to Constantinople. In one instance they managed to evade the vigilance of the guards by enclosing their missive in a hollow cane and sending it by the hand of a beggar. In the uncertainty that ensued the Emperor treated both Cyril and Nestorius, together with Memnon the Bishop of Ephesus, as alike deposed from office.

In the meantime the council tried to get on with other business. In order to secure some kind of uniformity in the doctrinal standard required of converts, it declared that no other creed than that of Nicea should be demanded of those seeking admission to the Church. A second item of practical

concern arose out of the claim of Antioch to exercise metro-political jurisdiction over the island of Cyprus. The Cypriotes maintained that they had always had the right of managing their own ecclesiastical affairs. The council ordered Antioch to refrain from any attempt at usurpation. In order to prevent such disputes in future and to stabilise the existing system of organisation, the council further decreed that henceforth no prelate was to take over the superintendence of any diocese that had not from the first been subject to his own see. This may have seemed to offer a chance of peace for the moment, but we shall see that twenty years later it was openly contradicted in the provisions made for Constantinople. Yet Cyprus at least has retained its autocephalous character to the present day.

The next move was made by the Imperial Commissioner in charge of the council, who arrived on the scene and arrested the three deposed bishops. With the leaders thus put out of action it was believed that more rapid progress towards agreement might be made. A formulary of reunion was composed in the hope that both sides would accept it, but in point of fact neither would give way. Theodosius made a last despairing effort by receiving a deputation from both parties. Being finally convinced that reconciliation was impossible, he dissolved the council. In these circumstances nothing was left but to abide by the resolutions of the majority. Memnon and Cyril were therefore allowed to return to their sees, but Nestorius was sent back in disgrace to the monastery from which he had come. In his stead Maximian was consecrated as Bishop of Constantinople. Four years later Nestorius was sent an exile to Egypt, and was harried from place to place until, worn out, he died in 451 shortly before the Council of Chalcedon.

But Nestorianism was very far from being dead. Its missions spread rapidly to the East, and before long established themselves as far as China. The support of Nestorian opinions became a point of national honour among some of the peoples in the East and assisted to arouse those mutual jealousies which did much to break up the Empire. It is a curious reflection that if Cyril had not been so precipitate

in composing his Twelve Anathemas and endeavouring to force them upon his opponents such a disaster might never have happened.

III

A heresy against which the Council of Ephesus directed several of its canons and which, as we have hinted, had a close affinity with Nestorianism, was that of Pelagianism. It has been said that 'the Nestorian Christ was the fitting Saviour of the Pelagian man'. Nestorianism had sought to show that Christ was a perfect man who was deemed worthy to be united with the divine Logos. It seemed to follow from this that a man could be perfect in the right of his own nature and without any extraordinary help from God. This is precisely what Pelagius claimed. Looking at the matter as a purely moral question he believed that the one thing necessary to enable people to bestir themselves to the heights of noble living was that they should realise the potentialities of their own nature. His teaching on the subject was worked out in opposition to the doctrine of Augustine, and in order that we may understand its full implications it will be necessary to give some consideration to the life and work of the great African doctor.

Augustine's teaching has been described as the highest attainment of religion since apostolic times. He did more than anyone else to raise the West intellectually above the East. He stood on the watershed between two worlds, the old classical antiquity which was just disappearing and the medieval world which was not yet born. He sums up in himself all that was best of the old culture and sends it forth endowed with all the richness of his vital personality to enliven the new. In the change from the one to the other his own personal experience is all-important; and it is that experience which was to direct the thought of mankind for many generations. Ecclesiastically Augustine may be said to be the father both of medieval Catholicism and of modern Protestantism. The Reformation itself is often described as the revolt of his doctrine of grace against his doctrine of the Church.

Augustine was born at Tagaste in Numidia in 354, the son of a pagan, Patricius, who was not converted until late in life, and of the saintly Monica, who like many good mothers could sometimes blind herself to moral issues in furthering the interests of her son. It is possible that the difference between his parents is reflected in the dual character of Augustine. He spent fourteen years at Carthage learning rhetoric, and there his illegitimate son Adeodatus was born in 372. A year afterwards he was turned to serious thoughts by the reading of Cicero's *Hortensius*. Then for nine years he was a follower of the Manicheans, but he was disillusioned when he met their sophistical leader Faustus. Symmachus, the pagan orator, invited him to take up a position as teacher of rhetoric at Milan, no doubt hoping that he would offset some of the Christian influences there. By this time he was a complete sceptic, but he was brought under the spell of Ambrose, and with many struggles set himself to live a more orderly life. For a period he sought relief in the philosophy of Neoplatonism, but he was profoundly moved when he came in contact with some Christian ascetics whom he found able to live a life after his own ideals without the aid of his own learning and philosophy. It was now that his conversion occurred in circumstances which are incomparably described by himself.

But when deep reflection had from the secret store (of memory) drawn and heaped together all my misery in the sight of my heart; there arose a mighty tempest, bringing a heavy downpour of tears. And that I might pour it all out, with its loud lamentations, I rose from Alypius. Solitude seemed to me better suited to the business of weeping; so I retired so far that even his presence could not be a restraint upon me. Thus was it then with me, and he perceived it; for something I suppose I had spoken, wherein the tones of my voice appeared choked with weeping, and so had risen up. He then remained where we were sitting, lost in amazement. I cast myself down I know not how, under a certain fig-tree, and gave rein to my tears; and the floods of mine eyes broke forth, 'an acceptable sacrifice to Thee' And not indeed in these words, yet to this purpose, spake I much unto Thee: 'and Thou, O Lord, how long? how long,

Lord, wilt Thou be angry, for ever? O remember not against us former iniquities', for I felt that I was holden by them. I kept on uttering wretched exclamations: How long? how long, 'to-morrow, and to-morrow?' Why not now? why not this hour make an end of my uncleanness?

Such words I spake the while I wept in most bitter contrition of my heart. And lo, from a neighbouring house I heard a voice, as of a boy or girl, I know not, singing and oft repeating, 'Take, read; take, read'. Instantly, with a changed countenance, I began to think most intently, whether boys in any kind of game used to sing such a phrase; nor could I remember ever to have heard the like. So checking the torrent of my tears, I arose; interpreting it to be no other than a Divine command, to open the book, and read the first chapter I should find. For I had heard of Anthony, that he had happened to come in during the reading of the Gospel, and had taken the passage read as a warning, spoken to himself, 'Go, sell all that thou hast, and give to the poor, and thou shalt have treasure in heaven, and come and follow me'; and by such oracle he was forthwith converted unto Thee. With such an inspiration then, I returned to the place where Alypius was sitting; for there had I laid the volume of the Apostle, when I arose thence. I seized, opened, and in silence read the passage upon which my eyes first fell: 'Not in rioting and drunkenness, not in chambering and wantonness, not in strife and envying: but put ye on the Lord Jesus Christ, and make not provision for the flesh to fulfil the lusts thereof.' No further would I read; nor was there need; for instantly at the end of this sentence, as though my heart were flooded with a light of peace, all the shadows of doubt melted away.

This was in 386, and the following year he was baptised. His mother died at Ostia while they were on the way back to Africa. He tried to found a monastery, but was persuaded to accept ordination. He was priested in 391 and four years later was consecrated as Coadjutor-Bishop of Hippo, succeeding as diocesan in 396. There he laboured for the space of a generation, dying at last in 430 while his city was suffering from the horrors of a siege by the Vandals.

One of the great troubles of Augustine's administration arose out of the conflict with the Donatists. After their revival under Julian these sectarians had begun quarrelling

with each other. Both Optatus and Augustine wrote treatises *
against them, but in spite of their internal divisions they
would not yield to argument. The government wished to
coerce them into peace, and at length in despair of any
other settlement Augustine was induced to agree. But
although he was willing thus to use force, it must be remembered in his favour that he would not admit the employment
against them of the death penalty. In 411 a great council
was summoned at Carthage which was attended by 279
Donatists and 286 Catholics. The imperial officer then gave
judgment against the Donatists and proceeded to enforce
his verdict. Four years later a law was promulgated forbidding their assemblies for worship. This was the real end of
Donatism. When the Vandals became masters of Africa
they had ceased to be of importance, and only a few lingered
on till the time of Gregory the Great.

In the meantime Augustine had engaged in much other
writing besides that of a controversial nature. About 400
he published his *Confessions*, one of the most popular books
of all time, from which we have quoted the account of his
conversion. With it he founded a new type of literature.
Over and above its surpassing interest as autobiography,
it gave a permanent place to the psychological method in
thought. In this respect it is in line with our modern systems,
the keynote of which has been described as a 'self-assured
subjectivity'. A book of a very different type is his *City of
God*, which took at least fourteen years (412–426) to write.
It is an attempt to answer the charge that the fall of Rome
and the calamities of the Empire were due to the forsaking
of the old religion and the embracing of Christianity. In
his reply Augustine gives his whole philosophy of history.
World events reflect a divine purpose and God's judgment
on nations can be discerned in their fortunes no less than
His judgment on individuals can be seen in the vicissitudes
of personal experience. But the fulfilment of God's blessing
must not be looked for in a secular society which has not
submitted fully to His sway. There are in fact two cities,
one earthly and one heavenly, which represent divergent
claims upon the love and allegiance of men. The strife

between these two was already begun in the struggle between the angels. At the moment they are represented by the two organisations of the State and the Church; and it is in the latter that the victory and the millennial reign of Christ are to be seen. It follows from this that the State is inferior to the Church. Later generations interpreted this in the sense that the State should be subject to the Church, and thus Augustine was made the parent of the medieval Papacy and the medieval Empire.

Augustine's theological views are set forth in his *De Trinitate* and *De Doctrina Christiana*. He completed the early development of Trinitarian doctrine by postulating the full equality of the three Persons. The subordinationism of the Origenist tradition now disappears. The Holy Spirit is believed to proceed from the Son as well as from the Father, and the threefold relation is that of the lover, the beloved and the love that flows between them. So close is their unity that the entire Trinity acts in the action of each Person, just as an individual acts as a complete person in every operation of memory, intelligence and will.

As against the Donatists Augustine developed his doctrine of the Church, defining it under what have ever since been regarded as the four characteristic notes of Unity, Holiness, Catholicity and Apostolicity. His doctrine of the ministry showed a considerable advance on that of his fellow African, Cyprian. Holy Orders are now described as belonging rather to the individual than to the office that he holds, they are a personal rather than an official possession. Thus a person who has been validly ordained to the priesthood is still a priest even though for a time he leaves the Church, and if he returns no further ordination is necessary to enable him to resume valid functions. In the same way the sacraments that he administers are independent of his moral character. Christ Himself is the true minister in each sacrament, so that it cannot be rendered invalid by the character of the minister who is His properly accredited agent. It is sometimes said that Augustine took an entirely subjective view of the method of the sacrament's working, holding that it is merely an outward signal of God's action

upon the soul. But this will not bear investigation. To his mind the subjective effect was dependent upon an objective gift. It is to him indeed that we owe the careful division of the sacrament into *sacramentum* (visible sign), *res sacramenti* (invisible grace), and *virtus sacramenti* (the effect of this grace in the life of the faithful). For the last to be successfully appropriated faith is necessary. But this does not involve for Augustine a logical contradiction between spirituality and formality; for the faith that is required is given in baptism. Although regular sacraments may be administered even among the sects, they become fully efficacious only within the Church, since it is in the Church alone that there is to be found the unity of the Spirit.

The necessity for this elaborate system of church and sacraments is to be found in Augustine's doctrine of man. Such supernatural means are necessary for salvation, because man in his natural condition since the fall of Adam is thoroughly depraved. He is simply a *massa perditionis*, and if left to himself would undoubtedly perish. But God has predestined some from all eternity to salvation. To them he gives His special grace not only to be called into His Church and to receive the help of His sacraments but also to use the sacraments effectively to their final perseverance. This predestination and this special gift of grace are both necessary for salvation, but once given they are alike irresistible. In Augustine's view this did not mean that man had no free will, but that God's love would play on him in such a way that he would quite voluntarily accept the aid that God held out to him.

This is a rough outline of the monumental system that was to affect Christian thinking for many centuries. By his *Confessions* Augustine gave an epoch-making impulse to both piety and philosophy; by his conflict with Donatism he established an equally important theory of the Church and ministry; in his *City of God* he laid down the lines of secular and ecclesiastical government; and in his doctrine of grace and predestination he started a controversy which has not yet completely died down. It is to the immediate reverberations of this last that we must now turn.

IV

Pelagius was a British monk, probably of Irish origin, who had settled in South Wales. He came to Rome about 400 and was shocked at the low state of morals in the capital, and especially at the apparent lack of effort on the part of the lapsed. In such a state of mind he was naturally perturbed by a sentence in Augustine's *Confessions*, 'Give what Thou commandest and command what Thou wilt', which seemed not only to put all initiative in the hands of God, but to deny altogether the possibility of any free exercise of a man's own will. Pelagius set himself to preach a more stirring morality. He believed that although most men are bad they are able to put themselves right if they will only make the effort. This belief he based upon a particular view of human nature. He denied original sin altogether; sin consists not in inheriting the nature of Adam but in following his example. Faith and effort alone are necessary if men are to succeed in their struggles. Pelagius did not deny that men received grace from God, but taught that such grace was part of the ordinary endowment of human nature and that nothing more than the natural endowment was necessary. There was at first no controversy over this teaching, perhaps because Augustine was busily occupied with the Donatist trouble. But when Rome was sacked in 410, and Pelagius took refuge in Carthage, he there laid considerable emphasis upon his view that man needs no extraordinary gift of grace to accomplish his salvation. This seemed to strike at the whole notion of redemption. It was really the Stoic philosophy of the day in a Christian dress.

Pelagius was supported and pushed still further in the expression of these views by his follower Celestius, another Irishman, who had been trained as a lawyer, but became a monk. He, too, came to Carthage, and there sought ordination, but he was refused on the ground of unorthodox teaching. He had stated:

(*a*) That Adam would have died even if he had never sinned;

(b) That his sin injured himself alone;
(c) That new-born children are as innocent as was Adam before his fall;
(d) That the whole race does not die in consequence of Adam's sin, nor rise in consequence of Christ's resurrection;
(e) That the Law may lead a man to heaven as well as the Gospel;
(f) That even before Christ came every man could live without sin.

Against this teaching Augustine wrote a number of treatises, the most famous of which is the *De Spiritu et Littera*. He relied upon his own experience of special grace, without which he was sure that he could never have recovered from his evil ways. He felt that grace was necessary to make the fallen will free, and that without this preliminary exercise of God's goodness man would never be able to take even the first step towards reformation. In addition to this there must be repeated gifts of grace to assist the struggler on his way. Grace must be both prevenient and concomitant.

Opinion was very divided between the two protagonists. In Rome Pelagius had won the sympathy of Rufinus, and when he left Carthage for the East he received much support from those who were inclined to the views of Nestorius. Theodore of Mopsuestia was particularly pleased with his teaching that sin does not reside in the nature but in the will. And Nestorius himself gave willing hospitality to the Pelagian leaders. There was indeed more likelihood of Pelagianism finding sympathy in the East than in the West, for the East was not so naturally engrossed in the moral problem, and also the very idea of grace was much less definite in the East than in the West. In the former it was difficult to distinguish the notion of grace from that of the influence of the Holy Spirit, but in the latter, very largely owing to Augustine's careful distinction between outward and inward parts of a sacrament, grace was now being conceived as a kind of physical force that could be conveyed through a material channel like water through a pipe. But

the natural affinities of Pelagianism in the East were offset by the authority of Jerome, who in this controversy entered the lists on the Augustinian side. Not that he took up the same position as Augustine. He did not believe that grace replaced the human will or that man was powerless in the grip of God. He held that divine grace co-operates with the human will, that is to say, he was a 'synergist'. With regard to Augustine's doctrine of predestination, he reduced it to the condition of mere foreknowledge. These views he set forth in the form of a dialogue when Pelagius and Celestius came to Palestine in 415.

In the general consensus of opinion the question of original sin was settled summarily by a reference to the practice of infant baptism. Why were children baptised before they could have committed any sin of their own? Obviously because they were sinful by nature. Since they were as yet incapable of exercising their own will, the sin washed away in baptism must reside not in their will but in their nature; and that nature they must have inherited from Adam. Thus, as Cyril had appealed to the Eucharist in order to settle a point of Christology, so the Augustinians appealed to baptism to settle a point of anthropology. But the controversy was not to be so easily settled as that.

Two African synods condemned the Pelagians in 416. Innocent I confirmed this condemnation just before he died. His successor, however, Zosimus, was a Greek and inclined to sympathy with Pelagius. When he was appealed to by Celestius he wavered. During his hesitation the Emperor Honorius stepped in and ordered Pelagius, in 418, to be exiled, and then the Pope was induced to join in the condemnation. But nineteen Italian bishops, with Julian of Eclanum at their head, refused to be so compliant, and would not sign the document of condemnation. Pelagius himself died two years later, and his opinions were formally and officially anathematised by the General Council of Ephesus in 431.

This, however, did not mean that the last had been heard of the subjects raised. After the African Church was destroyed by the Vandals the intellectual leadership passed to South Gaul, where the young monastic institutions were showing

signs of vigorous life. Among them was felt considerable difficulty in accepting Augustine's teaching, and Cassian in particular denied that divine grace was irresistible. He asserted that man's will always remains free. He even went further and said that man, unaided by any special gift of grace, can take the first step to his own salvation. Thus he denied the necessity of prevenient grace. This teaching was continued by Vincent of Lérins, who in his *Commonitorium* said that Augustine's teaching did not satisfy his canon of catholicity—*quod semper, quod ubique, quod ab omnibus*. The name given to these teachers and their followers has been since the sixteenth century that of Semi-Pelagians. Their views have never been accepted in their entirety, and the general teaching of the Church could perhaps best be described as Semi-Augustinianism. Against Pelagians she has asserted the necessity of supernatural grace; against Semi-Pelagians the necessity of prevenient grace, but Augustine's doctrine of the irresistibility of grace, although it has been the burden of much Calvinistic teaching, she has never accepted. The value of the controversy in directing thought to the respective parts played by God and man in the latter's salvation has been very great. It has been said that 'in no other controversy can we learn so much about the connexion and the contrast between morality and religion'. But essentially it goes back beyond theology proper to philosophy, and forms part of the fundamental, and perhaps insoluble, problem of free will and determinism.

CHAPTER XXI

THE PAPACY AND THE CHRISTOLOGICAL QUESTION

DURING all this time there was considerable development in the higher departments of ecclesiastical organisation. As long ago as the fourth century the Council of Nicea had recognised in the bishops of the provincial capitals a right of jurisdiction over the rest of the bishops within the province. Among the bishops who thus had metropolitical authority there were three whose special privileges were recognised, namely Rome, Alexandria and Antioch.

In the general disgust at the vacillation of the numerous synods and councils that followed after Nicea it was felt necessary to find some other canon of orthodoxy than that of an uncertain creed. Consequently the custom arose of naming certain great bishops as centres of communion for the rest. Already the Emperor Aurelian, in settling the question of Church property that arose in connexion with the case of Paul of Samosata, had adjudged it to the bishop who was in communion with the bishops of Rome and Italy. Later the Emperor Theodosius in his first edict, when he defined Catholicity as being belief in the Trinity, laid it down as a rule that they alone were to be accounted orthodox who not only held that faith but were also in communion with the bishops of Rome and Alexandria. The next step was that at the General Council of Constantinople in 381 Constantinople itself was placed among the leading sees and given an honorary precedence after Rome, because it was the New Rome, thus displacing Alexandria. Finally at the great Council of Chalcedon in 451 Rome, Constantinople, Alexandria, Antioch and Jerusalem were recognised as the five Patriarchates, the bishops of which

had the title of Great Father or Patriarch of the whole Church. Constantinople was thus given official authority in place of the *de facto* authority it had begun to exercise, including appellate jurisdiction for the whole of the East, just as it had already been conceded to Rome for the West. The effect of this was not merely to set Constantinople on an official equality with Rome, but to make it the rival of Rome in the effort to exercise supremacy over the whole Church throughout the world.

That Rome did aspire to this position was now sufficiently obvious. A great step forward had been made when Damasus, in 381, had based his authority not on the fact that he was the successor of Peter, but on the belief that he was the impersonation of Peter. The theory that Peter lives again ideally in each successive Pope made easier the claim to exercise all the rights and functions of Peter. It was unfortunate for Damasus that his own authority was challenged by Ursinus, a rival to his see, and that the strife between them led to such disgraceful scenes that the whole world was profoundly shocked. The Council of Chalcedon dealt with this claim in its own way by setting up against Rome a competitor in the shape of Constantinople.

I

During the fifth century the prestige of the Roman see varied to some extent with the personal qualities of the successive Popes. In Innocent I (402–417) Rome possessed a leader of very great ability, who was not afraid to make the fullest claims for his office. On his accession he successfully demanded the rights of jurisdiction over Eastern Illyricum, although for civil purposes that province now belonged to the eastern half of the Empire. His position was made all the more important when in 404 Honorius moved his seat of government from Rome to Ravenna. This position he improved by encouraging the growing custom for other sees to appeal to Rome for decisions on matters of law, a custom which was made natural by the growing prestige of Innocent himself. He deservedly gained a reputation for justice and courage by his championship

of Chrysostom, although it is to be noted that Chrysostom's own appeal was addressed to the Bishops of Rome, Aquileia and Milan. In the same way he earned a reputation for orthodoxy by supporting Augustine against the Pelagians. And here is to be seen a characteristic example of the way in which Innocent could use such a controversy to forward the claims of his own see. In answering the letter from the Council of Carthage, communicating to him the action the bishops had decided to take in the case of Celestius, he expressly commended them for referring the matter to the see of that apostle from whom all episcopal authority was derived.

Nevertheless he was not always successful when he intervened in the affairs of other churches. When Antioch tried to usurp the ecclesiastical jurisdiction over the island of Cyprus, which was now growing in importance, he tried to lay down the principle that ecclesiastical authority need not follow the shifting requirements of civil government, and this he used as an argument in favour of Antioch. But as we have seen, the claim of Antioch was not allowed, and although Innocent's principle received a large measure of assent in after years, for the time being it was felt wise to delimit the spheres of Church government along the same lines as those of secular authority.

Not all the Roman bishops handled the question of appeals with the same ability as Innocent. To act as a judge in other men's affairs may seem to increase one's own importance, but it may also provide an opportunity for making ludicrous mistakes. So the two succeeding Popes found to their cost in the case of Apiarius. This person was a priest of Sicca, in Africa, who in 417 was deposed by his diocesan, and appealed against the sentence to Zosimus of Rome. The Pope, quoting the famous canon of Sardica on the subject of appeals as if it came from Nicea, ordered Apiarius to be reinstated. The African bishops, however, instead of complying with the order, replied that they would investigate the authority of this alleged canon of Nicea. Meanwhile Zosimus died and Apiarius confessed his guilt of those misdemeanours for which he had been deposed. He was then restored to his priestly functions, but not to his former

cure at Sicca. Then came the answer from the Eastern bishops to the effect that the canon quoted by Zosimus was not to be found among the canons of the Council of Nicea.

Apiarius, however, again fell into the same sins and was again removed from office, and again appealed to the Pope. Coelestine, the new tenant of the papal see, took the same line as his predecessor and demanded the priest's restoration. But again Apiarius confessed, and much confusion fell on the papal legates who had demanded the carrying into effect of Coelestine's decision. The African bishops thereupon wrote to Coelestine the letter *Optaremus*, which in effect invited the Pope henceforth to mind his own business.

A better day dawned for the Papacy when Leo I began to rule (440–461). Leo was one of the greatest of all ecclesiastical statesmen, and has been called the Father of the Papacy. The whole world was fortunate in having at Rome the one really great man of his day during the invasions of Attila and Gaiseric. He was the only person who could exercise an effective influence on the barbarians. When Attila was invading Italy in 452, Leo met him at Venice and persuaded him to turn back.

Leo was thoroughly aware of his own power and was determined to use it and extend it for the benefit of the Church. He was fully persuaded that as successor and mystical impersonator of Peter, the Pope was supreme over all Churches. Indeed in him Peter was still present in his own see and was the source both of sacerdotal grace and of ecclesiastical authority. So ruthless was Leo in the exercise of what he believed to be his rights, that he even deprived of all metropolitical authority in Gaul the saintly Hilary of Arles, because he had dared to depose from office a bishop who had appealed to the Pope. His action in this matter was vindicated in a rescript by Valentinian III, in 445. Thus, as Dr. Kidd says, a papal autocracy was riveted on the Western Empire by the whole force of the civil law. He would be blind to the facts of history who did not realise that in one respect at least this was a great gain. It was the prestige of the Papacy more than any other single factor which tamed the barbarian and preserved for future

generations the best elements of the ancient civilisation in the West.

In the East Leo's authority was not so generally respected. It is true that, as we shall see, he was able to set the tone of Christological decisions, but his policy in the matter of the councils between 449 and 451 was more than once rejected, and it was against his express wishes that at Chalcedon the see of Constantinople was given jurisdiction over Pontus, Thrace and Asia Minor. Hence developed a rivalry between Rome and Constantinople which ultimately led to the schism between East and West.

II

The eastern half of the Empire was at this time suffering from troubles with the barbarians just as was the West, and the pious but weak Emperor Theodosius was quite incapable of coping with them. The principal enemies were the Huns, under their ferocious king Attila. To deal with them was left a woman in the person of Theodosius' far abler sister Pulcheria, who succeeded him in 450. She married herself to the general Marcian, and so raised into power the only soldier who was capable of checking the barbarians. She was harassed not only by external enemies, but also by the continuance of ecclesiastical controversy. The Eastern bishops as a whole had never reconciled themselves to the deposition of Nestorius, and they had a particular objection to the anathemas enunciated by Cyril. The latter, however, was determined to gain what advantage he could out of the controversy and adopted most reprehensible methods, at one time running his church of Alexandria into a debt of £60,000 in order to bribe the entourage of Pulcheria. The church of Antioch endeavoured to mediate in the dispute and eventually sent Paul of Emesa to Alexandria with a formulary of reunion. Paul was well received by Cyril, who took him into communion, and in 432 even allowed him to preach in Alexandria. Although Cyril did not withdraw his anathemas, some of his supporters thought that he was going too far in a Nestorian direction. In order

to satisfy them and ward off their suspicions, he was led to use a somewhat unguarded expression, speaking of the 'one incarnate nature of the Word of God'. This, however, did not immediately excite fresh turmoil. After the mission of Paul of Emesa there followed a decade of theological peace until the death of Cyril in 444.

The unfortunate phrase, however, found an echo in the teaching of Eutyches, the archimandrite of a monastery of three hundred monks near Constantinople. He exaggerated Cyril's doctrine so far as to say that at the Incarnation the Godhead and the manhood were 'blended and confused' in Christ. This implied that there were two natures before the Incarnation and only one nature after it, and from this implication Eutyches did not shrink. Such teaching was hotly opposed by Flavian, the Bishop of Constantinople, but Eutyches had the support both of the monks and also of his godson, Chrysaphius, the powerful favourite of Theodosius II. Flavian had omitted to bribe this courtier, who was consequently at the complete disposal of Eutyches and his ally, Dioscorus, the nephew and successor of Cyril at Alexandria. With such support the party of Eutyches was at first victorious, and penalties began to fall heavily upon the friends of Nestorius. Irenaeus, Bishop of Tyre, was banished, as was also Ibas of Edessa, while Theodoret of Cyrus was confined to his diocese.

This Theodoret has been described as the Augustine of the East. He was a great pastor as well as a first-class theologian, and had won back ten thousand Marcionites to the Catholic fold. But he incurred the wrath of the Eutychians by writing a dialogue, *Eranistes*, or the Beggarman, in which he had held up their views to ridicule. Their wrath was further inflamed when Flavian summoned a synod at Constantinople in 448, at which Eutyches was condemned. Both parties now sought support at Rome.

The traditional alliance of Rome was with Alexandria, but the very unpleasant character and the ambition of Dioscorus made this friendship no longer possible. Leo's reply took the form of a Tome, or summary of Christian doctrine, on the subject. This was in essence a restatement

of the formula 'two natures in one person'. It contains the following important points:

(a) Christ is the true Son of God and is yet of real human birth;

(b) The two natures of Godhead and manhood meet in Him and remain without confusion in the one Person;

(c) Each nature thus retains its own sphere of action;

(d) Nevertheless the properties of each nature are all alike available for the one Person;

(e) To say that there were two natures before the union is as foolish as to say that there is only one after it.

Leo believed that this statement of his should be enough to settle the question, and that therefore no council would be needed. However, through the influence of Dioscoros and Chrysaphius at court a council was summoned and met at Ephesus in 449. The composition of this council was anti-Nestorian. Theodoret and Ibas were debarred but the abbot Barsumas was summoned, this being the first time that a monk was given a seat at a council. The papal legates brought Leo's Tome to Flavian, but Dioscorus presided and the Pope's letter was not read. There were about 130 bishops present and their behaviour was such that Leo nicknamed the gathering *Latrocinium* or Robbers' Council. Eutyches was restored and Flavian was deposed, receiving such injuries at the hands of the monks as to cause his death. So great was the terror inspired that even of the papal legates only one was strong enough to voice his objection to the proceedings. The council, such as it was, ended in a complete victory for Dioscorus and the Alexandrian Christology. The chief representatives of the opposite views, Theodoret and Ibas, were deprived. And Dioscorus was strong enough in the support of Theodosius the Emperor to excommunicate Leo himself. Nevertheless Theodoret made a formal appeal to Leo, who now did his best to get another council summoned.

The situation was changed with dramatic suddenness when Theodosius fell from his horse and died (450). Pulcheria reversed her brother's policy and removed Chrysa-

phius by execution. In that very year a synod met at Constantinople, anathematised Eutyches, and restored some of the exiled bishops to their sees. Leo was more or less content with this and now shrank from the holding of another general council unless it could meet in the West. He was, however, again overruled, and it was determined to summon a great council. The first intention was to hold it at Nicea, but Marcian wished to be near the capital in case of alarm from the Huns, and it was decided that the council should be held at Chalcedon (451). As a preliminary caution all monks were ordered away from the vicinity of the main routes to the city so that it might be safe for the bishops to travel.

It was the largest council yet held; there were between 520 and 630 bishops present, but all except the papal legates and two refugees from Africa were Eastern. The imperial officers arranged the agenda and the papal legates sat beside them in the place of honour. Dioscorus was made to take his seat among the accused. The Palestinian bishops deserted him, leaving him with only twelve supporters. His teaching was condemned and he was himself sent into exile in Paphlagonia, where three years later he died. The Tome of Leo was accepted as dogma, and the council would have been glad to leave the matter there. But Marcian was anxious that the council should itself put forward an official definition of the faith, and a committee was appointed to draw it up. At first the only phrase upon which the committee could agree was that Christ was 'of two natures'. The imperial commissioners were not content with that, because, as they justly objected, Dioscorus could have said the same. The matter was referred to the Emperor, and was then sent to the committee for a fresh discussion. They now agreed to the formula 'in two natures'. This was what had been wanted all the time, for it asserted that the two natures in Christ remained distinct, and thus put an end to all Eutychianism in authoritative Church teaching. The phrase was inserted into an elaborate *Definition*, for the solemn reading of which Marcian and Pulcheria came in state to the council.

Du Bose sums up the doctrinal position by saying that

now 'for the first time along with the Athanasian statement
of the real divinity of the incarnate Lord there was posited
something like a corresponding and adequate statement
of the reality and actuality of His humanity'. Its keynote
was taken from the Tome of Leo, *'totus in suis, totus in
nostris'*. Jesus Christ was consubstantial with the Father as
touching His Godhead and consubstantial with us as touching His manhood. The two natures remain in Him without
confusion, without change, without division, without
separation. It was thus an essentially Roman formula forced
on the East by the imperial authority. It has all the Roman
directness in stating plainly the doctrine to be believed.
But it was unsatisfactory in that it explained nothing. In
recent times it has been said to represent the bankruptcy of
Greek theological thought. Certainly there are very few
modern scholars who would be content with a Christology
that viewed the two natures of our Lord as acting in a kind
of balance, so that when one is in operation the other is in
abeyance. Happily in this particular the Chalcedonian
Definition is a good deal less extreme than Leo's famous
Tome.

Its effect upon the ecclesiastical politics of the East was
profound. Alexandria remained unconvinced and retained
her essentially monophysite teaching. Her defeat on the
Christological question meant a grave loss of prestige and
carried with it a feeling of inferiority in comparison with
her rival, Constantinople. This difference between Alexandria and the centre of the Empire was most unfortunate,
as it coincided with the rising nationalism of the border
countries. This is the real origin of the separated Eastern
Churches, such as the Coptic, Armenian and Syrian. It did
more to break up the Empire than the attacks of the
barbarians.

In addition to fixing the terms of settlement to the theological difficulty the council also did other important
business. Theodoret and Ibas were restored; monks were
placed under the jurisdiction of the bishops; it was ordered
that clergy should not engage in trade or forsake the church
in which they had been ordained; disputes between clergy

and their bishops were to be taken to their exarch or to the Bishop of Constantinople; and, as we have seen, the patriarchal administration was advanced by putting Palestine under the control of Jerusalem and placing Pontus, Asia and Thrace under the jurisdiction of Constantinople. This sums up the work of the fourth Oecumenical Council. It is clear that in spite of the somewhat unworthy methods employed and of the real evils that resulted some valuable decisions were reached, and a definition of faith was laid down which, if it did not explain Christian doctrine, at least stated plainly the limits within which alone a satisfactory doctrine could be formulated.

A noteworthy attempt to re-establish the theological prestige of the Council has been made by Dr. R. V. Sellers in his book "The Council of Chalcedon" (S.P.C.K) 1954. He affirms that the famous *Definition* is a real contribution to Christology inasmuch as it combines and reconciles the three main traditions of Alexandria, Antioch and Rome.

CHAPTER XXII

THE OUTSKIRTS OF EMPIRE

IF the events connected with the last two general councils have led us to feel how far Christianity in the fifth century fell below its own early standards, we shall find the balance redressed when we consider the fortunes of the Church on the borderland between the Empire and the uncivilised world.

I

Armenia was the first country in which Christianity became the established religion. Since 69 B.C., when it was captured by Lucullus, the land between the upper waters of the Euphrates and Tigris had been reckoned part of Roman territory, although it was governed by its own native princes.

It was converted to Christianity by Gregory the Illuminator (257–331), an Armenian prince who as an infant had been carried away to Caesarea and there brought up in the Christian faith. The ruling prince of Armenia at the time of its conversion was Tiridates. He had made a determination to oppose the spread of Mazdaism by adopting the religion of his powerful Roman neighbours. He therefore sent Gregory, who had returned to his native country, back to Caesarea to obtain consecration as bishop (302). Gregory brought teachers from Cappadocia, Nisibis, and Edessa, but the work was hampered by the absence of a proper Armenian script until the fifth century, and the liturgy was conducted at first in Greek and Syriac. Nevertheless the new Christian Church was frankly national. The people were converted *en bloc*; the temples were turned into churches and the pagan priests were ordained into the Christian ministry.

Of this national Church Gregory became the Catholicos, that is to say the head of a practically independent church, owing only a slight duty of homage to another ecclesiastic. In this case the outside authority was that of Caesarea, whose influence during the early years was very great because of the hasty and imperfect way in which the conversion of the country had been carried out. The position of Catholicos, which was only less in dignity than that of Patriarch, was regarded in Armenia as hereditary, on the pattern of the Jewish High Priesthood. Gregory's grandson, Joussik, on succeeding to the office found it necessary to tighten up the organisation and to reform the manners of the people. For this excess of zeal he was murdered by order of the king Divan. There followed a period of rivalry between King and Catholicos. Joussik's grandson, Narses, who was brought up at Caesarea under Basil, tried to initiate a new reform but met the fate of his forebear, being poisoned by King Pap (373). Now ensued a pagan reaction, and many of the old idolatrous customs were restored. Basil sent a commission to set in order the affairs of the Church but he could not find suitable men for bishops. King Pap presented his own candidate, a certain Faustus, whom Basil would not accept. Faustus thereupon secured consecration at the hands of Anthimus of Tyana, and thus Armenia was set free from the tutelage of Caesarea.

A new epoch in the history of the Armenian Church started with the annexation of the greater part of the country by Persia in 387. The Church was at this time ruled by a descendant of Gregory named Isaac. He, with the monk Mesrob, constructed an Armenian alphabet, and began the foundation of an Armenian literature by translating the Septuagint. But in the middle of the fifth century King Jazdgerd II turned pagan and tried to make his people embrace the religion of Ormuzd. Seven hundred Magi were sent to superintend the conversion of the country and there followed a serious persecution. To this period belongs the martyrdom of the Leontian Christians, a body of forty soldiers who were left naked to freeze on an ice-bound lake. Toleration was introduced under Jazdgerd's

successor, but favour was shown only to apostates. It was not until after a revolt in 481 that religious equality was secured.

The Armenians were no more successful in escaping heresy than in avoiding persecution. Since the Emperor Marcian gave them no help in their struggles they had no interest in the Council of Chalcedon, and since the hated Persians took the Nestorian side in the current disputes it was inevitable that the Armenians should take the opposite view. They have ever since been reckoned Monophysites. But since they condemn Eutyches, and since their language cannot distinguish between Nature and Person, they can hardly be said to have been guilty of more than a technical error.

II. PERSIA

Persian Christianity came chiefly from Edessa, which, as a separate princedom between Armenia and Persia proper, formed the gateway to the East and North-east. This was the home of Syriac Christianity, and the place where the Peshitto version of the Bible was produced. It was the centre in which Semitic thought fought its battle with Hellenism for the honour of providing a mould for the development of Christian doctrine. Had it not lent itself to some aberrations in the early years, it might have left a more permanent impression than it ultimately succeeded in doing. But it was here that Bardesanes, the Gnostic, received much support, and here again that Tatian, the fierce disciple of Justin Martyr, nearly replaced the Four Gospels with his Diatessaron. When these extreme views had been shed, Edessa developed its thought on Antiochene lines, and Theodoret of Cyrus, Diodore of Tarsus and its own Bishop Ibas built up the type of theology which was widely reckoned as Nestorian. With Edessa was associated in this respect the neighbouring city of Nisibis. These did not, as is sometimes thought, provide a home for two different schools, but one school, which was transferred from Nisibis to Edessa in 363, and then was moved back to Nisibis in 489. Such is the ancestry of what we now know as the Assyrian Church, and the two cities share the honour of starting

the missions to China and India, the history of which is hard to trace but which certainly had a great, if temporary, success. *

The organisation of the Church in Persia is somewhat mysterious. Christians seem to have been grouped in communities consisting of ascetics of both sexes and including the usual orders of bishop, priest, and deacon, but what was the relation between these 'Children of the Covenant', as they called themselves, and ordinary Christians is not clear. Probably their organisation would be found, if sufficient details were available, to offer a close parallel to that of the Celtic Church of Ireland. At first they seem to have enjoyed a quiet history. In spite of the prevailing Mazdaism they were tolerated, and in 333 we find Constantine recommending them to the good offices of the Persian king Sapor II. When, however, Sapor began his wars with Constantine and tried to recover his lost provinces, all Christians, just because they were co-religionists of the Romans, became potential enemies, and they were made to endure forty years of persecution. A hundred of the faithful suffered martyrdom in the first massacre on Good Friday, 341, and by the end of Sapor's reign in 379 the names of no fewer than 16,000 martyrs were recorded.

During a period of peace the Church was re-organised at the synod of Seleucia-Ctesiphon in 410, under the Patriarch of Antioch but with its own Catholicos at Seleucia. Persecution again broke out during the wars with Rome under Bahram V. It was necessary for Persian Christians to show themselves loyal nationalists; they also desired to improve their position in Persia by strengthening their own local organisation. For both reasons they declared themselves independent of Antioch at the synod of Marcabta in 424. For the same reasons they refused to accept orthodoxy as defined at Chalcedon, and declared themselves Nestorian in 484; not indeed that they followed Nestorius, but that they accepted the teaching of Ibas and Theodoret. Thus it is to be noticed that Nestorianism, like Arianism, when condemned within the Empire began to flourish outside.

III. BRITAIN

The beginnings of Christianity in the British Isles are shrouded in the mists of legend. Stories connected with the names of S. Paul, Joseph of Arimathea, Bran and Lucius can, as far as we are concerned, be left to the sphere of ecclesiastical romance. Scientific deductions may be made from the following facts: Irenaeus, giving a list of Christian lands about the year 176, does not mention Britain, but Tertullian (*c*. 208) and Origen (239) both number Britain among the countries in which the gospel has been preached. It may therefore be concluded that Christianity reached Britain somewhere about the end of the second century. Whence it came is not certain but the probability is that it arrived *viâ* Gaul, and some have suggested that it came as the result of the persecution at Lyons and Vienne. This, however, is neither certain nor necessary. In the absence of the name of any great missionary it is likely that it travelled in the train of soldiers and merchants who recognised the duty enjoined upon every follower of Christ to work for the extension of His kingdom.

The notices of Christianity during the Roman occupation are only fragmentary. The first martyr seems to have been the Roman soldier Alban, but it is uncertain whether he perished during the Decian or the Diocletian persecution. Constantine was declared Emperor at York in 306, and one at least of his recent biographers thinks that by that time he was already a Christian. In 314 three British bishops, those of York, London, and probably Lincoln, were present at the Council of Arles, and it is noteworthy that all three towns were Roman camps. Athanasius asserts that British bishops were among those who defended him by signing the letter of the Council of Sardica in 343, and we know that in 359 three British bishops availed themselves of the imperial transport facilities for their journey to the Council of Ariminum. Chrysostom and Jerome join with Athanasius in attesting the orthodoxy of the British Church, but about 400 Victricius of Rouen came over to settle some personal quarrel among the bishops, and by 410 Britain had been

responsible for producing the heresiarch Pelagius. It is therefore possible that the British Church was tainted with both the Arian and the Pelagian heresies. Other delegates from Gaul were Germanus of Auxerre and Lupus of Troyes, who were sent over to win Britain to orthodoxy in 429. A conference was held at Verulam (S. Albans), after which it is said that the British won their famous Alleluia victory against the Picts. Apparently false teaching did not die out at once, for Germanus returned to Britain in 447 to complete his work of restoration.

Interesting questions arise about the position and condition of the Early Church in Britain. How far was it the Church of the people and how far that of their Roman masters? It is quite likely that it was a genuinely native Church, for the bishops are described as British, and Harnack points out that Christianity never became the religion of the camp. It has been suggested that it may have been the religion of the wealthy landowners, but against that we must set the facts that some of the bishops had to accept imperial aid for their transport to continental councils and that they were too poor to build their churches of stone. With regard to the organisation of the Church in Britain it has often been assumed that it must have followed the same tribal lines as were characteristic of Ireland. But the evidence seems to point the other way. It is significant that the bishops whom we have mentioned are known by the name of their sees. It is possible that there were some unattached bishops, like Fastidius, a semi-Pelagian writer, who has no diocese to his name. Nevertheless it is probable that the organisation was generally diocesan.

In the fall of the Roman Empire the British Church was less fortunate than that of some other lands. The Jutes and Saxons had not been christianised like the Goths, and they showed a special rage against the churches and their priests. This explains both the destruction of all traces of Christianity in the conquered territory and the fact that British Christians made no attempt to convert their neighbours. The British indeed seem to have been either destroyed or pushed into the west of the island. Nevertheless they were still sufficiently

in touch with the continent about 455 to accept, at the request of Pope Leo, the Roman cycle for the finding of Easter. Unfortunately for them Rome twice after that changed her basis of calculation, and consequently, when Augustine arrived in 597 there was a discrepancy between the customs of the two Christian bodies which made immediate co-operation somewhat difficult.

Of affairs in Scotland we know very little. The South Picts, who were in closest contact with the British, were evangelised by a missionary named Ninian about 397. His stone church was sufficiently remarkable to have left its memorial in the name of Whithern or White House. Such Christians as existed there during our period were finally driven out into Ireland.

Of Ireland a good deal more is known, although we can only guess how Christianity first found an entry into the country. Two possibilities present themselves: it may have come direct from Britain, or it may have come in the company of Greek merchants from the neighbourhood of Lyons. But at any rate it must have been already there when in 431 Pope Coelestine sent Palladius, who had been a deacon of Germanus, to 'the Scots who believed in Christ'. A more famous evangelist was Patrick, son of a British deacon, who at the age of sixteen was caught by pirates and taken captive to Ireland. After many years he escaped, and desiring to bring the gospel to those among whom he had dwelt so long, he received ordination, and returning in 432 laboured in Ireland until his death in 461.

Roman arms and organisation had not broken down the tribal system in Ireland, and it was perhaps natural that the Christian Church should develop there along tribal lines. Dioceses as territorial units do not seem to have existed, but running parallel with the tribe was an organisation of Christian ascetics within which were to be found one or more bishops. Although this organisation was peculiar, it is not to be supposed that Ireland lost all touch with continental Christianity. Patrick himself obtained episcopal consecration from Martin of Tours, and Irish merchants were holding communications with far parts

of the Empire when the British were completely cut off. This was of benefit to the continent itself, for in Ireland sprang up wonderful schools of art and learning which supplied Europe with its greatest treasures in days when the barbarians had caused the eclipse of such pursuits elsewhere.

CHAPTER XXIII

THE BEGINNING OF THE DARK AGES

I

POLITICALLY the fifth century saw the break-up of the Roman Empire, the consolidation of the barbarian gains, and the separation between East and West. In the East the emperors, although they were continually on the defensive against the barbarians, managed to maintain their own authority because their power was not rivalled by that of excessively able generals within their own forces. But in the West the story was very different. In the first quarter of the century the Visigoths made good their settlement in the south of Gaul, and in the second the Vandals settled in Africa, while there were continual inroads of Huns in Gaul and Italy. The defence against these adversaries was undertaken by barbarian generals in Roman service, who gradually displaced the emperors and finally dispensed with them altogether.

Half-way through the century, however, the hero was no barbarian, but Aetius, 'the last of the Romans', who recovered Gaul, checked the Visigoths, and kept the Vandals out of Italy. In the year of the Council of Chalcedon he had assisted at the repulse of Attila in the battle of the Mauriac Plain outside Troyes. The Roman advantage was not pressed home and the following year Attila destroyed Aquileia. It was after this that Pope Leo, with two members of the Senate, induced the Hunnish king to turn back from his advance on Rome. The fate of the imperial city was not long delayed. Gaiseric, the Vandal king, had already taken Carthage, and had since been busy consolidating the barbarian forces. Consequently when Attila died and Aetius was assassinated by the jealous Valentinian III (454), he was able to proceed to the sack of Rome in 455.

At the entreaty, so it is said, of Pope Leo the Vandals contented themselves with plunder, and vacated the city after a fortnight. The next *magister militum*, successor of Stilicho and Aetius, was Ricimer, but unlike them he was a German. Nevertheless he had sufficient reverence for Roman policy to set up one emperor after another. This reverence did not carry him so far as to preserve Rome inviolate, and when his own power was threatened he took the occasion of a civil war to capture the city in 472, thus bringing about the third fall of Rome within the century. Ricimer died in the same year and his place was effectively filled by one of his officers, Odovacar, who was not beset by the scruples of his master.

In 476 Odovacar was elected king of the Germanic tribes in Italy, and promptly deposed Romulus Augustulus, the last Emperor of the West. This did not mean any violent change in the system of government, because Zeno, the Eastern Emperor, now became nominally the ruler over the whole Empire. Nevertheless Odovacar bore the title of king, which his soldiers had bestowed upon him, although to the Romans he was no more than *patricius*. But he actually did rule in the West, and with him a new era began.

After seventeen years this somewhat ambiguous kingship was seized by the Ostrogoth Theodoric, who first defeated, and then murdered Odovacar. He set himself to appoint Roman officials and to preserve as far as possible the Roman system of government, but he made the kingdom of Italy an established fact, though like his predecessor he helped to build a bridge between the old and the new worlds by distributing a third of the public lands belonging to the Treasury among his soldiers.

In the meantime the Empire had managed to preserve itself in the East. In 457 Marcian had been succeeded by Leo, who set a precedent in receiving his coronation at the hand of the Patriarch of Constantinople. Warned by the fate which befel his Western colleagues at the hand of Ricimer, Leo was determined not to allow the power of his own military commander to grow excessive. In order to

prevent this happening he sought the aid of the Isaurians, who provided him with a bodyguard under the command of Zeno, and ultimately secured the murder of Aspar, the *magister militum*. This Zeno afterwards became Emperor, and made peace with the Vandals, who under Gaiseric had played an evil part in the history of both East and West. Owing to the unpopularity of his Isaurian favourites, Zeno was driven for a time to take refuge in his own country, by the usurper Basiliscus, but he made an effective return and continued to reign in comparative security until 491. This he did in spite of many troubles with the Goths, which were only ended when Theodoric withdrew from the gates of Constantinople to challenge Odovacar for the kingdom of Italy. Zeno was succeeded by Anastasius, a silentiary who shortly before had been a candidate for the see of Antioch, but proved a sufficiently astute ruler to retain his title until 518.

II

Ecclesiastical affairs during the latter half of the fifth century reflected in many respects this political situation. Particularly was this so in the growing separation between East and West. The Council of Chalcedon had left to posterity two special causes of difficulty. Theologically it had failed to reconcile Pope Leo to the Christology of Cyril, and on the institutional side it had caused a breach between Rome and Constantinople. In outlining the jurisdiction of the patriarchates it acted on the assumption that the organisation of the Church should follow that of the State. Roman interests had caused to be inserted into the sixth canon of the Council of Nicea a gloss to the effect that 'the Church of Rome has always had the pre-eminence', but this pre-eminence did not apply to jurisdiction, and Chalcedon gave to Constantinople the chief authority in the East because it was the seat of government. But if that principle had applied in the West it would have meant that the Bishop of Ravenna would have ruled over the Bishop of Rome. Consequently although Leo was induced to declare his assent to the doctrinal decisions of the Council

of Chalcedon he would by no means accept its decisions on jurisdiction.

Obviously in this disagreement there was cause for very considerable anxiety. It only required two resolute bishops to bring matters to a head. Such were not long in being found, when in 471 Acacius was appointed Bishop of Constantinople. During the papacy of Simplicius he had little trouble in consolidating his power, avoiding open conflict with the Pope by the simple expedient of refusing to answer his letters. But when in 483 Felix III became Pope the crisis arrived. A point of dispute was found in the position of Peter Mongus or the Stammerer, who, though an avowed Monophysite, had been supported as Bishop of Alexandria by Acacius. Felix sent a deputation ordering Acacius to appear and answer the complaint lodged against him by the rival claimant to the see of Alexandria, John Talaia. Far from so doing Acacius promptly placed the name of Peter Mongus on the diptychs. The Pope was unfortunate in the legates to whom he entrusted this business, for they fraternised with the enemy. For this, although two of them were bishops, they were excommunicated on their return by a synod of seventy-seven bishops. But a far more important step was taken by the synod in presuming to declare the Patriarch of Constantinople deposed (July 28, 484). The letter despatched by the Pope to inform Acacius of this sentence announced that he had no longer the right to the name of priest or to the exercise of sacerdotal functions, and that there was no possibility of his ever being released from the anathema. To serve such a writ was naturally a matter of some difficulty, but it was conveyed secretly to certain monks in Constantinople who were in antagonism to the Patriarch, and during service at S. Sophia one of them managed to pin it to Acacius' pallium. Needless to say, this document had little effect in the East, but it consummated the ecclesiastical separation between East and West, the actual schism lasting till 519.

Before the century had run out Rome itself was once again in the throes of schism. In 498 there was a disputed election, Laurentius and Symmachus being favoured by

rival factions. It is interesting to notice that the matter was referred to the King, Theodoric, though he was a Goth and an Arian. He declared that the candidate who had the majority vote was to be regarded as elected. Thereupon Symmachus became Pope, while Laurentius was compensated with the bishopric of Nuceria. However, this was not the end of the matter. Various charges were brought against Symmachus and a strong effort was made to depose him. The King ordered the Pope to answer these charges before himself, and on his refusal saw to it that properly constituted synods met to deal with the matter. Of these there were no less than five, some of them of a very disorderly nature, and it was only at Theodoric's direct command that a final judgment was made. This went in favour of Symmachus.

Thus even in the West there was at this time a much closer association between the Church and the State than is sometimes recognised. A further illustration can be found in the number of public officials who were induced to accept the office of bishop. Paulinus of Nola had been the consular official of Campania before he was ordained; Sidonius Apollinaris was Prefect of Rome before he became Bishop of Auvergne; and Germanus of Auxerre, whose intervention rescued Britain from heresy, also came from the civil service. Experience in affairs was excellent training for a bishop, and a good bishop was of great value to the government. Ever since 408 the Western bishops had exercised certain rights of civil jurisdiction. In his own see-town the bishop was generally recognised as *defensor civitatis*, a position which often, if not always, made him the most acceptable mediator between the citizens and their barbarian conquerors. One particular duty that often fell to his lot was the redemption of captives. Thus when Epiphanius pointed out to Theodoric that the lands of Liguria lay uncultivated because so many of the men had been carried away captive by the Burgundians, the King placed money at his disposal and the bishop bought back the men to the number of six thousand. On the other hand an evil result of this connexion was seen in the facility with which a conqueror or triumphant claimant to office would remove his rival by

compelling him to take Orders. What was probably the
first instance of this occurred in 474 when Julius Nepos,
Emperor of the West, had his unsuccessful rival, Glycerius,
consecrated Bishop of Salona. Later Marcian, who rose
against Zeno, was captured and ordained, but this did not
prevent his subsequent escape and proclamation as Emperor.
And even Anastasius, who succeeded Zeno, compelled
Longinus, his predecessor's brother, to be ordained. It is
obvious that here, as elsewhere, the close intermingling of
the affairs of Church and State was fraught with possibilities
of evil as well as of good.

III

When we turn to the theological controversies of the
period we have again to consider the dubious legacy of
Chalcedon. That council, as we have seen, failed to reconcile
Rome with Alexandria. By acknowledging our Lord 'in'
two natures rather than 'of' two natures it had expressly
closed the door to all who believed that in the Incarnate
there was only one resultant nature of God-made-man.
This, no doubt, was inevitable, but it was unfortunate that
nothing was done to conciliate these Monophysites, since
there was an overwhelming number of them in Egypt,
especially among the native population. When Dioscorus,
the notorious Alexandrian bishop who favoured these
views, was driven into exile, his successor Proterius was
appointed through the instrumentality of the ruling class,
which was mainly Greek. Here was an excellent opportunity
for anyone with a talent for intrigue.

The occasion was seized by Timothy Aelurus ('the Cat').
He, when Dioscorus died at Gangra, got himself elected
bishop, and caused the body of Proterius to be dragged
through the city streets and then burnt. He was driven out
later and replaced by another Timothy (Salophaciol, or
'White Turban'), but he returned on the crest of the Monophysite wave that came in with Basiliscus. He started the
succession of Monophysite bishops in Alexandria, of whom
one, Peter Mongus, was the cause of the schism between
East and West, and with him effectively began that Coptic

Church which has remained the native Egyptian expression of Christianity to the present day.

A somewhat similar disaster for the cause of unity and orthodoxy befell at Antioch. There the leadership of the Monophysites was undertaken by a former monk, Peter the Fuller, who secured consecration as bishop in 471. He enjoyed a stormy episcopate, being exiled three times, but he was supported by the same violent measures that prevailed at Alexandria. One of his orthodox rivals, Stephen, was waylaid in a suburban church and stabbed to death with pointed reeds. But Peter was capable of subtler methods. It is to him that we owe the introduction of the Nicene Creed into the Eucharist. As so employed it emphasised the Monophysites' repudiation of Chalcedon, since they desired no other creed than that of Nicea. Another liturgical innovation made by Peter consisted of an emendation of the Trisagion. To the words, 'Holy God, Holy and Mighty, Holy and Immortal,' he added the phrase 'crucified for us', which audaciously affirmed the unity of nature at its most vulnerable point, and gave his followers a battle-cry with which they could shout down their opponents both in church and in the street.

It was inevitable that, when not only the unity of the Church was threatened but also that of the Empire, government should take a hand. Basiliscus, during his short usurpation, took up whole-heartedly the Monophysite position and despatched an encyclical to the bishops demanding their adherence. But that raised so great a storm that he was compelled to withdraw it, and even so failed to preserve his power. When Zeno returned he set himself to restore order by going back behind Chalcedon to the point where ways had diverged. This attempt was embodied in the famous *Henoticon* or Union Document of 482, which seems to have been largely the work of Acacius of Constantinople and Peter Mongus of Alexandria. In this both Nestorius and Eutyches were condemned but the Twelve Anathemas of Cyril were approved. It says that Christ is one and not two, and it admits neither division nor confusion nor unreal appearance. The true character of the document can be

seen from its careful omission of any reference to 'nature', whether one or two. For this reason it aroused strenuous opposition at Rome, which stood steadfastly by the Tome of Leo. Acacius, as the chief author of the document, incurred the special enmity of the Popes. Thus the ground was prepared for the schism of 484. Zeno's policy having failed, Anastasius tried to improve upon it, and make terms with Rome. All his efforts, however, failed, and peace was only effected by his successor Justin in 519 on the condition of the deletion of Acacius' name from the diptychs and the anathematising of Monophysites.

Such was the fate of the Henoticon in the West. In the East, however, its fortunes were more diverse. At Antioch Peter the Fuller, whose Monophysite proclivities were notorious, accepted it. If it seem strange that Antioch should have yielded to a theology so unlike that of its famous school, the reason is to be found in the fact that the centre of the Antiochene theology had now shifted to Edessa. There the school which had been started after the surrender of Nisibis to the Persians in 363 had consistently developed a Nestorian type of theology, although that fact had not prevented some of its leaders from anathematising Nestorius himself. It is true that this tendency had sometimes brought them into opposition to the bishops of the see. Rabbulas, for instance, who became bishop in 412, was an ardent supporter of Cyril, and tried to bring his people into line with what he believed to be the policy of the Empire. He, however, was succeeded by Ibas (435) and then the Nestorian influence, deriving itself not from Nestorius but from Theodore of Mopsuestia, came in full tide. The most important teacher of this type was a pupil of Ibas, named Barsumas. He with a number of others suffered exile when a Monophysite bishop, Nonnus, succeeded to Ibas. They returned, however, and Barsumas became Bishop of Nisibis. There he welcomed his old friends in 489, when Zeno, fearing the Nestorian influence of Edessa, closed the school in that city. Barsumas won support from the Persian government by showing how opposed were he and his friends to the theology of Zeno and the Byzantine 'Romans', and thus

was confirmed the separation of that Persian Nestorian Church which, as we have already seen, during its period of brilliance spread as far afield as India and China.

While the Persian, or as it is now more usually styled, the Assyrian Church, was thus becoming Nestorian, the Armenian was fast becoming Monophysite. This was partly due to revolt against the tendencies of its neighbour, but also to the influence of Monophysite bishops of Antioch. The acceptance of the Monophysite position was confirmed at the time when Zeno was seeking to enforce the Henoticon and had closed the school at Edessa. In 491 the Catholicos Babken summoned a council at Valarschapat, which condemned both the Tome of Leo and the Council of Chalcedon. After the healing of the schism between Rome and Constantinople in 519 there followed a period of persecution for the Monophysites, but later their church was reorganised by Jacob Barodaeus, for which reason the West Syrian Monophysites are often known as Jacobites.

IV

During the second half of the fifth century the Church was served by a number of able men who stood out from the general mediocrity and preserved the best traditions of the old world from the universal chaos. Of these, one of the most picturesque figures is Sidonius Apollinaris (431–489). Son-in-law of the Emperor Avitus, he had had a considerable career in the civil service before he became Bishop of Arverna[1] (c. 470), a city which was the last outpost of the Roman Empire against the conquests of Euric, King of the Visigoths. Sidonius did everything possible to aid the defence of the city, but to no purpose; it had to be surrendered in order to save Provence. For his patriotism the bishop was exiled by the conqueror, but he made his submission and was later allowed to return to his see. He has left us in his letters vivid accounts of the court of Euric and a valuable mass of information on the civil and ecclesiastical organisation of the time.

Another bishop who proved less tractable and was only

[1] Now Clermont-Ferrand.

restored to his see after Euric's death was Faustus of Riez
(*c.* 400–485). It was he whom the Imperial Government
used in its negotiations with Euric, and he was also a
theologian of note. He was British by birth, and before
becoming bishop had been head of the famous monastery
at Lérins. As such he showed himself a representative of
the school later known as the Semi-Pelagians. This is
clearly seen in his book on *The Grace of God and Free
Will*, written at the request of a council assembled at Arles,
before which, as diocesan, he had delated one of his priests,
Lucidus, an extreme Augustinian. It is Pelagius rather than
Augustine whom Faustus openly castigates in this writing,
but the actual doctrine taught is much nearer to that of his
compatriot than to that of the Bishop of Hippo. Predestination he rejects, and grace he regards as the external help
that may come to us from the hearing of sermons and so
on; yet he does acknowledge original sin and believes that
by reason of it freewill has been somewhat impaired,
though not altogether destroyed.

Another instance of the way in which the Church protected the people during the barbarian invasions is afforded
by the career of S. Severinus, who established a kind of
theocracy in Noricum when that district was left without
a ruler and unprotected by Rome. He had a special care
for the poor, and by insisting on the proper payment of
tithes by the wealthier people he was able to support those
who had suffered most from the ills attendant upon war
and from natural calamities. It was he who in his hermit
days is said to have foretold the greatness of Odovacar,
a circumstance that led the German king to treat him
with great respect when the prophecy was fulfilled.

Boethius, the greatest of the writers of the period, has
been called 'the last of the Roman philosophers and the
first scholastic'. His best-known books are the *De Trinitate*
and the *De Consolatione*. The former was written as a protest
against Arianism, which owing to the successes of the Goths
was still showing considerable power. Perhaps his greatest
contribution to theology was his definition of the term
person, 'the individual substance of a rational nature', which

through Thomas Aquinas became authoritative. In the year 523 the Emperor Justin proscribed Arianism throughout the Empire. This act naturally caused some perturbation to Theodoric, King of Italy, and his Goths, and brought suspicion on those Romans who were likely to sympathise with the Emperor. Boethius, thought to be implicated in a plot, was thrown into prison. It was then that he turned to philosophy for relief, and wrote the *De Consolatione* before his death in 525.

* Salvian was a writer who came into prominence through his effort to do what Augustine had already attempted, namely, explain why God permitted all the evils that were happening in the world. In his *De Gubernatione* Salvian makes out that while the Romans were an evil and degenerate race the barbarians were virtuous and vigorous. God was simply giving the prize to the better man. In another work, *Ad Ecclesiam*, Salvian recommends an extreme form of charity, asserting that every Christian should leave his goods to the Church and to the poor. As he himself had set the example by retaining for himself, even in his lifetime, only what was absolutely necessary, he had perhaps earned the right to express a revolutionary opinion.

The reign of Theodoric saw something like a Christian literary revival. On this account it received the approbation of Ennodius, Bishop of Pavia, who regarded rhetoric as the queen of the arts. At this time the monk Cassiodorus tried to establish a school of Christian literature at Rome. But in one respect the literary artists of the time fail us: they number among them no true historian; the best that even Epiphanius could do was to summarise the histories of Socrates, Sozomen and Theodoret, which have little information to give us on the fifth century.

By this time a situation far more important for the future of Christianity than any that had arisen in the sphere of literature or of theological controversy had been created in Gaul. The Franks, 'a federation of armed adventurers', were ruled over by the fierce but ambitious king Clovis. He was married to Clotilde, a Christian and a Catholic. Their first two children were sickly, and the mother hoped by their

baptism to secure not only their safety but the consequent conversion of the king. One child, however, died and the other survived only with difficulty. Clovis was not yet convinced. Later in a critical engagement with the Alemanni, he called for aid upon 'the God of Clotilde'. Victory was vouchsafed, and he showed his gratitude by embracing the Catholic faith. In 496 on Christmas Day he was baptised by the Bishop Remigius at Rheims with no fewer than three thousand of his warriors. The bishops recognised in him 'the new Constantine'. He was indeed the only ruler at this time whose orthodoxy could not be doubted, and he speedily set himself to spread his rule and his faith both among his pagan neighbours and among the Arian Goths. Thus the Church, which had conquered the civilised world at the beginning of the fourth century and had seen that world crumble to dust during the fifth, set herself to build it up anew at the beginning of the sixth. With the Franks there 'entered into the Church the people which was to found the pontifical State, raise the Pope to royal rank, and by establishing the Carolingian empire, constitute the Christianity of the Middle Ages'.

SELECT BOOK LIST

BACKGROUND

ANGUS, S. *The Environment of Early Christianity.*
BARKER, E. *Alexander to Constantine.*
BIGG, C. *The Church's Task under the Roman Empire.*
COCHRANE, C. N. *Christianity and Classical Culture.*
DILL, S. *Roman Society from Nero to Marcus Aurelius.*
DIX, G. *The Jew and the Greek.*
GLOVER, T. R. *The Influence of Christ in the Ancient World.*
    The Conflict of Religions in the Early Roman Empire.
HALLIDAY, W. R. *The Pagan Background of Early Christianity.*
JAEGER, W. *Early Christianity and Greek Paideia.*
MOORE, G. F. *Judaism in the First Centuries of the Christian Era.*
    2 vols.
PEROWNE, STEWART. *Hadrian.*
RAMSAY, W. *The Church in the Roman Empire.*
ZERNOV, N. *Eastern Christendom.*

LITERATURE

Introductions

ALTANER, B. *Patrology.*
CROSS, F. L. *Early Christian Fathers.*
DE LABRIOLLE. *Christian Latin Literature.*
GRANT, R. M. *The Letter and the Spirit.*
STEVENSON, J. *Studies in Eusebius.*
SWETE, H. B. *Patristic Study.*
TIXERONT, J. *Handbook of Patrology* (St. Louis, U.S.A.).
WALLACE-HADRILL, D. S. *Eusebius of Caesarea.*

Translations

BARRETT, C. K. *The New Testament Background: Selected Documents.*
BETTENSON, H. *The Early Christian Fathers* (selections).
BLAKENEY, E. H. *Lactantius' Epitome.*
DIX, G. *Canons of Hippolytus.*
DODDS, MARCUS. *Augustine's City of God.*
DRIVER AND HODGSON. *Bazaar of Heracleides.*
EASTON, B. S. *Apostolic Tradition of Hippolytus.*
EVANS, E. *Tertullian's Treatise on the Resurrection.*
    Tertullian's Treatise against Praxeas.
JAMES, M. R. *The Apocryphal New Testament.*
KIDD, B. J. *Documents Illustrative of the History of the Church.*
    2 vols.

LAWLOR AND OULTON. *Eusebius' Ecclesiastical History* (Translation and Notes). 2 vols.
QUASTEN AND PLUMPE. *Ancient Christian Writers.*
ROBERTS AND DONALDSON. *Ante-Nicene Christian Library.*
S.P.C.K. *Translations of Christian Literature.*
STEVENSON, J. *A New Eusebius.*
WACE AND SCHAFF. *Nicene and Post-Nicene Fathers.*

HISTORIES AND BROCHURES

BAYNES, N. H. *Constantine the Great and the Christian Church* (British Academy Proceedings, Vol. xv).
BAYNES AND MOSS. *Byzantium.*
BIGG, C. *The Origins of Christianity.*
BRANDON, S. G. F. *The Fall of Jerusalem and the Christian Church.*
BURN, A. E. *The Council of Nicea.*
Cambridge Medieval History. Vol. i.
CARRINGTON, PHILIP. *The Early Christian Church* (first two centuries). 2 vols.
CLARKE, C. P. S. *Church History from Nero to Constantine.*
DUCHESNE, L. *The Early History of the Christian Church.* 3 vols.
EDMUNDSON, G. *The Church in Rome in the First Century.*
EVERY, GEORGE. *The Byzantine Patriarchate.*
FOAKES-JACKSON, F. J. *History of the Christian Church to 461.*
GWATKIN, H. M. *Early Church History to 313.*
KIDD, B. J. *A History of the Church to 461.* 3 vols.
    The Churches of Eastern Christendom.
    The Roman Primacy to 461.
LANDON, E. H. *Manual of Councils of the Catholic Church.* 2 vols.
LATOURETTE, K. S. *A History of the Expansion of Christianity.* Vol. i.
LIETZMANN, H. *A History of the Early Church.* 4 vols.
PULLAN, L. *The Church of the Fathers.*
WAND, J. W. C. *First Century Christianity.*
ZANKOV, S. *The Eastern Orthodox Church.*

ORGANISATION

BARTLETT, J. V. *Church-life and Church-order during First Four Centuries.*
DOBSCHUTZ, E. VON. *Christian Life in the Primitive Church.*
EVERY, G. *The Byzantine Patriarchate.*
GORE, C. *The Church and the Ministry.*
GREENSLADE, S. L. *Schism in the Early Church.*
HATCH, E. *The Organisation of the Early Christian Churches.*
HESS, H. *The Canons of the Council of Sardica.*
HORT, F. J. A. *The Christian Ecclesia.*

HARNACK, A. *The Constitution and Laws of the Church.*
JENKINS AND MACKENZIE (editors). *Episcopacy Ancient and Modern.*
KIRK, K. E. *The Apostolic Ministry.*
LIGHTFOOT, J. B. *The Christian Ministry.*
STREETER, B. H. *The Primitive Church.*
SWETE, H. B. (editor). *The Early History of the Church and Ministry.*
WAND, J. W. C. *The Four Councils.*
WORDSWORTH, J. *The Ministry of Grace.*

PERSECUTIONS

GWATKIN, H. M. Article on *Persecutions* in Hastings' *Encyclopedia of Religion and Ethics.* Vol. IX.
HARDY, E. G. *Christianity and the Roman Government.*
MASON, A. J. *The Persecution of Diocletian.*
MERRILL, E. T. *Essays in Early Christian History.*
WORKMAN, H. B. *Persecution in the Early Church.*

DOCTRINE

BARTLETT AND CARLYLE. *Christianity in History.*
BETHUNE-BAKER, J. F. *Introduction to the Early History of Christian Doctrine.*
DU BOSE, W. P. *The Ecumenical Councils.*
GWATKIN, H. M. *Studies in Arianism.*
KELLY, J. N. D. *Early Christian Creeds.*
   Early Christian Doctrine.
McGIFFERT, A. C. *A History of Christian Thought.* 2 vols.
MOZLEY, K. *Introduction to Theology.*
PRESTIGE, G. L. *God in Patristic Thought.*
   Fathers and Heretics.
RAVEN, C. E. *Apollinarianism.*
SELLERS, R. V. *The Council of Chalcedon.*
TURNER, H. F. W. *The Patristic Doctrine of Redemption.*
WAND, J. W. C. *The Four Great Heresies.*

GNOSTICISM

BLACKMAN, E. C. *Marcion and his Influence.*
BURKITT, F. C. *Church and Gnosis.*
CROSS, F. L. *The Jung Codex.*
GÄRTNER, BERTIL. *The Theology of the Gospel of Thomas.*
GRANT, R. M. *Gnosticism—an Anthology.*
WILSON, R. McL. *Studies in the Gospel of Thomas.*
   The Gnostic Problem.

SOCIAL AND RELIGIOUS LIFE

ALLWORTHY, T. B. *Women in the Apostolic Church.*
CADOUX, C. J. *The Early Church and the World.*
CASE, S. J. *The Social Origins of Christianity* (Chicago University Press).
DAVIES, J. G. *Daily Life in the Early Church.*
  Social Life of Early Christians.
  The Making of the Church.
HARNACK, A. *The Mission and Expansion of Christianity in the First Three Centuries.*
KALTHOFF, A. *The Rise of Christianity.*
KIRK, K. E. *The Vision of God.*
LECKY, W. E. H. *History of European Morals.*
NOCK, A. D. *Conversion.*
SCULLARD, H. H. *Early Christian Ethics in the West.*
STAUFFER, E. *Christ and the Caesars.*
TROELTSCH, E. *The Social Teaching of the Christian Churches.* 2 vols.
UHLHORN, J. G. W. *Christian Charity in the Ancient Church.*
WELSFORD, A. E. *Life in the Early Church.*

WORSHIP

BRIGHTMAN AND HAMMOND. *Liturgies Eastern and Western.* 2 vols.
DIX, G. *The Shape of the Liturgy.*
DUCHESNE, L. *Christian Worship.*
FORTESCUE, A. *The Mass.*
KLAUSER, T. *The Western Liturgy.*
SRAWLEY, J. H. *The Early History of the Liturgy.*
WARREN, F. E. *The Liturgy and Ritual of the Ante-Nicene Church.*

ART

BARNES, A. S. *The Early Church in the Light of the Monuments.*
DAVIES, J. G. *Origin and Development of Early Christian Church Architecture.*
LOWRIE, W. *Christian Art and Archaeology.*
STRZYGOWSKI, J. *Origin of Christian Church Art.*

BIOGRAPHIES

ATTWATER, DONALD. *St. John Chrysostom.*
BENSON, E. W. *Cyprian.*
BETHUNE-BAKER, J. F. *Nestorius.*
BURCKHARDT, J. *The Age of Constantine the Great.*
CAMPENHAUSEN, HANS VON. *The Fathers of the Greek Church.*
CORWIN, V. *St. Ignatius and Christianity in Antioch.*

FOAKES-JACKSON, F. J. *Eusebius Pamphili.*
HOMES DUDDEN. *Saint Ambrose.* 2 vols.
JALLAND, T. G. *Life and Times of Leo the Great.*
JONES, A. H. M. *Constantine and the Conversion of Europe.*
KING, N. Q. *The Emperor Theodosius and the Establishment of Christianity.*
SELLERS, R. V. *Eustathius of Antioch.*
SMITH AND WACE. *Dictionary of Christian Biography.* 4 vols.
S.P.C.K. *The Fathers for English Readers.*
TOLLINTON, R. B. *Clement of Alexandria.* 2 vols.
WAND, J. W. C. *The Greek Doctors.*
    The Latin Doctors.

ADDITIONS (1974)

BARLEY AND HANSON. *Christianity in Britain 300 to 700.*
BARNARD, L. W. *Studies in Apostolic Fathers and their Background.*
BETTENSON, H. *Later Christian Fathers.*
BROWN, P. *Augustine of Hippo.*
——. *Religion and Society in the Age of St Augustine.*
CAMPENHAUSEN, H. VON. *Fathers of the Latin Church.*
——. *Ecclesiastical Authority and Spiritual Power.*
CHADWICK, H. *The Early Church.*
CULLMANN, O. *Early Christian Worship.*
DANIELOU, J. *The Christian Centuries* (First 600 years).
——. *History of Early Christian Doctrine.*
DAVIES, J. G. *Early Christian Church.*
EVANS, R. F. *Pelagius.*
FOERSTER, W. *Gnosis* (Texts in translation).
FREND, W. H. C. *The Early Church.*
——. *Martyrdom and Persecution in the Early Church.*
——. *Rise of the Monophysite.*
LAMPE, G. W. H. *Greek Patristic Lexicon.*
MOMIGLIANO, H. (ed.). *Conflict between Christianity and Paganism in the 4th century.*
STEVENSON, J. *Creeds, Councils and Controversies.*
WILES, M. *The Christian Fathers.*
WILLIAMSON, G. A. *Eusebius 'History of the Church' translated.*

TABLE OF EMPERORS OF ROME

A.D.

14– 37 Tiberius.
37– 41 Caius (Caligula).
41– 54 Claudius.
54– 68 Nero.
68– 69 { Galba. / Otho. / Vitellius.

FLAVIAN EMPERORS

69– 79 Vespasian.
79– 81 Titus.
81– 96 Domitian.

96– 98 Nerva.
98–117 Trajan.

THE ANTONINES

117–138 Hadrian.
138–161 Antoninus Fius.
161–180 Marcus Aurelius.
180–192 Commodus.

193 { Pertinax. / Didius Julianus.
193–211 Septimius Severus.
211–217 Geta and Caracalla.
217–218 Macrinus.
218–222 Heliogabalus.
222–235 Alexander Severus.
235–237 Maximin the Thracian.
237–238 The two Gordians.
238–244 Gordianus III.

244–249 Philip the Arabian.
249–251 Decius.
251–252 Gallus.
252 Volusianus.
253 Aemilianus.
254–259 Valerian.
259–268 Gallienus.
268–270 Claudius II.
270–275 Aurelian.
275 Tacitus.
276–282 Probus.
282 Caius.
283 Carinus and Numerian.
284–286 Diocletian alone.
286–292 Diocletian and Maximian.
292–304 { Diocletian and Maximian, *Augusti*. / Constantius and Galerius, *Caesars*.
305 { Constantius and Galerius, *Augusti*. / Severus and Maximin Daza, *Caesars*.
306 Constantine, *Caesar*.
307–313 { Galerius, Maximin Daza, Constantine and Licinius, Maximian *restored* (usurper), Maxentius (usurper).

313–323 {Constantine.
        {Licinius.
323–337 Constantine I, alone.
337–340 {Constantine II.
337–350 {Constans.
337   {Constantius.

350–361 Constantius alone.
350–354 Gallus, *Caesar*.
354–361 Julian, *Caesar*.
361–363 Julian.
363   Jovian.
For the remainder see p. 205.

67(?) Linus.
76(?) Anencletus.
88(?) Clement.
97(?) Euarestus.
105(?) Alexander.
115(?) Sixtus I.
125(?) Telesphorus.
136(?) Hyginus.
140(?) Pius I.
155(?) Anicetus.
166(?) Soter.
175(?) Eleutherus.
193 Victor.
199 Zephyrinus.
219 Callistus I
        (Hippolytus).
223 Urban I.
230 Pontianus.
235 Anteros.
236 Fabian.
251 Cornelius
        (Novatian).
252 Lucius.
253 Stephen.
257 Sixtus II.
259 Dionysius.
269 Felix I.
275 Eutychianus.
283 Caius.

296 Marcellinus I.
304–308 *Vacant*.
308 Marcellus I.
311 Eusebius.
311 Miltiades.
314 Silvester.
336 Marcus.
337 Julius.
352 Liberius
        (Felix II).
366 Damasus
        (Ursinus).
384 Siricius.
398 Anastasius.
402 Innocent I.
417 Zosimus.
418 Boniface I
        (Eulalius).
422 Coelestine I.
432 Sixtus III.
441 Leo I.
461 Hilary.
468 Simplicius.
483 Felix III.
492 Gelasius I.
496 Anastasius II.
498 Symmachus
        (Laurentius).
514 Hormisdas.

TABLE A

PRINCIPAL DATES TO 500

GENERAL	CHURCH and STATE	HERESY and SCHISM	SYNODS and COUNCILS	WRITINGS
6/7 Census of Quirinius: Revolt of Judas	42 Persecution of Herod Agrippa I — Martyrdom of James Son of Zebedee 44 Death of Herod Agrippa I		49 Jerusalem Conference	
49/ Expulsion of the Jews from Rome by Claudius 50 62 Martyrdom of James the Just	64 Persecution of Nero—Rome ?Martyrdom of Peter and Paul			
70 Destruction of Jerusalem—Titus	95 ?Persecution of Domitian—Rome and Asia 104 Martyrdom of Simeon 112 Correspondence of Pliny and Trajan c115 Martyrdom of Ignatius 125 Hadrian's Rescript	c95 Ebionites: Cerinthus c100 Gnosticism -200 c120 Saturninus (Antioch) c125 Basilides (Alexandria) c135 Valentinus (Alexandria and Rome) 140 Marcion (Rome) c170 Bardesanes (Edessa)		96 *Epistle of Clement* c100 *The Didache* c115 Ignatius—*Epistles* c116 Polycarp—*Epistle to the Philippians* c126 Quadratus—*Apology* c130 *Epistle of Barnabas* (?c75) c140 Aristides—*Apology* c150 *Shepherd* of Hermas (?c100) c150 *Letter to Diognetus* c150 Justin—*Apology* c150 *Pistis Sophia* c150 Marcion—*Canon of N.T.* c152 Tatian—*Oration to the Greeks*
132 Revolt of Bar-Cochba 135 Jerusalem becomes Aelia Capitolina				

155 Anicetus and Polycarp—Easter controversy	156 Martyrdom of Polycarp	c157 Montanism	c157 *Martyrium Polycarpi*
c160 Hegesippus			c160 Ptolemaeus—*Letter to Flora*
	163 Martyrdom of Justin		173 Tatian—*Diatessaron*
			175 Melito—*Apology*
			c175 Celsus—*True Word*
		175 Asia—Synods condemn Montanism	
177 Irenaeus—Bishop of Lyons	177 Persecution at Lyons and Vienne		177 Athenagoras—*Legatio pro Christianis*
	Martyrdom of Blandina and others		180 Theophilus—*Ad Autolycum*
	180 Martyrs of Scilli		180 Minucius Felix—*Octavius* (?225)
			185 Irenaeus—*Adversus Haereses*
			190 Clement—*Address to the Greeks*
190 Clement—Head of Catechetical School at Alexandria		190 Monarchianism at Rome	
193 Tertullian of Carthage			c195 Clement—*Tutor*
c197 Victor and Polycrates—Easter controversy			197 Tertullian—*Apology*
			200 Tertullian—*De Praescriptiones*
202 Persecution of Septimius Severus	Martyrdom—Perpetua and Felicitas		Clement—*Miscellanies*
203 Origen—Head of Catechetical School at Alexandria	205 Tertullian becomes Montanist		
	211 First Long Peace	217 Hippolytus—Schism at Rome	
			c220 Hippolytus—*Apostolic Tradition*
			220 Tertullian—*Adversus Praxean*
			c230 Origen—*Hexapla; De Principiis*
		242 Manicheism	c230 Hippolytus—*Refutation (Philosophumena)*

TABLE A—Continued

PRINCIPAL DATES TO 500

GENERAL	CHURCH and STATE	HERESY and SCHISM	SYNODS and COUNCILS	WRITINGS
247 Dionysius—Bishop of Alexandria				c250 Origen—Contra Celsum
248 Cyprian—Bishop of Carthage				c250 Didascalia
	250 Persecution of Decius Martyrdom of Fabian			251 Cyprian—De Unitate
		251 Novatianist Schism	251 Carthage (The Lapsed)	
		255 Baptismal Controversy —Carthage and Rome -256	255 Carthage (Baptism) -256	
	257 Persecution of Valerian			
	258 Martyrdom of Cyprian and Sixtus II			
	260 Gallienus — Edict of Toleration Second Long Peace	260 Paul of Samosata— Bishop of Antioch (Monarchianism)		c260 Dionysius Alex.—Refutation and Defence
				c275 Apostolic Church Order
285 Anthony—Eremitic Monasticism				
293 Foundation of the Tetrarchy				
302 Gregory the Illuminator —Catholicos of Armenia				
303 Persecution of Diocletian —General				
305 Anthony—Semi-eremitic Monasticism	305 Persecution of Galerius —East			
	311 Galerius—Edict of Toleration	311 Meletian Schism (Egypt)		311 Eusebius—Martyrs of Palestine
	311 Persecution of Maximin Daza	311 Donatist Schism		
312 Battle of Milvian Bridge	313 'Edict' of Milan		314 Arles (Donatism and Baptism)	317 Athanasius—De Incarnatione
		318 Arian Controversy begins	321 Synod at Alexandria condemns Arius	

323	Constantine—sole Emperor	323	Constantine intervenes in Arian dispute						324	Eusebius—*Ecclesiastical History*
c325	Ammonius — Semi-eremitic Monasticism					325	NICÆA—1st Oecumenical Council (see Table B)			
c325	Pachomius — Monasticism proper									
328	Athanasius — Bishop of Alexandria									
330	Foundation of New Rome (Constantinople)			330	Eustathius of Antioch deposed Antiochene Schism	335	Tyre—Athanasius condemned			
		336	First Exile of Athanasius	336	Marcellus of Ancyra deposed Death of Arius					
337	Constantius — Emperor in East									
339	Monasticism introduced in West by Athanasius	339	Second Exile of Athanasius							
339	Eusebius, Bishop of Constantinople	339	Persecution in Persia							
						341	Antioch (Arianism)			
341	Ulfilas—Mission to the Goths					343	Sardica (Arianism)			
						344	Antioch (Arianism)			
351	Constantius—Sole Emperor									
						353	Arles (Arianism)			
c353	Hilary—Bishop of Poitiers					355	Milan (Arianism)			
		356	Third Exile of Athanasius			357	Sirmium (Arianism)	See Table C	c357	Hilary—*De Synodis* and *De Trinitate*
						358	Ancyra (Arianism)			
						359	Sirmium (Arianism)			
						359	Ariminum, W. (Arianism) Seleucia, E. (Arianism)			
				360	Macedonianism	360	Constantinople (Arianism)			
		361	Julian and the Pagan Reaction							
		362	Fourth Exile of Athanasius			362	Alexandria (Arianism)			
		365	Valens—Persecution of Orthodox							
		365	Fifth Exile of Athanasius							

TABLE A—*Continued*
PRINCIPAL DATES TO 500

GENERAL	CHURCH and STATE	HERESY and SCHISM	SYNODS and COUNCILS	WRITINGS
370 Basil—Bishop of Caesarea-in-Cappadocia		370 Priscillianism		
372 Gregory — Bishop of Nyssa		c370 Apollinarianism		
372 Gregory Naz.—Bishop of Sasima				
372 Martin—Bishop of Tours				c375 *Apostolic Constitutions*
373 Death of Athanasius				
374 Ambrose — Bishop of Milan				
379 Theodosius, Emperor				
381 Gregory Naz.—Bishop of Constantinople	380 Gratian's Rescript	381 Arian Controversy ends	380 Saragossa (Priscillianism)	380 Gregory Naz. — *Five Orations*
382 Jerome at Rome	382 Gratian — Removal of 'Altar of Victory'		381 CONSTANTINOPLE — 2nd Oecumenical Council (see Table B)	382 Jerome—*Vulgate* begun
385 Jerome at Bethlehem	385 Ambrose and Justina			
386 Conversion of Augustine				
386 Chrysostom—preacher of Antioch				
	390 Ambrose and Theodosius	392 Theodore — Bishop of Mopsuestia		
396 Augustine—Bishop of Hippo				
397 Ninian—Apostle of the Picts				
398 Chrysostom—Bishop of Constantinople		c400 Pelagius and Celestius at Rome		c400 Augustine—*Confessions*
400 Theophilus—Bishop of Alexandria, and the 'Tall Brothers'				
402 Innocent I—Bishop of Rome			403 Synod of the Oak (Chrysostom)	
404 Western Capital moved to Ravenna				

409 Synesius—Bishop of Ptolemais (Cyrene)				
410 Alaric—Capture of Rome				
410 Honoratus — foundation of the Monastery of Lérins				
412 Cyril—Bishop of Alexandria			411 Carthage (Donatism)	412 Augustine—*City of God* begun
			412 Carthage (Pelagianism)	
		414 End of Antiochene Schism		
		415 Pelagius in Palestine	416 Africa and Rome -418 (Pelagianism)	
417 Case of Apiarius				
422 Coelestine — Bishop of Rome				
		428 Nestorian Controversy	430 Rome and Alexandria (Nestorianism)	
		429 Cassian—Semi-Pelagianism	431 EPHESUS — 3rd Oecumenical Council (See Table B)	
431 Palladius—Ireland				434 Vincent of Lérins—*Commonitorium*
432 Patrick—Ireland				
440 Leo I—Bishop of Rome		440 Eutychian Controversy		
	445 Rescript of Valentinian III			446 Theodoret—*Eranistes*
			448 Constantinople (Eutychianism)	448 Leo—*Tome*
			449 Ephesus (*Latrocinium*)	
	c450 Persecution in Armenia		451 CHALCEDON (4th Oecumenical Council (See Table B)	
452 Attila—Invasion of Italy				
455 Gaiseric—Sack of Rome				
472 Ricimer—Capture of Rome				
		482 Zeno's *Henoticon*		
		484 Acacian Schism (Rome and Constantinople)		
		484 Separation of Persian Nestorian Church		
		491 Armenian Church condemns Chalcedon		
	496 Conversion of Clovis			

Note: For periods—episcopates, persecutions, controversies, schisms etc.—the initial date only is given.

277

TABLE B

FIRST FOUR OECUMENICAL COUNCILS

Date	Place	Proceedings
325	Nicea	1. Arianism—condemned by the formulation of the Nicene Creed as a test of orthodoxy 2. Meletian Schism (Egypt)—attempt to heal 3. Easter Question—discussed 4. Canons—ecclesiastical discipline and organisation
381	Constantinople	1. Arianism—settlement of the controversy by the re-affirmation of the Nicene Creed 2. Macedonianism—condemned 3. Apollinarianism—condemned 4. Antiochene Schism—attempt to heal 5. Canons: (a) Constantinople placed in order of precedence next after Rome (b) Provinces grouped into 'dioceses'
431	Ephesus	1. Nestorianism—condemned 2. Pelagianism—condemned 3. Cyprus—made independent of Antioch
451	Chalcedon	1. Dioscorus—condemned and deposed 2. Creeds—Nicene re-affirmed, and 'Niceno-Constantinopolitan' affirmed 3. Tome of Leo—approved as dogma 4. Definition of the Faith—formulated A statement of the Catholic doctrine of 'One Christ in two Natures', ruling out Apollinarianism, Nestorianism, and Eutychianism 5. Canons: (a) Jurisdiction of the Patriarchate of Constantinople defined (b) Division of Christendom into five Patriarchates—Rome, Constantinople, Alexandria, Antioch, Jerusalem—completed

TABLE C

ARIAN CONTROVERSY COUNCILS

Date	Place	Proceedings	Results
325	Nicæa	Adopted Nicene Creed (*homoousios*)	Arian reaction
341	Antioch	Adopted 'Creed of the Dedication' (omits *homoousios*)	Consecration of Ulfilas as Bishop of Goths
343	Sardica	1. Re-affirmed Nicene Creed 2. Canons *re* appellate jurisdiction of see of Rome. (Easterns withdrew to Philippopolis and condemned Athanasius)	Breach between East and West
344	Antioch	1. Adopted 'Macrostich' (first appearance of *homoios*) 2. Condemned Photinus	Period of peace until Constantius becomes sole Emperor
353	Arles	Western bishops forced to condemn Athanasius	Anomoean victory
355	Milan	Confirmation of Arles. Bishops given option of signing or exile	Homoousians overcome in the West
357	Sirmium	Adopted the 'Blasphemy' Creed (forbids the use of either *homoousios* or *homoiousios*) Hosius and ? Liberius forced to sign.	Reaction against Anomoean Arianism
358	Ancyra	The 'Blasphemy' condemned by Semi-Arians (Homoiousians)	Banishment of leading Anomoeans

TABLE C—*Continued*
ARIAN CONTROVERSY COUNCILS

Date	Place	Proceedings	Results
359	Sirmium	Adopted the 'Dated Creed'	Revised at Nicé
359	Ariminum (West)	1. Orthodox—rejected 'Dated Creed' 2. Homoeans—accepted 'Dated Creed'	All eventually sign Creed of Nicé (modified 'Dated Creed')
	Seleucia (East)	1. Semi-Arians—rejected 'Dated Creed' 2. Homoeans—withdrew	
360	Constantinople	Ratified Creed of Nicé as official creed of the whole Church	1. Victory of Homoean Arianism (cf. Jerome's remark) 2. Homoousians and Homoiousians tend to draw together
362	Alexandria	1. Re-affirmed Nicene Creed 2. Condemned Macedonianism 3. Explained the terms *ousia* and *hypostasis*	1. Cappadocians take the lead in the East 2. Explanation of terms leads to understanding between E. and W. supporters of Nicene Creed
381	CONSTANTINOPLE	1. Re-affirmed Nicene Creed 2. Condemned Macedonianism	Orthodox victory. Arianism suppressed except among the Goths

Note: THE PARTIES IN THE CONTROVERSY

1. Homoousians (Orthodox) 'Son of one substance with the Father'
2. Homoiousians (Semi-Arian) 'Son of like substance with the Father'
3. Homoeans (Arian) 'Son like the Father'
4. Anomoeans (Ultra-Arian) 'Son unlike the Father'

280

ADDITIONAL NOTES

page 6, line 2

It is upon the Essenes that the famous discoveries at Qumran are believed to have thrown much light. The so-called Dead Sea Scrolls reveal the presence of a highly disciplined community living in a fortress-monastery from the time of Alexander Jannaeus (103 B.C.) till the Roman advance on Jerusalem in A.D. 68. They practised a baptism of initiation, and in anticipation of the Messianic banquet shared in community meals of bread and wine. They seem to have expected two Messiahs, one priestly, the other royal, and they had a great veneration for their founder, the Teacher of Righteousness; but who he was there is so far nothing to show.

page 14, line 36

About A.D. 49. Described in Acts 15.

page 25, line 7

Recent opinion seems to have settled for a date within the first century. (Cross, *Early Christian Fathers*, p. 11.)

page 30, line 22

That there was a President seems confirmed by archaeological evidence. 'Moses' Seat' was a substantial structure in which the presiding elder sat facing the congregation with his colleagues on either side. (Sukenik, *Ancient Synagogues*, pp. 20, 38, 40.)

page 35, line 5

Some of Simon Bar-Cochbar's own letters, together with other documentary evidence, have been found in caves at Wadi Murabba'At near Qumran. It appears that the site was occupied by a detachment of Bar-Cochbar's forces between A.D. 132–5, when it served as a garrison on the route to Jerusalem. (I. F. Bruce, *Second Thoughts on the Dead Sea Scrolls*, pp. 53 ff.)

page 41, line 9

This Fragment is named after L. A. Muratori who published it (after its discovery in an eighth-century MS) in 1740. It gives a list of the New Testament books received towards the end of the second century, but since it is mutilated its omissions are not to be taken as conclusive evidence.

page 44, line 33

In view of what follows it should be noticed that in recent years attention has been focused on the early and less articulated forms of Gnosticism. In fact the term is now most often used of a type of thought that was already widely diffused in the New Testament period, and is believed to be attacked in Colossians and to have influenced the thought of the Fourth Gospel. Many of the writings belonging to the 'apocryphal New Testament' derive from this school of thought. Fresh interest was aroused by the discovery in 1945 of a small library of Gnostic literature at Nag-Hamadi on the Upper Nile. This collection of twelve codices included the now famous *Gospel of Thomas* (*c.* A.D. 150), which consists entirely of alleged sayings of Jesus and is closely parallel to the reconstructed Q document apparently used by the first and third evangelists to supplement Mark. The background thought of all these non-canonical documents is a syncretism of Jewish, Hellenistic and Christian elements in various degrees. Man is a divine being imprisoned in a mortal body and enchained by fate. From this bondage he can be delivered if he has the right kind of knowledge. The Gnostics claimed to have the key to the mystery. [See R. McL. Wilson, *The Gnostic Problem* (1958) and *Studies in the Gospel of Thomas* (1960), F. C. Cross, *The Jung Codex* (1955), Bertil Gärtner, *The Theology of the Gospel of Thomas* (1961).]

page 59, line 37

This did not mean that agreement was at once reached as to the contents of the canon. The first authority to use the same complete list of New Testament books as ourselves was St. Athanasius. But by that time the canon of the *gospels* had long been closed.

page 60, line 32

Recently there has been recovered his *Treatise on the Pasch*, described by F. L. Cross as a Christian Paschal Haggadah, that is, a Christian adaptation to the events of Good Friday and Easter Day of the explanation of the Passover usually given by the head of a Jewish household. (*Early Christian Fathers*, pp. 104 ff.)

page 61, line 16

He also wrote a book *On the Resurrection*, seeking to prove its possibility, its actuality, and its consonance with the divine justice.

page 70, line 18

F. L. Cross suggests that our ignorance may be due to the prevalence of Gnosticism in Alexandria during the first century-and-a-half. The later orthodox churchmen drew a decent veil over such tainted beginnings. (*Early Christian Fathers*, p. 117.)

page 74, line 27

A good deal of work has been done in recent years on Origen's methods as critic and exegete. It is clear that he was not particularly interested in the factual aspect of history and that he was prepared to go a long way in 'extreme' criticism in order to find room for his allegorical method of interpretation. It is also evident that he used canons of literary criticism that were much canvassed among the rhetoricians of his day. (R. M. Grant, *Earliest Lives of Jesus*, 1961. Hanson, *Origen's Doctrine of Tradition*, 1954.)

page 76, line 21

Two other works deserve special mention: the *Philocalia*, an anthology of his writings compiled by Gregory Nazianzen and Basil of Caesarea for their monks; and the *Discussion with Heracleides*, discovered in a disused quarry in 1941, an unique shorthand record of an informal conversation between a number of bishops and Origen on various theological topics.

page 79, line 33

This is asserted by Jerome but is now doubted.

page 81, line 16

Among these should be especially noted the treatise *On Baptism*, which couples anointing and laying on of hands with the actual baptism and is the earliest brochure we have on a Christian sacrament, and also the treatise *On Prayer* which is our earliest commentary on the Lord's Prayer.

page 92, line 31

It must be admitted that this view has not won current favour. Agape and Eucharist are still believed to have had a common origin, even if not to have been originally identical.

page 101, line 27

Commodianus' date is much disputed. Today scholars place it variously between the middle of the third and of the fifth centuries.

page 102, line 5

August 29, 251.

page 107, line 15

In addition to the *De Trinitate* there are to be reckoned to Novatian a treatise proving that the Jewish regulations with regard to food do not apply to Christians (*De Cibis Judaicis*), an attack on the theatre (*De Spectaculis*) and a dissertation on the benefit of modesty (*De Bono Pudicitiae*).

page 127, line 30

Christianity was officially established in Armenia by King Tiridates III in 301. Georgia was converted soon after, largely as the result of the teaching of the slave-girl Nina, and was proclaimed Christian in 330.

page 128, line 25

He was of African birth and had been a pupil of another African rhetorician, Arnobius, who was converted to Christianity as an old man and then, about 303, the time of the Diocletian persecution, wrote an apology for his new faith, the *Adversus Nationes*.

page 147, line 26

An alternative interpretation is 'dwellers around the shrines' (i.e. beggars who lived on the charity of the worshippers), see J. G. Davies, *The Making of the Church*, 1960, p. 90.

page 155, line 24

Other books by Athanasius are *Oratio contra Gentes*, an introduction to the *De Incarnatione*; the *Tres Orationes contra Arianos* (the first of which defends the Nicene christology and the other two discuss the scripture texts alleged by the Arians); a number of polemical works, of which the most important are the Apology against the Arians and the Apology to the Emperor Constantius; and the Festal Letters, of which the thirty-ninth gives for the first time precisely the same list of canonical scriptures that is in force today.

page 170, line 10

This attack was answered by Cyril of Alexandria in a great work of thirty books, of which only the first ten survive in full.

page 175, line 5

One of the most interesting of his books is the *Admonitions to Young Men*, in which he encourages the use of the pagan classics as an element in Christian education. Extant also are several hundred letters on a great variety of topics.

page 175, line 24

Another interesting example of Gregory of Nyssa's style is the *De Vita Moysis* in which the life of Moses is used to symbolise the mystical ascent of the soul to God. It is also thought to be Gregory's answer to the charge that he is 'interpolating a foreign philosophy into the Bible'. (W. Jaeger, *Early Christianity and Greek Paideia*, p. 81.)

page 176, line 8

There are also forty other Orations as well as many poems written with a deliberately literary intention. The Cappadocians did more than any other fathers since Clement and Origen to wed Greek culture to Christian faith.

page 186, line 18

Cyril, Bishop of Jerusalem, although consecrated by the Arian Acacius of Caesarea, had been three times exiled for his faithfulness to the principles of Nicea. His best known writing is the twenty-four *Catecheses* or addresses to catechumens taken down in shorthand as delivered and later published.

page 190, line 12

Lucifer was an exile from his native Sardinia, because he had refused to abandon Athanasius. He was extremely and even violently orthodox, yet died (*c.* 370) in the schism he had created.

page 195, line 31

To this Macarius were attributed fifty homilies which are of importance as examples of early Christian mysticism. But the authorship is doubtful and the homilies are even believed to reflect the heresy of the Messalians, a school of quietists, condemned at Ephesus in 431. (Altaner, *Patrology*, p. 305.)

page 205, line 5

Other Latin hymn writers of the period were Ausonius (*c.* 310–*c.* 392), tutor to Valentinian's son Gratian, who hovered on the border-line between paganism and Christianity, and Prudentius (348–*c.* 408), the greatest poet of the Christian west, whose best known hymns 'Bethlehem, of noblest cities', 'Servant of God, remember' and 'Of the Father's heart begotten', with half a dozen others are to be found in the English Hymnal. Here may also be mentioned Nicetas, Bishop of Remesiana in Dacia at the turn of the fourth to the fifth centuries (not to be confused with Nicetas, the Gothic martyr) who is by some reputable scholars believed to have been the author of the *Te Deum.*

page 206, line 17

Even the later Alexandrian scholars began to drop the use of allegorism in their more scholarly works and to have recourse to it only for purposes of edification (Altaner, *Patrology*, p. 299). An example of the ardent yet discriminating veneration for Origen can be seen in Didymus the Blind, who, having lost his sight at the age of four and remaining a layman, nevertheless was head of the catechetical school at Alexandria for more than fifty years until his death about the end of the fourth century.

page 210, line 10

This Epiphanius was a strong traditionalist. He did his utmost to prevent Greek culture from penetrating the Church, thus showing opposition not only to Origen but to the line taken by the Cappadocians. His two best known works are the *Ancoratus* and the *Panarion*.

page 211, line 4

In days when knowledge of Greek was declining in the west he did a good service in translating eastern books into Latin, including Eusebius' *Church History*. It is he who gives us the first Latin version of the Apostles' Creed.

page 212, paragraph 2

Our store of Chrysostom's writings has recently been enriched by the discovery, in 1955 on Mt. Athos, of a manuscript containing eight catechetical lectures by him.

page 227, line 1

Bishop of Milevis in Numidia. In 365 he wrote a considerable book against the Donatist bishop Parmenian, attacking the schismatics' practice of re-baptism and their fanaticism in destroying altars and chalices.

page 230, line 29

The literary works of heretics are now rare because they were normally destroyed by the orthodox, but a surprisingly large number of minor writings, fourteen in all, seem to have survived in Pelagius' case (see Altaner, *Patrology*, p. 440).

page 239, line 27

Altaner (*Patrology*, p. 398) says that he 'may be considered the leading exegete of the Antiochene school and the greatest Greek interpreter of Scripture in Christian antiquity'.

page 247, line 3

The earliest of the Syrian Church fathers was Aphraates. He wrote on Christian virtues and doctrine in twenty-three short treatises about the middle of the fourth century, using the text of Tatian's *Diatessaron*. He was a bishop from the province of Adiabene and had been a monk in the monastery of St. Matthew, north of Nineveh. He was an eye-witness of some of the worst persecutions in Persia. Contemporary with Aphraates was the more famous Ephraem the Syrian (*d.* 373), a deacon and the reputed founder of the Persian School at Edessa. He wrote much on scriptural, ethical and devotional subjects and is generally considered the greatest of the Syrian poets. (English Hymnal, 194.)

page 262, line 10

Salvian was born about 400 and died in 480.

INDEX

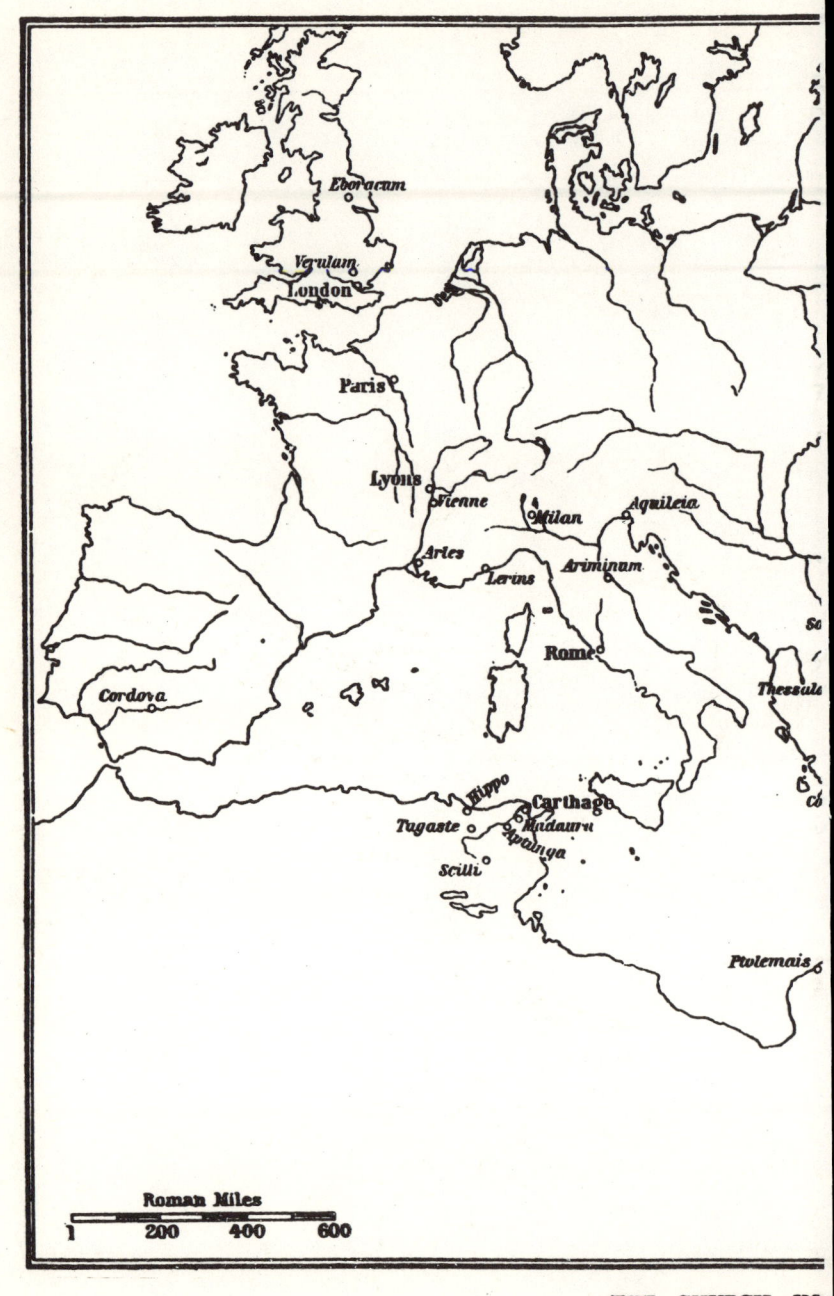

Roman Miles

1   200   400   600

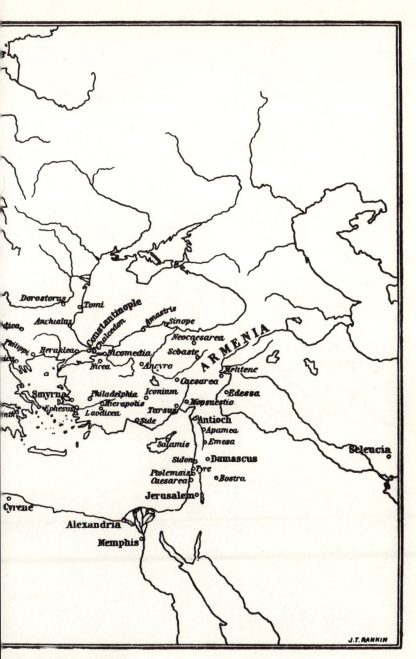

THE ROMAN EMPIRE

BRITISH
CHURCH

ARMORICA

PATRIARCHATE

ILLYRICUM

DALMATIA

MOE

OF ROM

Roman Miles

0   200   400   600

PATRIARCHATES

DACIA MOESIA

PATRIARCHATE OF CONSTANTINOPLE

ARMENIA

PERSIA

PATRIARCHATE OF ANTIOCH

PATRIARCHATE OF JERUSALEM

ARABIA

BYA

PATRIARCHATE OF ALEXANDRIA

J.T. RANKIN

SAXONS

SAXONS

FRANKS

BURGUNDIANS

OSTROGOTHS

LOM

SUEVI

VISIGOTHS

VANDALS

Roman Miles

0   200   400   600

BARBARIANS

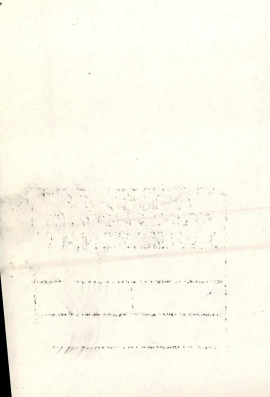

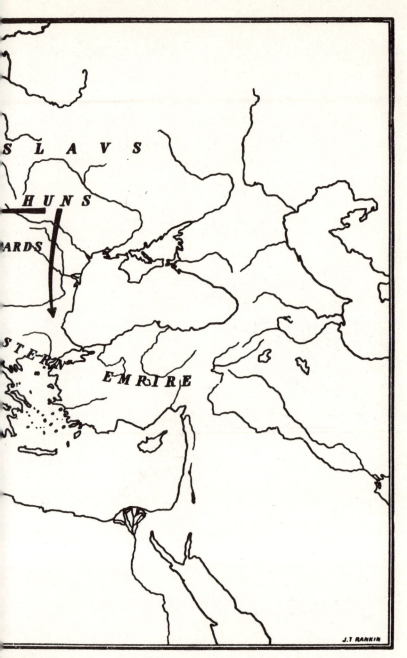

S L A V S

HUNS

ARDS

STERN

EMPIRE

. 500